YOU
CAN
HEAL
YOUR
PET

Praise for *You Can Heal Your Pet*:

'Warm-hearted, compassionate and eminently practical, You Can Heal Your Pet combines mainstream veterinary advice with complementary wisdom. Every pet-lover should have a copy of this book in their home!'

DAVID MICHIE, AUTHOR OF THE DALAI LAMA'S CAT AND THE ART OF PURRING

'Dr Rohini Sathish is a very compassionate, experienced and extremely competent veterinary surgeon. As a natural health veterinary surgeon myself, I would sincerely recommend this book to all pet owners and breeders.'

DR PAUL BOLAND BVSc MRCVS

'Modern medicine has advanced greatly with regards to diagnosis of diseases but is lagging behind in treatment options for some. I believe this book can offer valuable complementary advice to every pet owner.'

DR S LOGESWARAN BVSC GP CERT (ENDO) MRCVS

YOU CAN HEAL YOUR PET

The Practical Guide to Holistic
Health and Veterinary Care

ELIZABETH WHITER and
DR ROHINI SATHISH MRCVS

HAY HOUSE

Carlsbad, California • New York City • London • Sydney
Johannesburg • Vancouver • Hong Kong • New Delhi

First published and distributed in the United Kingdom by:
Hay House UK Ltd, Astley House, 33 Notting Hill Gate, London W11 3JQ
Tel: +44 (0)20 3675 2450; Fax: +44 (0)20 3675 2451
www.hayhouse.co.uk

Published and distributed in the United States of America by:
Hay House Inc., PO Box 5100, Carlsbad, CA 92018-5100
Tel: (1) 760 431 7695 or (800) 654 5126
Fax: (1) 760 431 6948 or (800) 650 5115
www.hayhouse.com

Published and distributed in Australia by:
Hay House Australia Ltd, 18/36 Ralph St, Alexandria NSW 2015
Tel: (61) 2 9669 4299; Fax: (61) 2 9669 4144
www.hayhouse.com.au

Published and distributed in the Republic of South Africa by:
Hay House SA (Pty) Ltd, PO Box 990, Witkoppen 2068
info@hayhouse.co.za; www.hayhouse.co.za

Published and distributed in India by:
Hay House Publishers India, Muskaan Complex, Plot No.3, B-2,
Vasant Kunj, New Delhi 110 070
Tel: (91) 11 4176 1620; Fax: (91) 11 4176 1630
www.hayhouse.co.in

Distributed in Canada by:
Raincoast Books, 2440 Viking Way, Richmond, B.C. V6V 1N2
Tel: (1) 604 448 7100; Fax: (1) 604 270 7161; www.raincoast.com

Text © Elizabeth Whiter and Dr Rohini Sathish, 2015

Interior images: p.1, 101, 249, 275 centre right and below left © Leesa Le May;
pp. 110–113 and 125–129 © Brian Clifford

A catalogue record for this book is available from the British Library.

ISBN: 978-1-78180-493-3

Printed and bound in Great Britain by TJ International Ltd, Padstow, Cornwall

Contents

Foreword

Healing.

As Guardians, we wish to do all we can to help heal our loved animals. It seems, therefore, that we would all have a very clear idea of what it is to heal. But, is it clear, really?

Thoughtfully, Elizabeth Whiter and Dr Rohini Sathish define this rich idea, and provide a wonderful compass and map for navigating the world of animal healing. Yet 'healing' as an idea is fertile soil yielding food for thought, so I would seed this soil here, as a starting point.

When we consider a healing of human or non-human animals, the physical body, the past, the psyche, the spirit, the earth, a relationship... what is the essence of a healing?

There are hidden esoteric wisdoms in language, so let's examine words. The word 'heal' is from the Old English *hælan*, which in turn is from an ancient word *hailjan*, meaning 'to make whole'. Dis-ease seems to arise from less wholeness.

Within a being, or a being-ness, we have parts, constituents and attributes... whether of the physical or meta-physical variety. These come and go at a certain harmonious rate, and disruption or disturbance in this manageable flux is experienced as dis-ease, sickness or trauma.

Health, therefore, emanates from integration, where a kind of completion emerges from pieces that fit well together, for an expected time. So a healing may be thought of as a re-integration.

These are the thoughts of a human mind, and being human is a wondrous thing. But, I suppose there are some drawbacks to our human-ness. Sometimes we do silly things. One of these silly things is forgetting that we are rather tiny in the scope of all that is. This forgetfulness can lead to hubris, or excessive pride.

There is an old saying: 'Those whom the gods would destroy, they first make proud.' Those of us in the medical establishment might be well served to write this on our foreheads in permanent ink. We forget that our viewpoints, the windows through which we see, are actually rather small keyholes. We forget about other Guardians.

We forget the limitation in our sight, in our vision of the cosmos. We forget there is more. We can oversimplify…we can favor contraction or stasis over expansion. And thus we may reject, out of hand, the in-sight through another keyhole, a different window.

In this we greatly err, for we may miss a particular aspect of the larger picture, a useful facet, another presencing of a thing that could be re-integrated in the healing. For that-which-is-truly-there has many aspects, and healing therefore must, by definition, promote a wholeness within the multiplicity of disparate parts. And first we must be willing to see this multiplicity, and to dismantle our hubris.

For these reasons, it is clear that my esteemed colleagues, the authors of this most useful book, are excellently on-point in presenting the many ways the reader may be a champion of animal healing. These many implements, this whole-istic and integrative approach, address the varied facets required in effective healing.

I hope you enjoy the illuminations of these pages, as I have, in your pursuit of the hailjan of your loved animals. For furnished here are thoughts and words that pave the way for the numinous deeds of creation and re-creation, those of the divine.

Dr Demian Dressler DVM
Veterinarian and author of the Dog Cancer Survival Guide

Preface

I believe that everything happens for a reason, and I have no doubt that meeting Elizabeth Whiter was no accident. I have been a successful veterinarian and surgeon for 21 years, and have been on lots of courses and gained extra proficiency to an advanced level in medicine and surgery, but when my own cat, Silky, was diagnosed with incurable cancer by oncologists I was deeply shaken and felt completely helpless.

In total desperation, I contacted many healers and complementary therapists online. Elizabeth Whiter was the only one who replied immediately. Her empathy, concern and support helped me immensely through a very difficult time. We remained in touch after Silky's passing, and I then went on to train as an Animal Healer with Elizabeth, which was an amazing, transformational journey. I now believe I am a complete veterinarian.

Elizabeth and I became really good friends. We realized we had similar values and a common vision, and also that we had a lot to learn from each other with regards to animal health. We both strongly believe that conventional veterinary medicine alone cannot ensure total animal wellbeing. There is a need to heal the *spirit*, too – to develop a spiritual understanding with every animal patient and the pet guardian.

An old proverb says: 'There is but ONE true Medicine, the medicine that heals the wounds of cosmos, spirit, psyche, soma, earth & time.' Elizabeth and I decided to write this book together to get this message across, and to demonstrate that it is possible to integrate conventional and complementary therapies for complete wellness.

Elizabeth is very committed and dedicated to her full-time animal healing work and has been a great pioneer, fundraiser and ambassador of complementary health for animals. She is the founder of the Healing Animals Organisation, where students from all over the world attend lectures and workshops and Diploma in Animal Healing courses.

I have found Elizabeth to be an inspirational trailblazer and a tireless crusader. I have tremendous admiration for her incredible dedication to her life's purpose – helping animals worldwide. I remember one year when she travelled to four different continents – as far as South Africa and Japan – to teach animal healing and work at animal outreach projects.

She also runs her own, very successful, complementary animal health and healing clinic, where she treats animals using a gentler approach with plant remedies, food advice, emotional wellbeing and environmental enrichment techniques. Her clinic is very popular and she is very much in demand because she is so involved and dedicated to helping pet guardians and their animals.

Elizabeth puts in a lot of effort in foraging, harvesting and preparing the best-quality herbal recipes and treatments for animals. I have watched her cook them and have tasted her wonderful animal recipes myself. I can say, hand on heart, that she is a truly fantastic chef: creative, enthusiastic and completely in her element while she is cooking.

Dr Rohini Sathish

I feel extremely privileged and excited to have written this book with Dr Rohini. She is kind and compassionate, and is one of the most genuine veterinarians I know. Nothing happens by chance, and fate intervened when I took a call from Rohini, asking if I could offer my services to help her sick cat, the beautiful Silky.

I could immediately tell that Rohini and I had a connection far greater than just a professional one. We were both united and committed to helping Silky, and thanks to her, Rohini and I are now the best of friends and work colleagues. I hugely respect Rohini's veterinary work in treating all animals with loving kindness and integrity, using conventional and complementary health side by side.

Rohini has proved to me why she is so loved by all of her practice clients. Her success lies in the fact that she sees beyond the immediate condition presented to her in her animal clinic and combines her conventional wisdom with her complementary healing skills, weighing up all the options and offering an integrated treatment plan to suit every individual patient. Dr Rohini is consistent and thorough; she has a super balance of logic and gut instinct and remains compassionate and kind to all animals and their carers.

Rohini later trained in the Diploma in Animal Healing: she is open-minded, focused and eager to learn new healing skills to add to her tool kit. She is a great listener with clients, and empathetic to every animal case.

It was with great delight that I offered Rohini the post of Veterinary Advisor to the Healing Animals Organisation, and she kindly accepted. The Organisation is involved in a number of outreach projects and fundraising events for animals in need, all over the world. Rohini is a committed and reliable team player, bringing her integrity and skill base to any situation and she always delivers. As Aristotle once said, 'Pleasure in the job puts perfection in the work'.

Team spirit is everything in our organization, and everybody has an important part to play – from volunteering to fundraising and offering healing. Rohini is a valued team player who is kind-hearted and gentle in spirit, and has a great sense of humour!

Elizabeth Whiter

Introduction

There is an old proverb that says: 'You never soar so high, as when you stoop down to help a child or an animal'. When this animal is your own cat or dog, it is *you* who can help and heal. You can help your pet in sickness and in health – with a bit of assistance from professionals like us. You can prevent your pet from falling ill in the first place, or support them through an illness, hasten their recovery and help them maintain their health afterwards. In fact, You Can Heal Your Pet.

We are both overjoyed to offer this book to you. It is a loving product of our life's work, vocation and dedication to serve animals in sickness and in health. We are both experts in our respective fields of veterinary and complementary animal therapies. We have worked together as an open-minded team on this book: spending sleepless nights on research, having endless discussions and sharing insights.

Between us we have more than 40 years of first-hand experience of treating animals. We have great respect and trust for each other's work and both believe that conventional medicine and complementary health need to go hand in hand to ensure total wellbeing. We are therefore very committed to working *together* in order to arrive at the best solution for each animal: almost like a couple of pet detectives trying to solve a case – looking at it from every perspective.

Ignorance may be bliss but knowledge is power, and empowering the modern pet owner is the driving force behind this book. Throughout, we hope to educate you, empathize with you and enable you to be exemplary pet guardians. We both felt greatly driven to write this unique book after noticing the amount of conflicting and confusing information available today; in fact, there is so much of it that we felt most of you wonderful pet guardians do not know which way to turn or who to trust.

Watching pet guardians like yourselves every single day in our animal clinics – as you struggle with choices – led us to come together and write this book. We hope that it will become your 'pet bible' and that you will refer to it time and again when you need help caring for your pet.

There are a lot of forums on pet-related topics on the internet. In fact, there is such a plethora of information available online these days that sometimes it can be truly overwhelming. We have really tried our best to provide you with clear and concise information in this book, including only the therapies and treatments that we have tried and tested ourselves, and are confident will work in most patients.

HOW TO USE THE BOOK

We gave a lot of thought to the structure of the book, so you can read the chapters in the order given. However, some of them – Chapter 2: *A–Z Food Recipes for Cats and Dogs*, Chapter 3: *A–Z Pet-Friendly Herbs* and Chapter 7: *A–Z Common Conditions in Cats and Dog*s – are designed and written in such a way that you can refer to them as and when a need arises. So, it is best that you read the book from beginning to end, but also feel free to dip in to these chapters when your pet shows a particular symptom.

You will find the word *diet* repeated a lot throughout this book. As Hippocrates said, 'Let food be thy medicine and medicine be thy food.' He knew the truth. We are *both* strongly united in the opinion that what goes into your pet in the form of food has the greatest impact on his or her wellbeing, and we decided to make *Food Is Medicine* the first chapter in the book for this very reason. This chapter, and Chapter 2: *A–Z Food Recipes for Cats and Dogs*, are full of top tips to help you take matters into your own hands and get cooking for your pet. The recipes featured have been tried and approved by our elite tasters – Morris, Lily, Frankie, Troy and Frodo, along with our animal clients over many, many years – and we are confident that your pets will absolutely love them too.

Where you source the ingredients for making healthy meals and snacks for your pet is also very important. This is where Chapter 4: *Harvesting Nature's Bounty for Your Pet* will be very useful. We are confident that you will love foraging for herbs and harvesting them yourself. Please have a go and have fun with transforming the culinary herbs listed into simple, natural topical treatments and yummy recipes, as shown in Chapter 2: *A–Z Food Recipes for Cats and Dogs* and Chapter 3: *A–Z Pet-Friendly Herbs*. They are so important for your pet's wellness and healing.

This book is called *You Can Heal Your Pet*, but what do we mean by healing? Healing is the process of making or becoming whole again. It refers to the restoration of good health, being repaired and then returning to balance. This is the destination, but your journey or the paths used to get there can be numerous. Hands-on healing, as described in this book, is a very practical and powerful way of helping your pet to heal.

In Chapter 5: *How to Give Healing to Your Pet* there are step-by-step guides to giving energy healing to your pet. These are fantastic for both you and your pet; they are for dealing with illness and then healing together so you can both become whole again. Yes – everything is possible for those who believe!

Scientists confirm that sharing your life with a companion animal is good for our health. One reason for this is that when we feel joy at being with our animal companions we set off a chain of events in the body. Endorphins are released and flood the body – these are the happy hormones, commonly known as serotonin and dopamine. Even just smiling at our pets results in more neurotransmitters being fired.

Studies show that when a person gives loving attention to their animal companion another hormone, oxytocin, kicks in. This same hormone is the one that rises when a woman has a baby, to increase the mother–child bond, and it also helps to reduce blood pressure and decrease levels of cortisol, a hormone related to stress and anxiety.

It is no wonder that many of us are gradually moving away from routine conventional medicine and towards more holistic therapies. Today, many mainstream practices, including those run by the National Health Service in the UK, are adding complementary therapies like acupuncture, healing, massage, meditation and yoga to their routine medical care, making it more holistic and integrated.

The reasoning behind this type of integrated holistic care is that, rather than focusing on illness alone, a proper wellness plan should also include prevention, rehabilitation and maintenance care. Complete healthcare now takes into consideration a person's current health condition and also their family circumstances, emotional wellbeing, diet, domestic issues and more, as all of these can impact a person's health.

This trend is also now evident in the pet health sector, as the pet guardians who have benefitted from complementary therapies themselves wish to see them available for their animals. *Integrated holistic veterinary care* is the way forward. We can all choose what sort of healthcare we want (or do not want) for ourselves, but when it comes to our pets, there is a surprising amount of regulation. For example, only a registered veterinarian is allowed to diagnose a condition, prescribe conventional veterinary medicine or practise acupuncture.

However, acupressure is one modality of healing that can be safely given by you to your pet – see Chapter 6: *Fingers and Thumbs*. It works on the same points on the body as acupuncture, but you do not need to panic about piercing a vein, an artery or a nerve as you are not using needles – only your fingers. Acupressure is straightforward and can be very effective.

You have probably realized that not all veterinarians believe in or approve of complementary therapies. To ensure that your pet gets the care you want, you need to pick a vet who is right for you and your pet, which is why we have included a chapter on this subject – Chapter 10: *How to Vet your Vet*. This is especially important if you have strong opinions regarding routine maintenance such as vaccines, which are strongly advocated by almost all conventional veterinarians.

It is our opinion that it is unrealistic to believe that diseases can be prevented just with vaccinations, and/or can be permanently cured just with medications. We strongly believe that well-informed pet guardians like you, who are willing to take equal responsibility with us in your pet's healthcare, are going to make all the difference.

Vaccination is a hot topic these days, and it is causing a lot of mental anguish. In Chapter 9: *The Vaccination Debate*, we guide you through making this important decision for your pet. We feel that while the primary vaccine course is necessary, the focus should then shift to strengthening your pet's natural defences by feeding a good *diet*. Read the chapter and then make a joint decision with your veterinarian.

We hope to assist the guardian in recognizing when there is a lack of holistic balance in their pet. It is about empowering you to feel confident you are making the right choices when it comes to maintaining the quality of your pet's life, and also helping you recognize any changes that indicate your animal is unwell.

We believe that this book will help you decide when veterinary intervention is a must, and when you can deal with issues yourselves. Chapter 7: *A–Z Common Conditions in Cats and Dogs* lists the conditions and diseases that are most often seen in cats and dogs today. Each entry explains the rationale behind the conventional veterinary treatment used and then, under the heading 'you', it describes your role as the pet guardian: showing what you can do and what you can make to support your pet through an illness, or to prevent it.

We all know that conventional medicine involves the use of pharmaceutical preparations – most of which have been developed from human generic drugs. Many of them are very effective, but they also have side effects. It is vital, therefore, that they are used with prudence and not overused or abused. This is why we included Chapter 8: *Which Drugs and Why*. We both feel very strongly that *you* as pet guardians should understand fully the most common classes of drugs used, so that you are able to make the right judgement call, in conjunction with your vet.

Sadly, these days some veterinary decisions are driven by monetary gain or are influenced by the pharmaceutical and pet food companies who have their own vested interests at heart. You, the pet guardian, therefore need the right knowledge and wisdom to make an informed choice, which we hope we have given you in this book.

Every animal and person is an individual with a distinct personality, so it is our aim to enrich every animal's time on this Earth, and assist its progression through life as the years roll by. Sadly most pet lives are far shorter than human ones. It should be our endeavour, duty and commitment therefore to have a 'tool kit' readily available at our fingertips to create the best possible life for them.

It is essential that we help our animals to adapt to the environment that we live in: bearing in mind that all dogs, for instance, are domesticated wolves and have evolved to their present breeds, crossbreeds, etc., over many years. In this context, emotional and mental wellbeing are of paramount importance and are an essential part of every animal's maintenance – in the same way that an engine requires regular servicing. You will find some very useful tips on how to enrich your pet's environment in Chapter 1.

Most importantly, one should never forget that animals never judge us – they simply give unconditional love. In return it is our obligation to nurture them and care for them as best as we possibly can, with the resources that we have. In the hands of the right vet and the right complementary therapist, veterinary care need not be cost prohibitive. Read on to see how you can take the best care of your pets – who give so much back to you and expect so little in return.

Finally, we would like our book to become the animal version of Louise Hay's acclaimed *You Can Heal Your Life*. We are both big fans of Louise and have always believed in her timeless message that we are each responsible for our own reality and 'dis-ease'. Just as our emotions can cause our ailments, so our emotions can affect our pet's emotions, and in turn, affect their health.

This is our opinion and our experience. You can unknowingly be the cause of your pet's illness, *but do not underestimate the power of your intentions*. Using this book, your hands and your pure intentions, You Can Heal Your Pet.

Good luck to you and your pets – You Can Do It.

Elizabeth & Rohini

Part I

HOLISTIC AND PRACTICAL PET CARE

Chapter 1

∿

Food Is Medicine – Nutrition, Diet and Lifestyle for Pets

A well-balanced diet is paramount for keeping our pets healthy, because good nutrition means more vital years for them. If we can create as natural a diet as possible for our cats and dogs – one that is very close to the diet that was eaten by their ancestors in the wild – they will be healthy, strong and fit.

In order to achieve this, a good balance of protein, fats, carbohydrates, vegetables, herbage, organic fibre and water, and sources of natural minerals and vitamins, is essential. Pet food should always be fresh and of high quality, and free-range or organic wherever possible.

Good nutrition is a key part of creating an optimum level of health for our pets, and as every animal is unique in its breed and type it is important that we assess a cat or dog's nutritional needs individually. We are the guardians of the animals that come into our care, and we owe it to them to provide the very best we can afford.

This section of the book is designed to help pet guardians make informed choices about their pets' nutrition, and to show how all the different ways of feeding have an important role to play. Whether you currently feed your pets with food that is home-cooked, raw, dried or canned (or both), no single way of feeding is the *only* way. An animal that eats well can live a long and active life, but one that consumes a poor diet can suffer health complaints.

The more we include natural foods and herbage in our pets' diets, the more they will thrive. They will have increased energy, a shiny coat, bright eyes, and a strong immune system. They will be alert and visibly happy and will enjoy their food more.

'AWARENESS' IS THE KEY TO GOOD PET HEALTH

Today there are numerous major pet health concerns manifesting as food sensitivities and allergies. There are hidden, toxic ingredients in some brands of pet food – including additives, colours, genetically modified substances and preservatives – and these can build up in the bodies of our beloved pets and cause them harm.

Animals that are fed cheap, processed pet foods can develop all sorts of ailments, including skin problems such as eczema, pruritis (itching), constipation, diarrhoea, wind, lethargy, and kidney and immune problems, to name but a few. It is equally important for me in my animal practice to test environmental and topical allergens and assess their impact on pets in today's modern world.

Dr Rohini and I believe that diet is key to an animal's wellness and longevity. Every cell in an animal's body needs fuel, and this comes from food and water, which is converted into energy. More than ever, it is important to create optimum health levels in the body by eating healthy food, and so the nutritional support we give our pets is vital.

Any nutritional improvements you can make to your pet's diet, however small, will enhance their overall health. Even if you are on a tight budget, you can feed some highly nutritious, reasonably priced storecupboard foods – I am going to 'bark' and 'meow' on about these later! In this chapter, I am going to share with you my tried-and-tasted, healthy home-cooked treats and meals, which are easy to prepare and will help supplement your pet's diet.

As a pet guardian with 35 years' experience of feeding my own cats and dogs – and in the last 16 years or so working in private practice with rescued animals, seniors and fussy eaters – I know how difficult it can be to weigh up time, money and the practicalities of introducing new foods to achieve a more natural, healthy diet. I realize, especially, how convenient it is to buy ready-made pet food at the supermarket, along with the rest of the family food shopping.

If you are feeding your pet canned food and biscuits, buy the highest quality you can afford. Economy ranges and supermarket own-brand varieties contain very few natural nutrients because the food is often cooked at a high temperature in order to preserve it for a longer shelf life, often destroying vital vitamins and minerals in the process. The manufacturers then replace these lost nutrients with synthetic and fortified ones.

Animal protein should be sourced from organic or free-range livestock that have had an opportunity to live part of the year outside, and graze freely. Many of the cheaper brands of pet food use factory-farmed animal derivatives that are not even fit for the human food chain. Some of these are contaminated with antibiotics, growth hormones and diseased parts; there is more on this below.

However, you should try not to change your pet's diet radically overnight. It is best to continue with your current feeding programme and slowly cut back on the quantities; this will allow you to introduce new foods bit by bit. It is important to monitor your pet's weight when you are offering new foods, so you can adjust quantities accordingly.

If you are in any doubt, see a veterinarian first, preferably one who practises integrative (conventional and complementary) medicine and specializes in natural food diets. A wide range of chronic conditions in cats and dogs respond favourably to food and nutritional changes.

THE NATURAL DIET FOR CATS AND DOGS

Let us now take a look at how history has shaped the way we feed our pet cats and dogs. At the beginning of the 20th century most domestic cats and dogs ate a near-natural diet. They hunted rabbits and small rodents, scavenged birds' eggs from nests, and were given scraps from their guardian's table – the remains of the Sunday roast, leftover soups and casseroles, bones, and cooked and raw vegetables.

Back then, pet guardians themselves were not eating processed foods; instead, the emphasis was on simple, home-cooked meals made with freshly harvested root vegetables, salads and legumes, and locally reared farm animals. Butchers were only too pleased to donate large meaty bones to locally employed hunting dogs and sight hounds, as well as working farm Border Collies and even smaller breeds such as Jack Russell Terriers and Dachshunds.

These dogs were lean and healthy and mainly earned their keep as working animals in the local community.

Cats too, the respected mice and rat catchers, would linger around the butcher's in the hope of a chicken wing, liver or carcass. With very few cars on the roads, domestic and feral farm cats wandered freely outdoors, day and night, hunting for prey. As natural-born hunters cats have an incredible ability to catch and eat their prey and would dine on rabbits, small birds, bats, voles, mice and rats at their leisure.

What went wrong?

If we fast-forward to the last 50 years or so, we see a takeover of our pets' diet by the pet food industry. After the world-changing events of the Second World War large numbers of people moved from rural communities to live and work in larger towns and cities, and their dogs and cats went with them.

They were valued as companions rather than working animals, and had to adapt to a brand new environment: one in which they could not hunt or self-select their dinner. Sadly, over the years the butcher's shop all but disappeared from our high streets – in part a result of the dominance of a new type of store: the supermarket.

Pet food manufacturers seized the opportunity to offer cheap pet food for the supermarkets to sell, much of it containing meat protein that was unfit for the human food chain. Livestock feed was often bulked out with grain, some of it genetically modified and grown using pesticides and herbicides for a higher yield. Commercial pet food was cooked at high temperatures, and during the process these chemicals turned into toxins that could be absorbed into the bloodstream, having a detrimental effect on all of the body's systems.

Gradually, more and more artificial colours, fats, and countless additives were added to pet food, as well as high levels of salt and sugar to make it palatable. It was also loaded with preservatives to help extend its shelf life. Some canned dog and cat food contained as little as 2 per cent meat, and was largely composed of animal derivatives and cereal. Yet demand grew and grew for ready-made pet food: it was cheap and convenient for guardians to buy and dogs and cats were eating it. Manufacturers responded and the pet food industry became a huge international business.

The winds of change

However, over time, thousands of animals started to become unwell, or even died, for no particular reason, and people started to ask questions about the content of commercial pet food. Animal feed manufacturers were governed by far fewer regulations than those that produced food for human consumption, and were therefore able to focus on quantity rather than quality, but gradually veterinarians and the public started to suspect that this wave of ill health might have something to do with the foods that pets were eating.

The list of ingredients on pet food packaging was often vague and guardians began to demand more clarity on the nutritional value and exact content of the food they were buying. Thankfully, this pressure exposed some of the pet food industry's double standards. In the 1980s a well-known pet food company had to redesign its cat food recipe when cats died after consuming it.

Apparently the product did not contain enough taurine – an amino acid derived from animal protein that cats must eat in order to survive. In this particular brand of cat food the meat content was so low it had to be bulked out with water and cereal, much cheaper components. During the manufacturing process the food was overheated, which damaged and destroyed much of the taurine it contained. Many of the cats that ate this feed eventually died of heart disease, and some were left blind.

More recently, another well-known pet manufacturer actually admitted on prime-time television that it adds red, green and yellow colouring to its dog food pellets – to 'brighten them up'. These artificial colours are not added to enhance a dog's nutrition, but for the benefit of its owners, as the pellets look more attractive in their pet's bowl.

Today, thankfully, the large pet food manufacturers are slowly cleaning up their act, due to public demand for better-quality food. And a small number of independent, family-owned pet food manufacturers who believe our animal companions deserve the equivalent of human-grade food are starting to emerge.

This growing band of ethical and passionate pet food companies are determined to produce high-quality wet and dried food for cats and dogs – made with natural ingredients, few additives and preservatives and no animal derivatives. These products may be more expensive and difficult to source on the high street but I applaud these companies for insisting on using free-range poultry, lamb and rabbit, sourcing the freshest organic vegetables and herbage, and campaigning for better welfare standards for the animals entering the food chain.

But there is still a long, long way to go, and I hope that consumers will continue to put pressure on the leading cheaper brands to improve their ingredients, even if we have to pay more. In the long run it will benefit our pets' health and their lifespan with us.

WHAT TO LOOK FOR IN A COMPLETE DRY AND WET PET FOOD

Shopping for a complete food for your pet can be quite confusing, as even the packaging can be misleading. With clever advertising and choice of words, even the most unappetizing foods can be made to look good. Manufacturers spend millions every year on product placement, and complete foods are competing against each other in a market that is now worth billions.

But often, pet guardians are led to believe they are buying a quality food when in fact most of the product development budget has been spent on getting the product onto supermarket shelves. I think it is a shame that the higher quality and more expensive pet foods – those that contain natural ingredients, clearly and comprehensively displayed on their packaging, as well as having a code of ethics on animal welfare to match – are not even stocked in supermarkets, because the profit margin is too low for the retailer.

Many pet foods are labelled as containing a balanced mix of nutrients, and some cheaper dried food products state they are a 'complete balanced food' and a premium brand. Unfortunately, when you take the food out of the packaging it looks like cardboard and tastes like it. I know this because I have experimented by eating small amounts of it myself! I am interested to see if I can detect certain sugars, salt and flavourings that can be addictive and difficult to wean some cats and dogs away from.

When I read food labels that contain enticing words such as 'natural' and 'healthy', I am immediately seduced and believe that the food will be good for my pets. These labels are always paired with an image of a beautifully healthy cat or dog, smiling out at me. The product's delicious-sounding contents are described as juicy, succulent and irresistible, and they almost have me salivating – just as my dogs do when I offer them a home-made sardine fishcake treat (you can find the recipe for this on page 51).

Marketing is king in the world of pet food – claims such as 'premium brand', 'complete' and 'balanced' are stated loud and clear on the front of nicely designed bags. Some manufacturers go the extra mile and use an expensive shiny metallic finish to the packaging, to emphasis that their product is the gold standard of pet food. It is not until you read the back of the bag and are presented with a minefield of scientific jargon and an incomprehensible list of food compounds that you wonder what is actually *in* the food.

On some food packaging a chemical breakdown of the food is given, but not the actual biological ingredients. So you can see the basic protein, carbohydrate, fat and fibre content, but not whether the product contains chicken, wheat, turkey fat or peas. Or sometimes it is a vague list of ingredients and nothing else. You are none the wiser as to what is actually in this bag of food.

Looking closely at pet food packaging

As I write this chapter I have in front of me a leading brand of complete dried dog food that I recently bought at the supermarket. Here is what the label says, word for word: *Composition: Cereals, meat and animal derivatives (26 per cent meat, 4 per cent beef), various sugars, vegetable protein extracts, oils and fats, minerals. With colourants, antioxidants and preservatives.*

In pre-packaged animal wet and dry foods, the ingredients are listed in descending order, with the largest quantity always shown first. Cereal is first on the list in the food label quoted above, but what percentage is it? Have several different grains been used? Are they genetically modified?

Second on the list is meat and animal derivatives. But what meat is it, exactly, and how is this 26 per cent made up? I am not even sure I know what 'animal derivatives' *means*. Is it animal parts not consumed by humans, like beaks, hooves, feathers, skin and bowels?

Okay, now we come to the 4 per cent beef – but what cut is it? Is it the carcass? It is all too vague. Next up are the 'various sugars'. We do not know which sugars, though, or the percentage of the ingredients they make up.

There are many different sugars used in pet food, among them cane sugar, corn syrup, beet, dextrin, dextrose and so on.

Oils and fats are up next; most of these are by-products collected from various sources, including highly heated corn oils and poultry and beef fat. To prevent these oils turning rancid in the heating process, artificial preservatives are added – despite a growing body of evidence that proves they can be harmful.

Top tip ✍

When you are buying a complete pet food remember to read the label first. In pre-packaged animal wet and dry food, ingredients are listed in descending order, with the largest quantity always shown first.

What is particularly worrying is that we do not know the long-term implications of feeding a complete food. There has not been any in-depth research into the effects of these cheaper processed foods. So if we give it to our pets on average twice a day, for 365 days a year, how will we know what effect it will have on their health?

Dr Rohini and I have examined a lot of wet-food packaging in an attempt to glean what exactly is in the product. We have seen that many brands contain a large percentage of moisture to bulk out the food content. The processors' rationale is simple: water is cheap and easy to source, and so the technique of adding water and additives is applied to a vast array of wet pet foods. Indeed, almost any low-grade, mass-produced processed meat product will have been treated this way.

Plant proteins are cheaper than good quality meat proteins so pet food companies make a higher profit margin through using grains such as soy, wheat and corn. Many of these low-grade grains are not fit for human consumption as they have been sprayed with pesticides to prevent them from going mouldy – they are only used for animal feed.

In any medium-sized UK supermarket you will find eight or more aisles stocked with everything for your household, from food and drink to cleaning materials. On average one aisle is devoted to animal feed – dry and wet food and pet treats. Most supermarkets only stock their own brand of pet food, and the cheaper versions of other brands. It is very rare to find a superior, high-quality pet food or a brand that is wholly organic, unless you are buying online or at a pet store.

On average there is a mark-up of up to 1,000 per cent on own-brand supermarket pet foods. The bottom line for a retail store is sales revenue – space is tight for any supermarket so to devote one eighth of their space to pet food must mean they are making a great deal of money, surely?

I completely understand that it is convenient to buy everything under one roof, including pet food; however, I am uncomfortable with the quality of some of the food being fed to our canine and feline friends, much of which could be detrimental to their health.

Pet food shops and online retailers

As I explained earlier, many of the supermarkets find it hard to stock the more expensive, higher quality pet food brands, due to the very small profit margin they will make on them. But I love the fact that we have choice in this area, and my allegiance lies with the pet food shops – which stock so many more brands.

They will happily order specialized and prescriptive foods for you and often have detailed product factsheets with a breakdown of all the ingredients, whether they are human-grade or not, and the manufacturer's code of ethics.

The more spacious outlets have freezers stocked with frozen complete raw foods, and meat such as minced (ground) beef (handy if you are preparing raw food yourself; more on this later). It is in your interest to know that your pet is being fed a wholesome, ethically derived and nutritious diet and is not eating ingredients that are unfit for human consumption.

It is true that it can be more expensive to feed your pet in this way; however, I value the fact that human-grade ingredients have been sourced and that animal welfare standards have been adhered to. If we as consumers can demonstrate how much this means to the health of our pets, perhaps it will provide enough pressure for the cheaper brands to change their ways for the better.

Top tip ✍

When sourcing high-quality dry food check the order of the ingredients on the label, and the percentages of any named proteins – for example, chicken. It is not good enough for a manufacturer merely to list these as 'animal protein', so write to them to ask for a detailed product factsheet.

SHARING YOUR FOOD KNOWLEDGE WITH YOUR VET

Some conventional vets recommend commercial pet foods because they are led to believe that all dietary needs can be met in a dried biscuit. At most vet schools pet food manufacturers will often sponsor the nutrition seminars and a sales representative will perform a very slick presentation on the pros of offering a complete dried food. They will often claim that it is as good or better than a home-cooked diet, or raw food.

I know this because four of my graduates from the Diploma in Animal Healing at The Healing Animals Organisation are veterinarians and all expressed concern at how little is taught at vet school about real food compounds; they told me that the bias is towards dried food above everything else.

They were delighted to learn so much more about home-cooked diets on my course. I teach that particular vegetables and culinary herbs can be used as part of a balanced diet, and that all animals are unique and have individual tastes and needs – not all 'paws' fit one type of food.

Top tip ✍

When buying prescriptive pet food from your veterinarian, compare the prices with online suppliers, who may be cheaper.

My vet students witnessed the animal guests on the course self-selecting certain culinary herbs, cooked and raw vegetables, animal protein, eggs and plant material and it was an eye-opener for them. But I think what really impressed them was the opportunity to talk with pet guardians face to face. Having been given some new ideas about food the vets loved sharing the simple and quick ways of enhancing an animal's diet – not by making radical changes to it but by adding healthy, real food snacks and meals made from storecupboard ingredients.

An example would be adding a can of sardines – full of omega-3 fatty acids, calcium, iron, potassium, vitamins B12, A, D, E and K6 – a couple of times a week. (Buy these in sunflower oil, tomato sauce or spring water, but steer clear of brine, as it has salt added). Or cutting down on the amount of dried food (especially if it is being fed 365 days a year) and maybe including one or two free-range eggs a week, plus some lightly cooked peas and carrots to increase the amount of roughage.

Some of the guardians were thrilled to have validated their love of preparing a fresh, home-cooked diet for their cats and dogs, and appreciated being encouraged to include free-range chicken, lightly cooked vegetables, cooked organic pulses, basmati rice and a sprinkling of unsalted ground-down nuts as a treat.

At last, these guardians had something in common to discuss with a vet – *real food*. They did not feel intimidated by scientific jargon, just encouraged and empowered as responsible pet guardians who know that nutritious food is the basis of good health for any animal.

Case study: adding real food to a dog's diet

In my practice I see many dogs that are seemingly uninterested in food. On one occasion I had a vet referral to see a beautiful Labradoodle called Boris. Pam, Boris's guardian, was worried her dog was showing signs of lethargy and boredom. He remained in his bed for long periods of time and sometimes seemed uninterested in going for a walk; he also often picked at his food, leaving it until the next day to finish it.

Boris's veterinarian had given him a thorough check over and physically he was fine. But Pam told me she felt Boris had 'lost his joie de vivre'. Boris and Pam came to my clinic, and after a lengthy consultation that explored everything from his medical history and day-to-day life to his canine buddies and other environmental factors, we moved on to the subject of diet.

Pam was feeding Boris a complete dried food, with freeze-dried potato and dried carrot as treats. Sometimes he would have a dog treat – a dry, bone-shaped kibble, primarily made of cereal. Pam was worried that Boris was leaving the dried food uneaten and was upset when one day he raided the waste bin and ate the remains of the Sunday roast chicken carcass: bones and all! She was confused by all the conflicting advice she had read on the internet about what to feed dogs and what not to. In the end, tired and fed up, she stuck with a recommended dry food and dry treats to be on the safe side.

In a food consultation I always have to hand a variety of real foods for pets to self-select. Pam was convinced I would not be able to entice Boris into eating anything. With a dog like Boris, who had been on dried foods for all of his four years, it is important not to change the diet radically and only slowly introduce new foods.

When doing this, each food type needs to be placed in a bowl and offered *one at a time*. Foods should not be mixed together, and likes and dislikes should be noted. (If foods were mixed up, tastes and smells could mask a particular food a pet does not like or need, and we would never know what was working.)

Top tip ✍

Offer new foods on a self-selection basis only: do not mix foods together. Offer individual items on a plate, one at a time, until you feel comfortable that your pet likes them. Then you can mix some of them together, e.g. vegetables.

For Boris I had several ceramic plates containing minute quantities of real food for him to try. First up was a bite-sized piece of cooked organic chicken breast, minus the skin. Boris sniffed the plate and then tucked in to the chicken, looking up at Pam for more. Then followed a sliver of hard-boiled egg (at this early stage raw egg could have upset his tummy).

Pam looked on, astonished, as Boris licked the plate clean. She muttered something about never having tried any of these foods, and how terrible she felt that she had denied Boris the right to eat something real and tasty. I assured her that she did not need to feel guilty, and now was as good a time as any to make some healthy changes.

It suddenly dawned on Pam why Boris had stolen the cooked chicken carcass from the bin. In the wild he would have hunted prey such as rabbits or wildfowl and stolen eggs from birds' nests. Okay, so in the natural world Boris would be eating raw proteins and not cooked, but it was lovely to see Pam witnessing a different perspective – Boris and putting his needs first. She also saw how, as a guardian, she could help give back to Boris some wholesome natural foods to create vitality and wellness.

Boris then wolfed down a small portion of lightly steamed vegetables – two florets of broccoli, a small potato, some diced carrot and a small handful of peas. Suddenly, Pam had a lightbulb moment. She could see a visible difference in Boris's behaviour; he appeared to grow in stature, and became inquisitive and interested in all the tastes and smells as he licked his lips in anticipation of the next tasty morsel. Pam began to think that it might have been the old, boring dried food that had been causing his depression.

By this stage Boris was wagging his tail; his eyes were sparkling with delight and he was alert – suddenly there was something more interesting for him to focus on. He sat bolt upright, patiently observing the various plates and giving Pam a 'what's next?' look. As Boris was eating minute portions of food I decided to continue with the food testing.

The organic chicken breast I had fed him had been poached in water the night before and left to cool. After setting the meat aside, I had tipped the resulting broth into a cup. Chicken broth is of great benefit to cats and dogs as it contains important vitamins and minerals. It is a great comfort to senior animals in particular, and those from rescue centres who need an extra boost of nutrients to support their immune system. I offered Boris a quarter of a cupful of the broth, and he lapped it up and licked the bowl clean.

Top tip ✍

Avoid feeding cooked chicken bones to cats or dogs as they can splinter and cause damage to the oesophagus and the lining of the stomach.

Pam asked me if she could use a cooked chicken carcass to make a broth for Boris. The answer was 'yes' – this is a very economical way of using up any remnants of meat left on the bones, including organs and gristle (the tough, elastic tissue attached to bone). All of this contains vitamin D and calcium, which are important nutrients for pets. Here is how to make the broth:

⚞ Make your own ⚟

Chicken broth for cats and dogs

1. Place a cooked chicken carcass in a large, lidded saucepan and add 550ml (1 pint) of water. Bring to the boil and then turn off the heat and leave to cool, preferably overnight, with the lid on.

2. Remove the chicken carcass and then strain the liquid (broth) into a glass container with a lid. Keep refrigerated and use within three days.

Extras: add vegetables such as carrots, green beans, courgettes (zucchini), potato, broccoli (florets and stalks) to the broth. When cooked, they will soften nicely and add fibre to your pet's diet.

Please note that cold chicken broth should *not* be used as a substitute for water. It is important to have fresh drinking water available at all times.

As I was writing up the food notes for Boris, Pam mentioned that she had noticed he was drinking quite a lot of water at home. I explained that as Boris was eating dried food, which has less moisture, it can increase thirst. In the natural world prey such as rodents and wildfowl are made up of at least 70 per cent water and cats and dogs would reabsorb this liquid through eating them.

Top tip ✍

Pour the chicken broth into ice cube trays and place in the freezer. In the summer months, dogs and cats (especially seniors and those in rehabilitation) can enjoy licking this nutritious, cool snack.

Pam and I discussed the ways in which real food can be incorporated into a dried-food diet. It is important not to cut out dried food entirely, but instead to reduce it by a small amount and replace it with, say, a small handful of fresh-cooked chicken and some lightly steamed vegetables (more if your dog is a large or giant breed). Over a period of weeks, gradually increase the amount of cooked real food and continue decreasing the dried food element. I suggested Pam had a go at making the K9/Feline Nature's Own Hotpot (*see recipe page 51*).

Pam was very eager to get started, but I reminded her that she needed to take things slowly and introduce new foods one at a time, as Boris might experience an upset tummy while he was adjusting to real food. If this happens when you try this food exercise with your pet, do not be alarmed and dismiss the exercise entirely. Just go back to the original diet you were feeding and start again slowly.

I also advised Pam to keep an eye on Boris's faeces while he was undergoing the change in diet: stools can loosen when softer cooked proteins and vegetable matter are eaten, and harden when raw bones are consumed. This is perfectly normal as it takes time for the digestive system to settle into a new routine.

Top tip ✍
Offer dogs both raw and lightly steamed vegetables. Some breeds will ignore raw vegetables and prefer to eat them cooked, and vice versa. Raw vegetables and fruit sometimes appear as undigested matter in a pet's faeces – this is perfectly normal. Include lightly cooked vegetables to add fibre to the diet, and to help the body absorb the raw foods more easily.

For Pam, a whole new world has opened up when it comes to feeding Boris. She has decided to cut back on the quantity of dried food she is feeding and supplement it with natural foods. She admits she does not cook much at home, but when she does she enjoys it. I am thrilled that she is taking this step; she is a busy lady but she feels confident that she will be able to build this into her schedule.

As for Boris, the proof has been in the eating, as he is now self-selecting a variety of new foods offered to him. Pam is also cooking some of my recipes and Boris is happily eating them too. A few weeks after the consultation Pam reported that Boris is a changed dog. He has more energy and enthusiasm, eats with gusto and looks for his lead every day, to go for a walk.

Top tip ✍
Keep a food journal to record which foods your pet eats and when. Include any that are left uneaten. Offer two new foods a couple times a week and increase slowly.

When cats and dogs come to my clinic for a consultation and they self-select a range of my home-cooked foods and treats, I also like to find out what kind of foods guardians are eating. This will determine how far they are willing to go when it comes to adding real foods to their pets' diet. We all lead busy lives, and what we are prepared to do has to fit in with our lifestyle.

STORECUPBOARD SUPERFOODS FOR PETS

When it comes to buying food and other items for my household, I shop at the supermarket like everyone else – I buy organic fruit and vegetables from there, along with grains, herbs, spices and so on. What I particularly like about food shopping today is that I can also purchase many of the 'storecupboard superfoods' I use to supplement my pets' diet. For example, I buy cans of own-brand sardines in sunflower oil, free-range eggs, basmati rice, frozen peas, beautiful bunches of organic carrots, sweet potatoes and courgettes (zucchini).

These days it is becoming expensive to feed ourselves, let alone our pets, but introducing some of these superfoods and my home-made meals and treats (*see the recipes in Chapters 2 and 3*) to your pet's diet can help you reduce your overall pet food bill. In my household there is a menagerie of animals to feed, and I want them to have the very best food I can afford. I may not buy an own-brand complete food from my supermarket, but I thank them for stocking natural foods I can use to feed both myself and my pets.

The superfoods shopping checklist

I love preparing and cooking the freshest ingredients I can lay my hands on, creating tasty meals that are wholesome, nutritious and economical. My animals have to fit in with my lifestyle, as I am not going to spend every waking hour making pet food. Equally I am not going to palm them off by giving them a commercial complete food twice a day when I know they will benefit from all the goodness contained in real food.

So I have devised a food plan that enables me to prepare and cook for myself and for my pets at the same time. While you are shopping for yourself and your family, use the following checklist to stock up on healthy food items to make pet meals and treats:

⇨ *At the supermarket*

- Fresh vegetables such as carrots, broccoli, green beans, Brussels sprouts, courgettes (zucchini), sweet potatoes, butternut squash, spinach.

- Free-range eggs.

- Free-range chicken.

- Minced (ground) beef and lamb.

- Fresh fish such as cod, salmon, mackerel.

- Canned fish such as sardines and mackerel (buy these in sunflower oil, tomato sauce or spring water, but steer clear of brine as it has added salt).

- Basmati rice, pulses.

- Organic plain yoghurt.

- Natural, unsalted nuts and seeds. Walnuts, almonds, pecans, hazelnuts, and sunflower and pumpkin seeds will need to be ground with a pestle and mortar before being added to food.
- Frozen foods such as peas, prawns and fish.

⇨ *At your local butcher*

I buy free-range meat from my butcher (who also gives me free of charge the chicken carcasses I use to make the broth recipe on page 15). Ask your butcher if you can have any unwanted fresh chicken carcasses. My three dogs – a large Boxer cross Bull Mastiff, a Norfolk Terrier cross and a Border Terrier cross – are fed raw free-range chicken wings and thighs, chicken breast and leg meat and venison; they also chew on large, raw, meaty lamb bones, which are a good source of calcium and help keep their teeth clean.

Top tip ✍
Avoid feeding cooked animal skin or trimmed fat, and crusts of bread or pizza – all of which have no nutritional value.

I supplement the meat element with my chicken broth – see recipe on page 15. I make a big pot twice a week, throwing in a range of seasonal vegetables and a handful or two of basmati rice. All the goodness is sealed into the broth, which lives in a large glass container with a Tupperware lid in the fridge for up to three days – or I freeze it in smaller containers and use it as and when I need it.

In the summer months my dogs sometimes have lightly cooked chicken, beef, salmon and trout, as when the weather is hot raw food may go off more quickly. When I am busy I supplement this with smaller quantities of canned fish such as pilchards, sardines or tuna in sunflower oil, which contain omega fatty acids noted for their anti-inflammatory properties. I also offer them my home-made herb-infused oils (*see recipe page 50*).

Top tip ✍
Forty per cent of a dog's diet should be free-range or organic meat and fish and the remaining 60 per cent should be made up of vegetables – lightly cooked and raw – grains, unsalted ground-down nuts and seeds, and fruit.

My dogs are companion animals and do not work for a living like their ancestors did a few hundred years ago, so I go easy on feeding them organ meat. For centuries, kidney, liver, heart, tripe, etc., were the main protein source for most working dogs and all are well-known 'heating' foods that give the body an extra boost of energy and nutrients. But with many of our pooches leading a more sedate lifestyle these days I recommend a small quantity of organ meat just once a week.

A couple of times a week my dogs love to have a free-range egg or two. One of them, Lily, has a sensitive tummy and she prefers her eggs hard-boiled or scrambled; the other two love to eat them raw. Take a look at my egg recipes on pages 44–46.

Top tip ✍

Feed dogs twice a day. Many dogs can become overweight if fed once a day as the body's metabolic rate can slow down to compensate for the lack of food.

Twice a month I bake a large batch of tasty and nutritious dog treats. They take just 35 minutes to prepare and cook, and can be cut into squares and frozen. There is a range of recipes for you to choose from in Chapter 2. These healthy snacks are a great training aid for positive reinforcement work, too. You can also try treats such as raw whole carrots, pieces of apple and banana, blackberries, blueberries, raspberries and ground-down nuts and seeds.

From time to time I feed my Woof Berry and Yoghurt treats (*see recipe, page 54*), which consist of natural organic yoghurt, blackberries and mashed ripe banana: live natural yoghurt helps restore the gut's natural flora and is great during and after a course of antibiotics.

FOOD ALLERGIES

Dr Rohini and I see a number of dogs and cats that may be suffering from sensitivities to certain foods. Quite often pets have been eating a particular type of food for a very long time and some of the biological compounds they contain can overload the body. For example, the high percentage of grain cereals in foods, along with a lack of high-quality animal protein and sufficient amino acids from animal sources, are factors in the increase in skin problems.

Many pet foods contain a high proportion of cereal, which is used to bulk it out, hence the increase in food allergies in some breeds.

Food allergies are simply defined as an immune system reaction caused by the ingestion of particular food substances. They can cause a wide range of symptoms in animals, and veterinary experts estimate that 15 per cent of all allergic skin disease in dogs and cats may be caused by food hypersensitivity.

This hypersensitivity appears to be the second most common cause of pruritis (itchy skin) skin disease in cats and the third most common cause in dogs. There does not appear to be any sex or breed predisposition, although in my practice I see a lot of German Shepherd Dogs and West Highland Terriers with food allergies.

Food allergies do not just affect the skin – they can also affect the gastrointestinal system and occasionally the nervous system. Typical skin symptoms include severe pruritis, hair loss, redness, skin infections and ear infections. Gastrointestinal signs include vomiting, diarrhoea (sometimes bloody) and straining and increased frequency of bowel movements. Rarely, seizures have been associated with food hypersensitivity. Food allergies have also been associated with hyperactivity, depression, irritability, arthritis and joint pain, asthma, chronic bronchitis, hypoglycaemia and sinusitis.

How to detect food allergies

If your pet has any of the above symptoms, and you think they could be food-related, check with your veterinarian first. Sometimes you can figure it out just by doing a bit of simple detective work. Check when the itching or other symptoms began to show up. Was it right after you changed your dog or cat foods? Go back to feeding the former food and if the symptoms clear up, you have your answer.

Food trials are the easiest way to figure out food allergies. I usually recommend a food elimination diet in the first instance. To do this, limit your pet to one protein source and one carbohydrate source to which they have previously had little or no exposure. For example, if your pet is on a basic dog or cat food that contains wheat, cereal and beef as its main ingredients you may want to choose either a home-made diet of fish and rice (a higher ratio of protein) or one of the prepared hypoallergenic diets of fish and rice.

One has to be patient as it can take many months to see a change: there have been reports of food elimination trials in which symptoms took six months to improve. In my practice, though, I usually see improvements within a fortnight. Once you have realized that your pet is sensitive to a particular pet food, it is then important to know which food is causing the allergy. Is it the carbohydrate source – such as wheat or cereal – or the protein source such as beef, chicken or fish? Or could it be something else, like flavourings, preservatives or artificial colours? All of these are possible culprits.

You can simply add one food source back in at a time, which is commonly known as a food provocation trial. For instance, if you add back wheat and the symptoms reoccur, you know that wheat is the offending allergen. The most common food allergens for pets include beef, chicken, pork, wheat, corn, soya beans, eggs and dairy products. (These foods are usually very cheap cuts of meat and dairy products packed with antibiotics that have suppressed the animal's immune system.)

If you prefer to feed branded pet food, experiment by changing over to a different brand, keeping a note of all the different ingredients and chemicals that are in the product. Some people choose to cook a home-made diet for their pet and detect individual foods to which they are allergic. A recipe that has been very successful for some of my clients, and one you can try, is the K9/Feline Nature's Own Hotpot (*page 51; please use only one protein source at a time – i.e. chicken – in the hotpot*).

Also be aware that certain toys and snacks, such as bones or other chews, may contain offending substances as well, and therefore need to be removed during food elimination trials. There are blood tests available for food allergies, but there is still some controversy about how reliable these actually are. Food allergies can also mimic other diseases, including other allergies such as inhalant or contact allergies and flea allergies, as well as parasitic infections.

Top tip ✍

Replace plastic feed and water bowls with ceramic or stainless steel ones, as harmful chemicals can leach from plastics into the drinking water and food our pets consume.

NUTRITION AND DIET FOR DOGS

Dogs are omnivores, with the balance towards being carnivore – in the wild dogs eat meat. When we go back in time and consider the diet of the ancestor of all dogs today – the wolf – we see that they ate deer, wildfowl and rabbit carcasses. This food provided everything the wolf needed to survive, including pre-digested vegetable matter found in the digestive tracts of their prey.

As carnivores, dogs have sharp and jagged teeth that are designed for tearing and ripping up meat. They also have a short and simple digestive tract that allows them easily to digest animal protein and fat and their stomach also contains strong hydrochloric acid, which can break down harmful bacteria and help it to fully digest animal proteins, bones and fat.

Many people ask me about feeding a raw food diet to dogs and I explain that it really depends on the individual animal and whether you as the guardian can commit to preparing the food yourself or buying it pre-prepared and ready to feed. A raw diet may not suit all dogs, as each animal is unique and has individual needs.

The BARF diet

One particular raw feeding practice that has become popular in recent years is the BARF diet (Biologically Appropriate Raw Food). BARF is a phrase coined in 1993 by the Australian veterinary surgeon Ian Billinghurst, who proposed that pet dogs could eat a raw food diet including bones and raw vegetable matter.

The BARF diet is based on the belief that carnivores do not just need to eat meat (in fact, this could potentially be unhealthy, as meat alone does not provide all the vitamins and minerals required). In the wild an animal eats all of its prey, including the organs, muscle meat, bone cartilage and stomach contents. Wild dogs may eat birds' eggs, berries, herbs and grasses too, and consume plant material to self-medicate.

The BARF diet can be fed to dogs in a number of ways. The purest form is to feed the whole, or part, of an animal – for example an entire chicken. However today it is more convenient for the pet guardian to buy chicken wings, legs and breast meat from the butcher's or a supermarket. One of the advantages of this way of feeding is that it is ideal for keeping a dog's teeth clean: chewing meat, sinew and bone provides a natural 'floss' for teeth and gums.

If you decide to prepare a raw food diet yourself, vegetable matter can be included to create a balance (see the vegetables listed in the shopping checklist above). Including vegetables in the diet replicates the way in which a wild dog will eat the stomach contents of its prey. You can source raw food in several ways. You can buy meat from your local butcher or, if you do not like the idea of preparing raw meat yourself, or time is a constraint, you can buy frozen, pre-prepared BARF food from specialist suppliers.

There are many online suppliers offering pet foods based on the BARF diet, including www.naturesmenu.co.uk and in the USA, www.bravopetfoods.com and www.primalpetfoods.com. These foods usually come in blocks containing minced (ground) meat that includes bone and cartilage, vegetables and herbage. If you choose to feed these BARF blocks, include some raw meaty bones in the weekly feeding regime, to keep your dog's teeth and gums clean and healthy.

You can also buy minced (ground) raw meat from pet stores such as Pets at Home in the UK (www.petsathome.com) and www.primalpetfoods.com in the USA. Always buy the best quality food that you can afford and ideally where you know the provenance. Suppliers of good quality meat will be very happy to share their sources with you.

Supplementing a raw diet

There are many nutritional supplements that can be added to a raw diet. However there are two that are commonly believed to be the most important – fish oils such as salmon or krill, and cold-pressed linseed oil (*see page 76*).

Fish oils and cold-pressed linseed oil are a good source of omega-3 fatty acids and vitamin E, which have been shown to help boost the immune system, control inflammation, help prevent heart disease and be beneficial in the treatment of cancer, arthritis and renal disease. Dosage depends on the size of your dog – offer 1 teaspoon a day to small breeds, 2 teaspoons to medium breeds and 3 teaspoons to large breeds.

Raw food preparation and hygiene

You will need to make a number of preparations before transferring your dog (or cat) to a raw diet. You will need to buy good-quality storage containers in which to keep your food, and a freezer. A good antibacterial chopping board is essential, as are a meat cleaver (to break up the BARF blocks) or a meat food processor.

Hygiene is an important aspect of raw feeding and food preparation areas should be kept spotlessly clean. Storage containers and bowls must be washed thoroughly after each feed. Even meat intended for human consumption can still carry bacteria, so it is advisable to wash hands and utensils after handling raw meat. Do not refreeze food once it has been defrosted.

CASE STUDY: THE BARF DIET IN PRACTICE

One of my Diploma in Animal Healing students, Lynne, decided to switch the diet of her dog, Millie, from a dried one to a BARF. Here, she tells us how she got on:

'There are several schools of thought about the best way to transfer your dog from a prepared food diet to a raw one. They range from going "cold turkey" and changing the food overnight, to a steady introduction over a week or so, gradually changing the percentage of one style of feed (dried food, say) to another, such as a home-cooked diet. The latter is the route I chose to take with Millie, who suffered no adverse effects (she does, however, have the constitution of an ox!)

'The most common advice is to feed around 2 to 3 per cent of your dog's body weight daily, divided into two meals. However, all dogs are different – they take varying amounts of exercise and have different metabolic rates – so this percentage is just a guide. See the table below for guidelines.'

Raw, BARF-prepared food feeding guidelines	
Dog's weight	Amount of food
11kg (25lb)	225–350g (8–12oz) daily, or two meals of 115–175g (4–6oz)
22kg (50lb)	450–675g (1–1½lb) daily, or two meals of 225–350g (8–12oz)
34kg (75lb)	680–900g (1½–2lb) daily, or two meals of 350–450g (12–16oz)
45kg (100lb)	900g–1.3kg (2–3lb) daily, or two meals of 450–675g (1–1½lb)

'I started off by feeding Millie 450g (1lb) of meat a day, split into two feeds; however she soon started to gain weight, so I reduced the ration to 280g (10oz).

She is currently on 225g (8oz) of meat a day (half the amount I fed her at the outset).'

Millie's BARF menu		
	Breakfast	Supper
Monday	Free-range egg	Chicken wings
Tuesday	Minced (ground) beef	Chicken backs
Wednesday	Free-range egg	Turkey necks
Thursday	Minced (ground) lamb	Pigs' trotters
Friday	Free-range egg	Chicken wings
Saturday	Minced (ground) beef	Lamb breast bones
Sunday	Free-range egg	Chicken backs
Note: as with any kind of feeding, fresh water should always be available.		

'I feed Millie the BARF-prepared food and then give her raw, meaty bones twice a week, primarily to clean her teeth. I feed marrow bones and rib bones, and I have just introduced lamb neck bones. I tried chicken wings, too, but she did not get as excited by them as she did the minced (ground) meat, and she also regurgitated them on a number of occasions. I think she ate them too quickly and did not chew them properly.

'Millie has been on the BARF diet for a number of months now and is thriving. She loves the food (no more lying there and just looking at the bowl). She looks fabulously well, too: her body shape has changed; she has got great muscle tone, and is "solid" but not at all fat. Her teeth have greatly improved, and her coat is beautifully soft.

'I was feeding her a quality dry food before the change, so I have not noticed a significant difference in the size of her faeces (which is often a pleasant side effect of the change). However, I have noticed that she drinks less water than she used to.

'Changing to a BARF diet is a little daunting at first – especially handling raw meat (not great if you are a vegetarian). You need to have the belief that you are doing the right thing and that you are feeding your dog a balanced and nutritious diet. It can also be a little frightening if you are not used to feeding your dog bones, especially if they vomit them back up on occasion.

'However, I would encourage anyone to change to a raw diet. It is feeding your dog as nature intended; it keeps their teeth clean, their immune system strong. For those dogs that suffer allergies associated with eating prepared food, it is a simple way to restore them to full health – there are no additives and preservatives in this diet.'

ENVIRONMENTAL, MENTAL AND EMOTIONAL WELLBEING FOR DOGS

Today, the vast majority of our canine companions live with us in the home (just a small minority of working dogs live in outdoor kennels). In the wild dogs such as wolves look after themselves in a pack – sleeping, hunting and eating together – but our domesticated dogs rely on us for food, shelter, exercise and companionship. It is our responsibility, therefore, to make sure our dogs have everything they need to lead a full and happy life.

My three dogs are part of my family and we welcome the fact that they have always chosen to share our living space. Most of the time they live in a spacious kitchen that is warm, sunny and well ventilated, with non-slip stone tile flooring throughout. They have an assortment of beds, each topped with a 100 per cent cotton duvet cover – these are easier to keep clean and less itchy than synthetic ones, and insects find it difficult to make a home in them.

For most of the day the dogs have access to a large, well-fenced garden covered with grass, shrubs, trees, a vegetable patch and herb gardens, and there is a stone patio where they can explore, play and sunbathe when it is warm and sunny. They have a regular daily routine of exercise, play and walks with me, or my husband when I am abroad working with animals.

Our dogs love to be with us as much as we love to be with them, and they even come away with us when we holiday in the UK. During the week they interact with my clients and their dogs, which enables them to stay socially active.

Not all dogs have had the best start in life. My three are all rescue animals who had issues of abandonment, physical and mental abuse, fear of traffic noise and agoraphobia. Over a period time, through dedication and commitment, we have aided their rehabilitation using healing, herbs, diet and positive-reward dog training.

If you are encountering any difficulties with your dog I thoroughly recommend you read Dr Rohini's *A–Z Common Conditions* chapter, which details many of the problems experienced by dogs, including aggression, anxiety, depression, fears and phobias. Your first port of call, though, is always your vet, who will thoroughly check over your pet and rule out any physical conditions.

I would now like to share with you a few of my favourite tips for keeping your dog physically, mentally and emotionally fit: these have helped the hundreds of dogs I have treated at my clinic or in their homes.

Lifestyle tips for dogs

- Keep to a routine: feed your dog twice a day and give at least one good walk daily. If more than one person in the household is training the dog, everyone needs to be singing from the same song sheet or your dog will become confused.

- Positive-reward dog training uses praise and rewards to see what motivates your dog into correctly following a command. (Offering one of my healthy dog biscuits can be really useful in one-on-one reward training (*see recipes in Chapter 2*).

- Offer a natural treat once in a while: a 100 per cent deer-antler dog chew (ethically sourced) is unprocessed, has no smell and is a great teeth cleaner. It will keep your dog amused for hours.

- Buy a Kong rubber dog toy, which is designed to be filled with your pet's favourite healthy treats. Many of my clients make my Woof Berry and Yoghurt dog treats (*see page 54*) Liver Cake K9 bake (*page 52*) or any of the dog biscuits featured in Chapter 2 for use with this toy. I recommend the medium or large Kong as dogs find it hard to lick the inside of the small version. The toys are available in the UK from leading pet shops and amazon.co.uk and in the USA from www.amazon.com.

- Dogs are social animals and they love to engage in the daily household activities and interact with us. If your dog(s) live inside, place comfy beds close to regular guardian activity, like the heart of the kitchen. Dogs that are isolated or shut away for long periods of time will develop insecurities, depression and behavioural issues.

- Invest in an orthopaedic or memory foam bed: seniors with joint problems, stiffness or muscular problems will find this invaluable. Although they are quite expensive, it is worth it in the long run for your pet's comfort and wellbeing. The beds are available in the UK from leading pet shops, www.amazon.co.uk and www.petsathome.com and in the USA from www.amazon.com and www.k9ballistics.com.

- Larger breeds of dog and seniors suffering from stiffness, arthritis and hip dysplasia really benefit from a ramp to get in and out of a vehicle. Source one that is anti-slip and preferably coated with rubber matting (many of my clients struggle to lift their dogs and consequently hurt themselves). Dog ramps are available in the UK from www.petplanet.co.uk and www.petsathome.com and in the USA from www.amazon.com and www.drsfostersmith.com.

- Fresh, plain water must be available at all times. If you ever have to add anything to water, such as remedies or medication, always offer it in a separate bowl so your pet can choose.

- Position comfortable bedding inside the house, near a window, so dogs can lie on it in full sunlight if they so wish, and absorb natural vitamin D from the sun's rays. Always have other bedding available if they want to retire elsewhere, especially when it is hot. If the weather is sunny and you have a secure garden place bedding outside, too, so your dog can relax in the sunlight; make sure there is a shaded area he or she can retire to.

- If you have laminate flooring, place rugs or runners on it, to encourage dogs to walk with ease. Dogs can become unsteady and slip on uncovered laminate flooring, leading to uncertainty and a lack of confidence.

- Have a CD of soft, relaxing music or a classical music radio station playing while you are out of the house. Alternatively, leave the TV on at a low volume. Many dogs love to watch TV, and some eventually doze off, just like us!

- Whatever the size of your garden, allow your dog to have access to sensory stimulation. Plant culinary herbs (in preparation for making some of the lovely pet treats featured in Chapters 2 and 3). Dogs have millions of smell receptors and love to spend time sniffing the air, the ground and the plants around them. Allow grasses like couch grass, or long blades of grass turf, to grow so dogs can chew on these and absorb the nutritional and health properties of chlorophyll in the tips of the plant.

- Plant a small rose bush with budding blooms – dogs love to smell the aroma of roses as it is relaxing and calming.

- Some dogs that live alone with a guardian can benefit from the presence of a canine friend in the household: they can provide friendship, confidence and comfort to each other. If it is not feasible to have another dog, some dogs enjoy the company of a cat. Read Chapter 11: *Give a Pet a Home*, as many rescue centres will have established whether or not a particular dog can live with another dog or cat.

NUTRITION AND DIET FOR CATS

Cats are obligate carnivores, which means they *must* eat meat as part of their overall diet. There are two main nutrients that cats need to survive – taurine and arachidonic acid – and these are found only in animal tissue. Taurine is an essential amino acid and arachidonic acid is an essential fatty acid; both are found in high quantities in meat and are practically non-existent in plant-based foods.

Cats require these food compounds in order to function properly. Taurine and arachidonic acid provide energy and are vital for growth and development; they are essential for healthy eyes and a fully functioning heart, producing new antibodies, hormones and tissues and helping form bile salts that aid the digestion of fats.

Taurine is found in animal flesh such as chicken, turkey, wildfowl, rabbit, lamb and beef, and to a lesser degree in fish and eggs. Even feral cats that live outdoors are not able to make taurine themselves, and need to source it from the prey they catch, such as mice, rats, other small rodents, rabbits, insects and small reptiles.

Top tip ✍

Another source of taurine is organ meat such as heart, liver and kidney. Feed this in small amounts, varying it weekly. Offer it raw or lightly poached in water (retain the liquid broth and offer that separately).

Cats are very different from dogs and must never be fed wet or dried dog food as it does not contain the level of protein they require. Nor must they have a vegetarian or vegan diet, as they will become very deficient in taurine, which could lead to blindness and death. In some cases cats existing on the cheaper processed brands of cat food exhibit signs of depression, lethargy, shortness of breath, a dull coat and a compromised immune system.

Top tip ✍

A few high-quality wet and dried food manufacturers offer high meat content in their products and a precise listing of natural ingredients. In the UK, try Lily's Kitchen, Applaws, Nature Diet, Nature Menu and Orijen. In the USA, try Taste of the Wild, Blue Buffalo, Orijen, Halo, Honest Kitchen, Canine Caviar and EVO Wild Craving.

In the wild cats hunt mice, small birds and rabbits, and will eat the stomach contents of their prey. I have witnessed my own cat, Rosie, hunting for food in a nearby field. She once killed a rabbit and dragged it back to our home before eating it whole, including the meat, the carcass, the liver, heart and muscle and bones. She even ate the stomach contents, which were full of natural fibre and roughage, including partially digested grasses, herbage, seeds, fruit and grains.

I felt terribly sad for this dear rabbit, but in the wild cats hunt for prey every day to survive; nature has provided everything a cat requires in its diet to stay healthy and alive. Some domestic and feral cats will even forage for fruit and nuts, and steal eggs from nesting birds to eat.

Top tip ✍

Sixty per cent of a cat's diet should be free-range or organic meat and fish, and the remaining 40 per cent should be made up of vegetables – lightly steamed or boiled (and/ or pureed raw) – plus seeds and nuts ground to a powder. Some breeds will ignore raw vegetables and prefer to eat them cooked, and vice versa.

Some cats love a varied diet and wherever possible it is good to offer foods that they can self-select. As cats can be fussy eaters, it is good to vary the types of food you offer, and experiment with different preparation techniques. Try lightly cooked and/or pureed raw vegetables, fruit, grains (cooked brown rice and pulses), nuts (ground down to powder), and eggs (lightly scrambled, hard-boiled or raw) a couple of times a week – some cats like the egg yolk and white blended together.

You could also try a probiotic like live, plain yoghurt to help the gut flora: this is great during and after a course of antibiotics, which destroy both harmful and beneficial bacteria in the gut. Always offer your cat fresh water. If you are worried about the quality of your tap water, offer filtered or natural mineral water.

Top tip ✍

When giving prescriptive pills to cats that are suspicious of medicine, try wrapping them in a small amount of Dairylea soft processed cheese, available in the UK (or Velveeta in the USA). Cats seem to love this cheese and tend not to spit out the secret medicine concealed within it!

The importance of Vitamin D

All animals need sunlight to manufacture vitamin D, including us. Today, many indoor pets do not receive enough sunlight to create the vitamin D they need for healthy bones and a strong immune system. I have encountered hundreds of cats at rescue centres and on home visits and observed that, when the sun is shining brightly, they always try to find a spot near a window to absorb its rays. Many of the cats I treat at rescue centres position themselves in the sun when I give healing to them.

I teach animal healing in Japan and in the capital city, Tokyo, many cats live in high-rise apartment blocks. It is crucial that these cats, and other housebound cats around the world, have access to large, sun-facing windows, ideally without coverings, so they get the benefit of the sunlight that penetrates the room during the day. I have observed how many cats will follow the sun's rays from window to window, thus giving themselves the option of sitting in full sunlight or not.

Top tip ✍

A sun-facing window is essential for creating the *purrfect* suntrap for house cats. Position furniture so cats can access the sun more readily if they need to climb onto a table, sofa or window ledge.

Adding natural food to your cat's diet

If you are feeding your cat a complete wet or dried food (or both), why not offer some nutritious natural foods too? You will be amazed at how much your cat enjoys trying something new. Very gradually, introduce some home-cooked (or raw) foods, and decrease the amount of processed foods – take it slowly and be patient with your cat's food choices.

Top tip ✍

Some cats like to eat pureed vegetable matter. Put lightly cooked vegetables, along with a little of the cooking water, in a blender and liquidize. Pureed vegetables are great for all cats, including seniors that have had teeth removed, fussy eaters or those recovering from surgery.

I will never forget the time I gave Oliver, my beautiful long-haired cat, a permanent home. The staff at the local RSPCA rescue centre, where he had been living for over a year, told me he loved sachet wet food and dry food twice a day, so I had my work cut out with his diet, as I was keen to offer him my home-cooked and raw recipes. I had to take a step back and assess Oliver's needs at that moment. He had to be introduced to new foods one at a time, so I slowly decreased the quantity of his wet and dry food.

When he first came to me, Oliver was obsessed with a leading brand of wet food that was full of sugar, preservatives and animal derivatives. I coined the phrase 'McDonald's cat', to describe him, because it was obvious he had spent a lifetime eating mainly processed food. This became even more evident when the vet showed me the tartar that had built up on his teeth – canned soft foods can stick to teeth and cause plaque.

Top tip ✍

Adding some of my chicken broth (*see page 15*) or the K9/Feline Nature's Own Hotpot (*page 51*) to the complete wet or dried food you are currently feeding your cat may help entice them to eat more natural foods.

If cats have been brought up from a young age to eat dry or wet foods they will be more wary about trying new foods offered to them. Quite often, natural foods may have to be disguised and added to some of their usual food in order for them to trust it.

Usually, doing this goes against the grain for me, as I believe animals should be able to self-select natural foods when we offer them. However, every cat is different and Oliver certainly showed me that. It took me almost a year to wean him off a highly processed diet and onto a healthy, balanced diet of home-cooked and raw foods, supplemented by a quality sachet and dried food.

But as I have explained, each cat is individual, and many of my clients worry about how fickle their cats are with food. Oliver was incredibly fussy, yet he was always interested in everything I put in front of him. Even if he sampled a mouthful and left the rest I always observed his likes and dislikes. He has been my greatest teacher in the importance of perseverance – sometimes I would think he did not like a particular food, but he would amaze me by coming back to it a couple of weeks later and eating it.

Top tip ✍

Cats can be very fussy in their eating habits and it takes perseverance and patience from the guardian. Do not dismiss a food such as lightly cooked chicken if your cat initially shows no interest in it. Offer it again another week. Or try serving it differently: tearing it up into small strips rather than dicing it into chunks, say, or maybe pouring over a little chicken broth to make it more appetizing.

Storecupboard superfoods for cats

Some of my clients do not want to handle raw or cooked animal protein; however they *are* keen to offer some natural storecupboard superfoods to help supplement the complete dry and wet food they are feeding their cat.

Most cats like to eat canned fish, such as sardines, mackerel or tuna. Buy these in sunflower oil, tomato sauce or spring water, rather than brine, which has salt added. Vary which type you feed, and offer small amounts, starting off with 1 teaspoon per feed time. Decant the contents of the can into a glass container with a close-fitting lid and keep it in the fridge. Use within three days.

Again, when you are introducing new foods, slowly decrease the amount of dried food you are feeding to balance out the diet. One economical, nutritious and tasty dish is my sardine fishcakes (*see recipe page 51*). Most cats I know adore this special treat.

Top tip ✍

When feeding prawns as a snack or treat, source wild prawns from the North Atlantic, and avoid the large farmed prawns from the Far East, which contain antibiotics and preservatives. Defrost frozen prawns at room temperature and wash before feeding.

Feeding dried food

Many clients come to me with concerns about feeding their cat a diet that is made up entirely of dried food. This kind of diet can sometimes be problematic, and there have been cases of kidney- and bladder-related conditions. Always speak to your veterinarian before going ahead, or get a second opinion from a holistic veterinarian specializing in natural food diets for cats.

I would always have a good-quality wet food available in a separate feeding bowl, to increase moisture content (mammals are composed of around 70 per cent water, including the prey cats would hunt in the wild). I would also have my chicken broth on hand (*see recipe page 15*), and plenty of fresh, filtered water in a separate bowl. Or I would recommend making a slow switch to a raw food diet.

Top tip ✍

Supplement your cat's diet by offering small amounts of my herb-infused food oils (*see page 50*). Cats love to self-select catmint, marigold, rosehip and chickweed.

Feeding real wet food

Pet guardians are becomingly increasingly aware of the importance of high-quality wet food in satisfying their cat's nutritional needs. When they make the switch to a higher-quality brand, though, some find their cats can become really fussy and refuse to eat it. A small band of manufacturers have been seriously listening to guardians and holistic vets and have come up with a 'halfway house' quality food to help cats make the transition from processed foods.

This food consists of lightly steamed meat and vegetables sealed in a pouch. It contains a minimum of 70 per cent real meat and is sugar free – processed foods typically contain 4 per cent real meat and are loaded with sugars. Have a look at www.naturesmenu.co.uk or www.primalpetfoods.com.

RAW FOOD FOR CATS

There are also companies who supply complete and balanced raw cat food. This usually comes in frozen blocks containing smaller, ready-made cubes that are easier to serve. The cubes contain minced (ground) meat – which includes bone and cartilage, vegetables and herbage – and are extremely handy if you do not like preparing raw food yourself, or have limited time available.

One particular manufacturer claims to use human-grade meat from ethically assured farms. The meat contains sufficient natural taurine, so it is not necessary to add a synthetic version back in – as is done with cheaper brands of cat food. The food is not processed, either, other than to mix the ingredients together and shape them into more manageable cubes, and it is subjected to safety bacteria tests before it leaves the factory. See www.naturesmenu.co.uk and in the USA, www.bravopetfoods.com and www.primalpetfoods.com.

If you do decide to feed these blocks you may like to include some raw chicken wings in the weekly feeding programme – to keep your cat's teeth and gums clean and healthy. Some of the feedback I have received from guardians who are feeding a raw diet to their cats reveals that they have observed calmer behaviour, improved appetite, better muscle tone and a reduction in ailments such as skin inflammation, digestive issues and urinary tract infections.

Top tip ✍

Cats who can be weaned off wet food and onto raw make a better transition than those who go from dry food to raw.

If you are feeding a combination of dried and wet food, add a little of my chicken broth to the dried and slowly increase the lightly cooked cubes mentioned above. There may be periods when your cat will switch back to eating dry for a while, and then seek out what you are eating!

MENTAL, EMOTIONAL AND ENVIRONMENTAL WELLBEING FOR CATS

There are some cats that live indoors 24/7 and are totally reliant on their guardians to service their nutritional and environmental needs. We would all love our cats to roam freely outside, and the majority of them do, but some cannot.

Like us, most of our pets, both dogs and cats, are living a full and long life. Older cats – who I like to refer to as 'seniors' – get to a time in their lives when they prefer to stay cosy and warm inside. If they have developed age-related conditions such as failing eyesight, depression or arthritis, they may feel vulnerable and find it hard to get around.

In fact, cats in any age group can find themselves housebound. Some are unable to go outside because they live in high-rise apartment blocks. Others live near busy main roads and could easily get knocked over and killed. Some cats *can* go outside but choose not to, while others do not like other cats visiting their garden and invading their territory and so prefer to stay indoors. There are also cats that are naturally scared of the outside world, as they have been brought up from birth to remain indoors and have never had an opportunity to go outside.

Whether cats are able to roam freely outside or not it is vital we bring some of the natural world *inside* to help them feel content and happy, and not stressed or anxious because they cannot go out. It is important that we do not deny our pets positive stimulation: they are entitled to this, as in the wild they would be nourishing themselves by self-selecting plant material, play hunting and exploring the outdoors.

ENVIRONMENTAL ENRICHMENT TIPS FOR CATS

I would like to share with you a few of my favourite tips for keeping your cat physically, mentally and emotionally fit: these have helped the hundreds of cats I have treated at my clinic or at their homes. Now I am going to be honest with you, some of the ideas below can be a bit messy for your home, but the benefits to your cat will be huge, and they will thank you big time!

- Natural, unsprayed fallen tree trunks and large branches from a wood or forest make excellent scratching posts; have a few dotted about the house.

- Make a catnip or valerian cat toy (*see pages 64 and 89 for instructions*).

- Have edible plants dotted around the home, including catnip and wheatgrass.

- Buy a 1m² roll (24in wide × 64.5in long) of grass turf from a good garden centre and place it in a deep-sided tray. Position near a window to absorb sunlight, and keep it watered. Cats love to roll on the grass, sit in it and even eat it.

- Create a 'cat snuggle space' inside your wardrobe, and keep a door open so your cat can access it; also, keep a few drawers open, as cats love to explore and have hiding places.

- Find the right water fountain: cats love to play and drink running water (many cats love to drink and play with a dripping tap in the bathroom or kitchen).

- Position comfortable furniture near a window, so cats can lie on it in full sunlight.

- Have soft, relaxing music or a classical music radio station playing while you are out.

- If you have two cats in the household place three cat litter trays around the home (use natural substrates that are not perfumed).

- Try to keep the space under beds clear, so cats can retreat there as a resting space and play area.

- Plant a small rose bush with budding blooms – cats love to smell the aroma of roses as it is relaxing and calming.

Exercise, agility and games

Play hide-and-seek with your cat. Some cats love to follow you around if you have dried catnip or a catnip plant in your hand (*page 64*) If your cat can climb, have a special food treat they love, like Catnip Feline biscuits (*page 41*), and place it somewhere high, or choose a high ledge on a cat tower, so they can use their natural hunting skills to grab, pounce, grasp and chew.

A laser light toy is great fun for you and your cat – I have observed that the ones with a red light are the most attractive to cats. Some of these toys even have a separate button that allows you to have the laser beamed as an image of a mouse or a paw. *Be mindful not to shine the light in your cat's eyes – always beam the light further ahead.*

Chapter 2

~~

A–Z Food Recipes for Cats and Dogs – Wholesome, Easy-to-Make Meals and Treats

I have always loved cooking and have a passion for creating tasty, nutritious meals for myself and my cats and dogs. All of the recipes included in this chapter are simple and quick to make and have been tried and tested on hundreds of my animal clients with great success. Many animal rescue centres and my Diploma in Animal Healing students make my cat and dog treats to sell at animal charity fundraising activities, and my recipes have even appeared on BBC television.

For a decade or so I have been perfecting recipes in which the ingredients are more than just a substance to fill an empty stomach when our pets are hungry. Real food is far more than that: it has a nutritional value that fuels the body with goodness, creates positive energy and restores and strengthens all the systems.

In my clinic I see animals at all stages of life – from puppies and kittens through to adolescents, adults and seniors. The diet and food routines of these pets may vary as they get older or develop certain ailments, so I have created a variety of food recipes packed full of vital nutrients and key vitamins and minerals to support the body and help in overall health. Please refer to the *A–Z Common Conditions* chapter to see the recipes Dr Rohini and I particularly recommend you tailor to your pet's condition.

These days I am seeing more pets that have been diagnosed with various stages of cancer, and so I cannot emphasize enough the importance of making for your dog some of the cancer-fighting recipes included below, such as the Combat Cancer Vegetable Harvest Bake and the Combat Cancer Turmeric and Chickpea treats.

In my first book, *The Animal Healer* (Hay House), I wrote about a most remarkable dog called Frosty who was diagnosed with cancer and given six weeks to live. Her wonderful guardians, Shaun and Christine, brought Frosty to see me. After gaining the permission of her oncologist vet I put some food changes in place for Frosty and she responded well. Her new diet consisted entirely of organic fresh produce, including free-range chicken and eggs, brightly coloured vegetables and fruits full of beta-carotene and lycopene – well-documented anti-cancer compounds.

It took patience, dedication and an outstanding commitment from Shaun and Christine to see things through, as Frosty battled against the ravages of chemotherapy and exhaustion. Yet she always looked forward to the food her guardians made for her every day, and this helped give her the strength and stamina to live. We believe this diet also helped minimize the side effects of her chemotherapy. Frosty fought back and lived a further two years, enjoying a full and active life with her guardians.

We can help change an animal's life for the better by changing the way they eat. Every cat and dog I have been a guardian to has relished eating real food. I honestly believe they appreciate it as much as I love making it. It is such fun making healthy dog and cat foods: even if you try just one recipe in this chapter as a treat for your pets, they will love you forever! Observing my dogs' interest in every stage of the cooking and eating process – they sniff the air and salivate at the smells wafting through the kitchen – is a joy to behold. Tastes and smells remain in our animals' memories throughout their lives, just as they do in our own.

Enjoy the recipes!

⚘ Bladderwrack K9/Feline sea biscuits ⚘

140g (5oz) self-raising flour
1 large free-range egg
85g (3oz) dried seaweed, such as bladderwrack, kombu or dulce
2 tablespoons bladderwrack-infused sunflower oil (*see recipe under herb-infused oil*)

Method: please use the instructions below for preparing and baking all the biscuit recipes in this chapter.

1. Preheat the oven to 190°C/375°F/Gas Mark 5. Grease a 20 × 29cm (8 × 11in) baking sheet.

2. Put the ingredients in a large bowl and mix them until they form a soft dough. Spread dough 1cm (½in) deep on the baking sheet. Bake for 25–30 minutes until just firm.

3. Remove from the oven and allow to cool. Cut into bite-sized squares.

4. Keep in an airtight, labelled container in the fridge for up to five days, or freeze for up to one month.

⚘ Calendula biscuits ⚘

175g (6oz) organic self-raising flour
1 large free-range egg
1 tablespoon unset (runny) honey
2 tablespoons calendula-infused sunflower oil (*see recipe under herb-infused oil below*)
3 tablespoons calendula petals, sieved from the infused oil

Method: see under Bladderwrack K9/Feline sea biscuits above

⚘ Catnip Feline biscuits ⚘

115g (4oz) dried catnip
115g (4oz) self-raising flour
1 free-range egg
2 tablespoons catnip-infused sunflower oil (*see recipe under herb-infused oil*)
1 tablespoon unset (runny) honey

Method: see under Bladderwrack K9/Feline sea biscuits above

৯৯ Chamomile Tea & Honey biscuits ৯৭

4 tablespoons cold chamomile tea (in a cup, steep two chamomile teabags in boiling water, then leave to cool)

115g (4oz) milled linseed meal

115g (4oz) self-raising flour

1 free-range egg

2 tablespoons chamomile-infused honey (*see recipe under herb-infused honey*)

Method: see under Bladderwrack K9/Feline sea biscuits on page 41

৯৯ Charcoal K9/Feline D-Tox biscuits ৯৭

115g (4oz) self-raising flour

85g (3oz) activated charcoal

2 free-range eggs

2 tablespoons unset (runny) honey

Method: see under Bladderwrack K9/Feline sea biscuits on page 41

In recent years, activated charcoal has been used to treat toxic ingestions, as it helps absorb poisons from the gastrointestinal tract. It is also useful in reducing the side effects of chemotherapy and radiotherapy. This recipe is helpful only with specific conditions, so it should not be fed as a regular treat.

৯৯ Chicken broth for cats and dogs ৯৭

1. Place a cooked chicken carcass in a large, lidded saucepan and add 550ml (1 pint) of water.

2. Bring to the boil and then turn off the heat and leave to cool, preferably overnight, with the lid on.

3. Remove the carcass and then strain the liquid (broth) into a glass container with a lid. Keep refrigerated and use within three days.

Extras: add vegetables such as carrots, green beans, courgettes (zucchini), potato, broccoli (florets and stalks) to the broth. When cooked, they will soften nicely and add fibre to your pet's diet.

❧ Combat Cancer Vegetable Harvest Bake ☙

A selection of fresh vegetables – such as pumpkin, squash, sweet potato, courgette (zucchini), carrot, cauliflower and beetroot.

1. Preheat the oven to 190°C/375°F/Gas Mark 5. Wash the vegetables thoroughly and chop into bite-sized pieces. Place on a baking sheet and drizzle with a little olive oil.
2. Bake in the oven for 40 minutes. Remove and allow to cool in the sheet.

Keep in an airtight container in the fridge for up to four days. Add a small handful to daily feed.

These vegetables are a rich source of iron, calcium, potassium, magnesium, zinc, vitamins A, B C, E, B6, beta-carotene and dietary fibre. Rich, deep-red vegetables such as beetroot contain betacyanin, a powerful anti-cancer agent. Feel free to feed this healthy recipe to your pet at any time.

❧ Combat Cancer Vegetable Combo ☙

A selection of prepared fresh vegetables – such as cauliflower, broccoli, cabbage, Brussels sprouts, kale, peas, spinach, Swiss chard.

1. Wash the vegetables thoroughly and chop into bite-sized pieces.
2. Lightly steam the vegetables. Remove from the steamer and allow to cool.
3. Keep in an airtight container in the fridge for up to four days. Add a small handful to daily feed.

These vegetables are a rich source of vitamins A, B, C, K, B6 and E, plus folic acid, calcium, magnesium and potassium. Feel free to feed this healthy recipe to your pet at any time.

❧ Combat Cancer Fruit Combo ☙

A selection of fresh fruit – such as blueberries, blackberries, strawberries, apple, banana, fig, raspberries, watermelon and kiwi.

1. Wash the fruit thoroughly and chop into bite-sized pieces (if using peaches, nectarines, apricots or other stoned fruit, remove stones).
2. Offer your pet a small handful of any of the above fruit – on a separate plate alongside their daily food. Allow them to self-select what they want.

These fruits are a rich source vitamins A, C, E, K, plus beta-carotene, calcium, magnesium, phosphorus and flavonoids such as lycopene and lutein (which are well-documented anti-cancer agents).

⚘ Combat Cancer Turmeric and Chickpea Treats for dogs ⚘

115g (4oz) chickpea flour
55g (2oz) self-raising flour
1 free-range egg
½ tablespoon turmeric
2 apples, grated

Method: see under Bladderwrack K9/Feline sea biscuits on page 41

EGGS FOR CATS AND DOGS

Every part of an egg is highly nutritious for dogs and cats, including the eggshell. In the wild dogs and cats steal eggs from birds' nests as they are a high-quality source of protein, especially when prey is difficult to find. Eggs are naturally rich in vitamins A, B2, B12 and D, plus iodine, selenium and phosphorus. They are an excellent and healthy snack to feed and add to home-made recipes.

Most dogs love all the egg recipes listed below; however some cats can be fussy and you may need to experiment to see which one is best for your cat. Always start off with cooked eggs if your pet is fed a diet of dried food, as raw could give them an upset tummy. You can gradually introduce a raw egg to meals when you have established your pet is happy with natural foods.

I usually boil half a dozen eggs at a time and keep them in the fridge until I need them. Apart from a midday or night-time nutritious snack, I use hard-boiled eggs for positive-reward dog training. They are also a very handy snack for pets with diabetes, as they maintain glucose levels without the spiking effects of grain-based treats.

⚘ Hard-boiled Egg K9/Feline treat ⚘

4 large free-range eggs

1. Add eggs to a pan of boiling water and boil for 10 minutes.

2. Leave eggs to cool, then remove the shell and offer one egg per dog or cat as a treat. Keep hard-boiled eggs with their shells on in the fridge for up to three days.

⚘ Eggshell K9/Feline Calcium treat ⚘

After you have used the yolk and white of an egg keep the shell. When you are using the oven to bake other things, pop the eggshells on a baking sheet and cook them in the oven for 20 minutes at 190°C/375°F/Gas Mark 5.

1. Once the shells have cooled, place them in a pestle and mortar or a coffee grinder and grind down to a fine, sand-like consistency.

2. Store in an airtight glass jar in the fridge for up to two weeks (label and date the jar).

3. Every few days, sprinkle a teaspoon over your pet's food, or add a tablespoon to one of the dog and cat biscuit recipes in this chapter.

The main ingredient of an eggshell is calcium – 1 teaspoon contains approximately 800–1000mg of calcium. The eggshell membrane is also used as a dietary supplement and has been shown to reduce the effects of osteoarthritis, stiffness and painful joints. The membrane contains proteins such as chondroitin sulphate, glucosamine and hyaluronic acid, well-known, over-the-counter compounds you can buy at the pharmacy to help with these conditions.

⚘ K9 herb omelette ⚘

4 large free-range eggs
1 large sprig of herbs, finely chopped: try chives, thyme, sage or mint
1 tablespoon light olive oil
1 large carrot, grated

1. Beat the eggs in a bowl and then add the herbs and carrot.

2. Pour the mixture into a lightly oiled, non-stick frying pan and cook over a high heat for 2–3 minutes, or until the entire egg and herb mixture is set and firm to the touch.

3. Remove from the oven and allow to cool. Cut into bite-sized squares.

4. Keep in an airtight container in the fridge for up to three days.

⚘ Scrambled eggs ⚘

2 large free-range eggs

1. Crack the eggs into a microwave-proof bowl or jug, then whisk together with a fork.

2. Place in a microwave and cook on high for 2 minutes. Allow to cool and then feed.

⚘ Garlic K9 biscuits ⚘

115g (4oz) oatmeal
85g (3oz) self-raising flour
1 free-range egg
2 cloves garlic, ground to a paste
1 tablespoon unset (runny) honey

Method: see under Bladderwrack K9/Feline sea biscuits on page 41

Please see alternative recipe below for cats, using chives instead of garlic

⚘ Chive Feline treats ⚘

1 small bunch chives, finely chopped
115g (4oz) self-raising flour
1 free-range egg
115g (4oz) can sardines in sunflower oil (use all of the oil in the can)

Method: see under Bladderwrack K9/Feline sea biscuits on page 41

⚘ Ginger K9 biscuits ⚘

115g (4oz) self-raising flour
115g (4oz) milled linseed meal
1 free-range egg
2 tablespoons ginger-infused honey (*see recipe under herb-infused honey*)
A piece of fresh root ginger (1cm/½in long), finely grated

Method: see under Bladderwrack K9/Feline sea biscuits on page 41

ᕥ Hedgerow Hip Bites for dogs ᕦ

225g (8oz) organic self-raising flour
2 large free-range eggs
4 good handfuls ripe autumn rosehips (remove pips)
2 tablespoons unset (runny) honey
2 tablespoons rosehip-infused sunflower oil (*see recipe under herb-infused oil*)

Method: see under Bladderwrack K9/Feline sea biscuits on page 41

Variation: substitute the rosehips for one large grated eating apple or one banana, or two handfuls of blackberries.

ELDERBERRIES

Elderberries are the fruit of the elder tree and are packed full of vitamins A and C, plus beta-carotene and antioxidants. Studies have found that elderberries are effective in easing the symptoms of respiratory conditions: the bioflavonoids and other proteins in the juice destroy the ability of cold and flu viruses to infect a cell.

In fact, scientists have so enthused about elderberries that elderberry juice was used to treat a flu epidemic in Panama in Central America in 1995, and the fruit is listed in the 2000 edition of Mosby's *Nursing Drug Reference* for colds, flu, yeast infections, nasal and chest congestion.

Elderberries are best picked in July and August, when they have a deep and rich purple colour. The following remedy is great for mild cold and cough-like symptoms and for senior dogs needing a boost of energy from the goodness of elderberries. I created it to help Carley, a dog trainer whose own dogs were suffering from colds, and it proved to be a great success, as Carley explains:

'My dogs came down with colds after a young puppy I was training developed a cough. My vet reassured me it was not serious and only rest was needed. Elizabeth was so helpful and made me the K9 Bark Berry cough remedy for all the sneezing dogs to take. They all loved it and so did I! It was delicious – and even better knowing it would really help relieve their symptoms. She also made them some garlic-infused honey to lick (see recipe below), which again they loved. Within a day, all the dogs' cold symptoms had cleared up. I can't thank Elizabeth enough for her help and advice.'

✌ K9 Bark Berry cough remedy ✌

1kg (2lbs 4oz) ripe elderberries
Cloves
Lemons
Sugar
Root ginger

1. Wash and de-stalk the berries. Place in a large pan with enough water to cover. Bring to the boil and simmer until berries are soft, about 30 minutes.

2. Strain the berries through a sieve and retain the cooking liquid. Then, for every 550ml (1 pint) of liquid add 10 cloves, the juice of one lemon and 200g (7oz) sugar.

3. Return to the heat without the berries, add a 2½-cm (1-in) piece of fresh ginger, and simmer until the sugar has dissolved. Boil hard for 8 minutes. Remove the cloves and ginger and let the liquid cool.

4. Pour into dark plastic 100ml (3½ fl oz) bottles, label and store in the fridge or freezer until needed.

HERB-INFUSED HONEY

Honey is a wonderful complement to your pet's diet when infused with herbs in the way shown in the following recipes. Honey contains mainly sugars: equal amounts of fructose and glucose, a tiny amount of sucrose and maltose and a little water. It can be ingested and also used topically. The pH of honey is commonly between 3.2 and 4.5 and this relatively acidic pH level prevents the growth of many bacteria. Because of its unique composition and chemical properties, honey is suitable for long-term storage and is easily assimilated, even after long preservation.

To maximize the longevity of a herb-infused honey it is important to limit its access to moisture. If exposed to moist air, honey's hydrophilic properties will attract moisture, which will eventually dilute it to the point that fermentation begins. Minimize excess water in herb-infused honey jars by harvesting fresh herbs on a hot, sunny afternoon.

Honey has antibacterial and antiseptic qualities. I often feed garlic-infused honey to my dogs, as garlic is a natural flea repellent. It is also good for first aid and shock. Allow cats and dogs to lick natural honey from your hand, as it is very calming and is recommended for pets that have been scared; it also helps animals that are in shock and traumatized.

Note: never let your pet ingest garlic on its own as it can burn the oesophagus.

⚘ Garlic-infused honey ⚘

1 jar unset (runny) honey
1 bulb garlic (use 6 cloves)

1. Strip the outer layer of skin from each of the garlic cloves. Gently prick the cloves all over and place in the jar of honey.

2. Put the jar in the fridge and leave to infuse for one week.

3. From time to time, agitate the jar by tipping it upside down – this help maximize the infusion process. After one week remove the garlic cloves. The honey will appear thinner in consistency and have a pungent garlic aroma.

4. Label and date the jar, and keep in the fridge. Use within six months.

5. Place ½ teaspoon garlic-infused honey on a clean plate, so pets can self-select.

⚘ Ginger-infused honey ⚘

1 jar unset (runny) honey
25g (1oz) piece of root ginger

1. Chop or slice the ginger and add to the honey jar; remove after one week.

2. Label and date the jar, and keep in the fridge. Use within six months

3. Offer ½ teaspoon ginger-infused honey to your pet on a clean plate.

⚘ Herb-infused honey ⚘

It is best to stick to one type of herb per jar of honey. Rosemary, sage, thyme and chamomile (leaves and flowers) work well.

1 jar unset (runny) honey
A sprig of a single herb

1. Using a cotton thread, wind round the stems of the herbs and secure tightly to make a bundle.

2. Immerse the herb bundle in the honey. When the herbs are tied it is easier to remove them from the honey jar after infusing. Remove herbs after one week.

3. Label and date the jar, and keep in the fridge. Use within six months

4. Offer ½ teaspoon herb-infused honey to your pet on a clean plate.

HERB-INFUSED OIL

Like the herb-infused honey, herb-infused oil is a tasty addition to your pet's diet. It is made by infusing a single type of dried herb and sunflower oil in a glass jar for a period of time – between four and six weeks – with the mixture being agitated (shaken vigorously) every day. The plant material is then removed by filtering the oil, leaving the oil with some of the therapeutic constituents and properties of the herb, and its colour.

Herb-infused oil can be added to the biscuit recipes listed above, but do not add it to your pet's regular food as he or she may not want it. Always offer separately – place ½ teaspoon of herb-infused oil on a clean plate and allow your pet to self-select the oil. This is lovely to offer as a healthy treat some time during the day, other than meal times.

If you would like to harvest and dry your own herbs please refer to Chapter 4: *Harvesting Nature's Bounty for your Pet* for more information. If you would like to purchase ready-made herb-infused oils, visit www.animalchoices.co.uk.

⚘ Herb-infused sunflower oil ⚘

Use only one herb per infusion.

50g (1¾oz) dried herb of your choice – *select one* of the following: catnip, chickweed, calendula (marigold), mint, nettle, rosehip or bladderwrack
500ml (18 fl oz) sunflower oil

1. Fill a dry, sterilized glass jar (*see top tip below*) with your chosen dried herb and cover completely with the sunflower oil – keep pouring until you reach the slope or shoulder of the jar, leaving a small space for the oil to breath.

2. Screw the lid on tightly and leave the jar in a warm place, or in direct sunlight, or on a sunny windowsill, for between four and six weeks – or until the oil has taken on the colour of the plant material. Shake the jar vigorously every day.

3. After the oil has infused strain the herb off into a sterilized measuring jug and put the oil in a (preferably dark) bottle.

4. Label and date the bottle and store in a cool, dry place. Use within three months. If unsure, smell and taste the oil and do not use it if it's rancid.

If you have a dishwasher you can sterilize jars and lids in it. Alternatively, place clean jars, measuring jugs and metal sieves in a pre-heated oven at 90°C (200°F) for 30 minutes. Allow to cool before using.

⋆ K9/Feline fishcakes ⋆

2 × 115g (4oz) cans sardines in sunflower oil
115g (4oz) self-raising flour
1 large free-range egg
1 tablespoon olive oil
1 heaped tablespoon unset (runny) honey

1. Preheat the oven to 190°C/375°F/Gas Mark 5. Grease a 24 × 21 × ¾cm (9 × 8 × ¼in) baking sheet.

2. Mash all the ingredients together in a large bowl, until they form a soft dough.

3. Spread dough evenly over the baking sheet, and bake for 15 minutes. Remove from the oven and allow to cool on the sheet. Cut into bite-sized squares.

4. Keep in an airtight glass container in the fridge for up to three days, or freeze for up to one month.

Variation: substitute sardines for the following: 1 × 215g (7½oz) can wild red salmon with juice or 1 × 150g (5½oz) can tuna in sunflower oil.

⋆ K9/Feline Nature's Own Hotpot ⋆

225g (8oz) free-range minced (ground) turkey or chicken, or chicken breast meat
1 large carrot, grated
1 handful French green beans (cut small)
1 handful basmati rice
1 medium potato, diced
1 handful frozen peas*
2 cabbage leaves, shredded

1. Place all the ingredients in a large pan and add enough water to cover.

2. Bring to the boil and then gently simmer for 30 minutes, until most of the liquid has been absorbed (top the pan up with water if it starts to dry out). Allow mixture to cool.

3. Keep in the fridge for up to three days, or freeze for up to one month.

* Frozen peas are a wonderful storecupboard superfood and a source of protein, vitamins B, C and K, phosphorus, potassium, zinc, carotenoids and folic acid. Add a handful of peas to any of the hot pot recipes at the cooking stage, to bulk out the fibre. Dogs and cats alike love lightly cooked peas.

⚸ Linseed K9/Feline biscuits ⚸

140g (5oz) milled linseed meal
85g (3oz) plain or self-raising flour
1 free-range egg
2 tablespoons unset (runny) honey
2 tablespoons light olive oil
2 level tablespoons dried eggshells (optional)

1. Preheat the oven to 190°C/375°F/Gas Mark 5. Grease a 24 × 21 × ¾cm (9 × 8 × ¼in) baking sheet.

2. Put the ingredients in a large bowl and mix them until they form a soft dough. Spread dough evenly over the baking sheet, and bake for 15 minutes. Remove from the oven, and allow to cool in the sheet. Cut into bite-sized squares.

3. Keep in an airtight, labelled container in the fridge for up to three days, or freeze for up to one month.

Variation: add a handful of finely chopped herbs: try sage, thyme or parsley.

⚸ Liver Cake K9/Feline Bake ⚸

450g (1lb) liver (chicken, lamb or beef) chopped into small pieces
280g (10oz) self-raising flour
2 free-range eggs
1 large handful finely chopped curly parsley

1. Place all the ingredients in a large blender or food mixer and mix until a soft dough is formed. Spread dough 1cm (½in) deep onto a baking sheet. Bake for 25–30 minutes until just firm.

2. Remove from the oven and allow to cool. Cut into bite-sized squares.

3. Keep in an airtight container for up to three days, or freeze for up to one month.

⚘ Mint K9 biscuits ⚘

175g (6oz) self-raising flour

1 free-range egg

2 tablespoons mint-infused sunflower oil (*see recipe under herb-infused oil*)

1 teaspoon unset (runny) honey

1 handful finely chopped fresh garden mint

Method: see under Bladderwrack K9/Feline sea biscuits above

⚘ Nettle K9 biscuits ⚘

175g (6oz) self-raising flour

1 free-range egg

2 tablespoons nettle-infused sunflower oil (*see recipe under herb-infused oil*)

1 teaspoon unset (runny) honey

1 handful finely chopped nettles

Method: see under Bladderwrack K9/Feline sea biscuits above

⚘ Prairie Woof Jacks ⚘

Oats are a key ingredient in these dog biscuits. Cultivated for food for thousands of years and with the highest source of plant protein of all cereals, oats are an excellent source of dietary fibre and great for anxious and stressed dogs as they help support the nervous system. Oats are packed with vitamins B1, B2, D and E.

4 tablespoons light olive oil

3 heaped tablespoons unset (runny) honey (natural, or infused with thyme or sage, see recipe above)

225g (8oz) oats or oatmeal

1 large apple, grated

2 handfuls ground natural nuts, i.e. walnut, cashew, pecan

1. Preheat the oven to 190°C/375°F/Gas Mark 5. Grease a 20 × 29cm (8 × 11in) baking sheet.

2. Heat the oil in a large pan for a couple of minutes and then stir in the honey. Add the oats, apple and nuts. Mix well until a soft dough is formed.

3. Spread dough 1cm (½in) deep onto the baking sheet, pressing down evenly with the back of a tablespoon. Bake for 20–25 minutes.

4. Remove from the oven and allow to cool in the sheet. Cut into bite-sized squares.

5. Keep in an airtight, labelled container in the fridge for up to five days, or freeze for up to one month.

⊰ Woof Berry and Yoghurt dog treats ⊱

Blackberries are one of the most abundant fruits in the UK and are best when harvested between late July and October. Try and pick them on a warm, sunny afternoon, when they are at their juiciest. Dogs adore blackberries as they contain lots of vitamin C. You can also freeze them and use them in the winter months.

If you have picked blackberries from a hedgerow for use in this recipe, place them on a sheet of baking paper for an hour to allow any moisture to evaporate and any insects that have taken up residence to vacate the berries!

500g (1lb 2oz) carton organic natural yoghurt*
200g (7oz) ripe blackberries
1 ripe banana, mashed
3 level tablespoons good quality smooth peanut butter*

1. Place all the ingredients in a large bowl and combine them until they form a mixture with a loose consistency.

2. Spoon the mixture into a silicon ice-cube tray or silicon cupcake moulds and place into a freezer.

3. After 2 hours the cubes should be firm to the touch. Pop one out as and when you want to offer your dog a treat.

In the summer my dogs and I adore licking these cubes, and they help keep us cool. In the winter months I let the cubes thaw for a few minutes before we eat them!

Variation: substitute raspberries, blueberries or strawberries for the blackberries.

I like to use a yoghurt brand with high animal welfare standards, with the cows that supply the milk allowed to graze outdoors for part of the year. Choose a peanut butter brand that contains a high percentage of peanuts – around 95 per cent – and no palm oil. A very good example of this is a brand called Sun-Pat, available in the UK and USA. Also available in the USA is Woodstock Farms Organic Peanut Butter.

Chapter 3

~~~

A–Z Pet-Friendly Herbs – Simple
Plant Remedies for Everyday Use

In this chapter I am delighted to be sharing my culinary herb recipes, top tips and natural plant remedies for pets. I have been using these for more than two decades, and they have been tried and tested on my own companion animals, at rescue centres all over the world and in my private practice.

The following alphabetical list of pet-friendly herbs provides the common and Latin names for the plant material I keep on hand in my kitchen and apothecary for use in natural healing, along with a clear explanation of the many ways in which each can be used and the common conditions they can treat. The featured herbs are my favourites.

I have also outlined which *parts* of the plant to use and have highlighted some of the medicinal compounds they contain – these are what makes the plants so special and allows them to be used to treat a range of everyday ailments while also providing important preventative measures. Also included are top tips for senior pets, housebound animals and those in rehabilitation from physical and emotional trauma, rescue and rehoming.

For more serious medical conditions these simple plant remedies are not a substitute for veterinary treatment, but make no mistake, conventional and holistic treatment go hand in hand – it is never one or the other and both are vital for treating the whole animal fully. We all want the very best for our pets and it is our duty to put them and what is best for them, first.

As a responsible guardian to the animals in my care, I would never diagnose or medicate a medical condition of theirs. Neither would I make a random phone call to someone to seek a diagnosis. A consultation with my vet is my first priority. She will make the diagnosis and together we will decide together the best course of action and a long-term plan. Using a combination of veterinary expertise, complementary treatments, a healthy diet and herbs for sensory wellbeing, we and our vets can be a winning team to help heal our animal companions.

Not all illnesses are simple physical problems and many can arise from an emotional imbalance or a dysfunctional lifestyle. Prescriptive medication is not necessarily going to solve this. Most illnesses will have other contributory factors: it might be stress – emotional or mental or both – or it might be behavioural or food-related. We need to investigate everything to get to the root of the problem and not just deal with what we can see on the surface.

USING HERBS IN YOUR PET'S DIET

Most of the herbs listed below have both medicinal and culinary virtues. When we use them in remedies to treat the animals in our care, it is important that they are kept as close to their natural state as possible, as in the natural world animals self-medicate with a variety of plant material to help them survive.

Enriching our pets' lives at home with a variety of positive stimulations that involve taste, smell and touch is both rewarding and mentally invigorating for them – in the same way that it is for us when we are exposed to fragrant aromas such as that of a rose. Personally, I feel love and happiness; and when I smell mint I feel more focused, and when I smell lavender I feel calm.

In the natural world animals are exposed to a huge variety of smells and they have an innate response to aromas, tastes and touch. They are even aware of how the external parts of a plant, flower or tree can affect their own body when they rub themselves up against it.

It is fascinating to observe how an animal responds to some of the remedies listed below. You may well observe a change in your pet's behaviour and body language when you use them, with signs of licking, chewing, yawning, sighing, appearing to stare into space, or becoming very relaxed. These are all indications that our animals are processing the aromas of the plants and beginning to chill out. Simply inhaling the aromas can be the trigger point to allowing healing to commence.

Dogs and cats have more than 300 million smell receptors (humans have just 6 million) and these can detect the tiniest vibration. All the senses are activated when they use these receptors, working on the physical, emotional and mental responses. There is much animal and human research showing that the aromatic smell of plant and herb material can affect the olfactory system: it reaches the bundles of nerve endings in the brain which, in animals, are associated with emotions, instinct and mood.

Cats and dogs are highly intelligent animals, and like us, they actually know what is best for them: after all, they looked after themselves for thousands of years before they came to live with us. We have taken away the opportunity for our companion animals to live entirely in the natural world and so they are reliant on us for most of their needs.

For me, then, it is gratifying to observe my cats and dogs self-select and munch on some of the grasses in our back garden, and know they are picking the succulent young shoots packed full of chlorophyll – which is such an important nutrient, rich in fibre that keeps the body healthy. I also like to bring some elements of the natural world *into* my house, where my pets live with me, and try to create as natural an environment as I can. In doing so I can maintain a balanced, joyful life for my pets.

Over the years, I have witnessed with my own eyes thousands of cats and dogs that were curious, interested and visibly appreciative of the positive intention and love that goes into creating something special for them. When we are happy and content our companion animals are happy and content too. Have fun making some of the remedies and treats below and enjoy this precious time with your animal companions.

🌿 ALOE VERA *(Aloe barbadensis)*
Parts used: the inner leaf gel immediately beneath the skin of the leaves.

Please note: all of the remedies containing aloe vera in this book are intended for external use only.

Common uses

Aloe vera is one of nature's most remarkable plants and has been valued by mankind for more than two millennia. It originated in Africa and has rapidly spread to parts of the globe where the climate is favourable: it needs sunshine and no frost. Some of my animal charity work takes me to Africa, the Mediterranean and Sri Lanka – places that offer the perfect location and the right conditions for aloes to thrive.

Growing to around 70–80cm (2–2½ft) high, with about 10 to 12 thick, broad and spiky leaves forming a rosette and tapering to a point, this majestic, dark green plant is the source of the base gel I use to treat skin problems *(see recipe below)*.

Top tip ✍

Aloes are easy to grow indoors as houseplants. Place them on windowsills to absorb full sunlight and water them a few times a week to keep them succulent. There are some 300 aloe plants dotted around my house!

Aloe vera plays a crucial role in helping animals with a number of skin conditions. Firstly it soothes and is cooling to the skin; it helps with minor wound healing, skin irritations, burns, cuts, scrapes, sunburn, eczema, flea and tick bites. As it contains around 98 per cent water it is the perfect base material for remedies for furry animals as it is easily absorbed when you apply it topically (on the skin). Aloe vera forms part of my first-aid kit at home and abroad as it is gentle and soothing and most dogs and cats like and trust it.

Key properties

Let us take a closer look at the leaf of the aloe vera, where all of its medicinal properties live. The leaf comprises the rind, the sap and the mucilage inner gel. The rind of aloe vera leaf is dark green and waxy. Below it are vascular bundles, or tubules, containing the 'sap' – the clear, jelly-like gel we are interested in using. Inside this is a mucilage layer, rich in polysaccharide sugars, which surrounds the inner gel (the water – the storage organ of the plant).

There are more than 75 known ingredients in the aloe vera leaf. Minerals include zinc, potassium, magnesium, calcium, sodium, copper, iron, manganese and chromium. Vitamins include A, C and E, together with the B group, and there is even a trace of vitamin B12, which is very rarely found in plants. Aloe vera possesses a powerful anti-inflammatory effect and broad antimicrobial activity. It contains powerful plant sterols – chemical compounds containing salicylic acid, which has painkilling and anti-inflammatory properties.

When applied topically, aloe gel has the ability to penetrate deep into the skin, where it stimulates and increases the activity of collagen and elastin, proteins that are part of the connective tissue that surrounds the body, enabling them to replicate themselves faster than they would normally. This speeds up the healing of the cell membranes, creating a healthy-looking skin and a barrier to insects, deterring them from laying their eggs in damaged skin. Research has shown that aloe vera can increase the rate of skin healing by about a third.

Top tip ✍

After making any topical remedy, test it on the back of your hand before using it on your pet. If after 10 minutes it still feels soft, cooling and gentle, proceed to applying it to your animal friend.

Dogs and cats with skin problems such as eczema and dermatitis respond well to aloe vera – especially the chronic variety in which there is often an allergic element. Since aloe vera contains natural antihistamines and antiseptic properties, mainly thanks to saponins (a soapy substance that acts as a cleansing agent), itchiness can be reduced, which in turn helps to soothe and calm the skin. Aloe vera complements conventional skin treatments as part of a long-term plan.

❧ Aloe vera basic gel ☙

A large handful of aloe vera leaves
½ teaspoon xanthan gum*
½ teaspoon vitamin C powder*

1. Break open the aloe vera leaves and scrape out the inner sap – this can be quite fiddly as the sap is slippery.

2. Place the sap in a blender, add 2 tablespoons of water, the xanthan gum and the vitamin C powder. Blend together until a thicker, gel-like consistency is achieved.

3.   Store in a labelled, airtight glass jar in the fridge for up to one month.

4.   Apply topically to affected area or itchy skin, avoiding the face and genitals.

* Vitamin C powder is a natural preservative you can buy in pharmacies or online. Xanthan gum is a natural thickener you can buy online (*see Resources section for stockists*).

To use the aloe vera basic gel, gently massage it between your fingers and apply it to the skin. Inevitably, you may have some fur in the way, but continue to work in and around the hair follicles. The gel is absorbed very quickly. It is excellent used 'neat' or as a remedy with added ingredients (see *Bladderwrack* below).

Top tip ✍

If you decide to purchase aloe vera from a shop, check the ingredients list on the packaging. A good-quality product will have aloe as its main ingredient and will be a cold stabilized gel, unfiltered and not concentrated. Unfortunately there are many products claiming to be aloe vera that actually contain very little of the plant, and these will therefore not be as effective.

❦ BLADDERWRACK *(Fucus vesiculosus)*

Parts used: whole plant.

Common uses and key properties

The common bladderwrack is part of the seaweed family and can be found washed up on beaches all over the world. There are hundreds of varieties of seaweed and almost all are edible: seaweed has been a source of food for animals and humans for thousands of years. It is packed full of beneficial nutrients, and fed in small amounts it is a wonderful food supplement for dogs and cats.

One of the main chemical compounds found in bladderwrack is iodine, used extensively to treat an underactive thyroid. It also contains organic (photo-synthetic) vitamins B and C, trace minerals, lipids, plant sterols, amino acids, omega-3 and omega-6 fatty acids, antioxidants, polyphenols and flavonoids. It is useful as an electrolyte when valuable salts have been depleted from the body.

In recent years seaweed taken internally has been promoted for weight loss in overweight animals (it stimulates thyroid activity), for boosting the immune system, decreasing blood sugar and cholesterol, increasing gastrointestinal tract function, and for decreasing the joint pain associated with arthritis. Seaweed is also believed to be a detoxifier and a useful healing agent.

Top tip ✍

When foraging for seaweed choose small coves and clean beaches where water is free from impurities – I steer clear of harbours, where motor boats are often tethered. After gathering bladderwrack, wash it thoroughly to remove all sand and hang it out on the washing line or in an airing cupboard to dry. When crispy, dry chop into 1cm (½in) pieces with a pair of scissors, then use a pestle and mortar or a coffee grinder to grind it to a fine sand. Place in a labelled, airtight glass jar.

Bladderwrack can be used externally in compresses to reduce inflammation and arthritic pain and can be added to aloe vera gel as a topical application (*see recipe below*) to help with stiff joints, ligament damage, lick and bed sores – especially if animals are convalescing or paralysed for long periods of time.

⊱ Make your own ⊰

Bladderwrack K9/Feline sea biscuits
See recipe page 41. These are a lovely treat and easy to make. If you would prefer to use culinary dried sea vegetables, there are many seaweed varieties, including sea lettuce (*Ulva lactuca*) and dulse (*Palmaria palmata*), which are available in some supermarkets and specialist food shops. Also try the UK-based seaweed supplier Seagreens: www.seagreens.co.uk.

Bladderwrack-infused sunflower oil
See recipe page 50. This cat- and dog-friendly oil is highly nutritious. It contains essential minerals and electrolytes and is a strong immune-system stimulant. It is nourishing and useful for overweight animals needing a thyroid boost.

Powdered bladderwrack for cats with gingivitis
Research has shown that 100 per cent powdered seaweed is good for cats with this dental condition, especially where plaque builds up on the teeth. I have noticed that you need to administer it for at least six months to see any results. *See Resources section (page 296) for where to buy bladderwrack.*

Aloe vera gel with seaweed
115g (4oz) dried bladderwrack
6 tablespoons aloe vera basic gel (*see recipe above*)
½ teaspoon xanthan gum

1. Place the bladderwrack in a cup, add boiling water and steep overnight until cool.

2. Strain the liquid and then place in a blender with the aloe vera basic gel and the xanthan gum. Blend to achieve a smooth gel.

3. Store in a labelled, airtight glass jar in the fridge for up to one month.

4. Apply topically to affected area or itchy skin, avoiding the face and genitals.

❀ CALENDULA/MARIGOLD *(Calendula officinalis)*
Parts used: petals and flower heads.

Common uses and key properties
If you see the word *officinalis* in the Latin name of a plant, it is a hint at its medicinal virtues. Calendula, or marigold, is a safe and gentle plant that is a great source of culinary delight and a panacea for all manner of ailments. It forms part of my main apothecary and first-aid kit as it has many actions – as a mild anti-inflammatory, a wound healer, a skin healer, an astringent and a nutritive. It is traditionally used for skin and gastric complaints.

Calendula contains essential oils, pro-vitamin A and carotenoids (colourful plant pigments that are powerful antioxidants supporting the immune system) – hence the fabulous signature colours of its bright orange or deep yellow flowers. The plant is used in ointments and creams for cuts, bruises, burns and ulcers. It is used internally for gastric ulcers and inflammation. Being rich in sulphur, calendula has excellent blood-cleansing and antifungal actions and acts as a liver stimulant. Animal research studies have shown the saponin compounds in the plant may possess anti-tumour properties.

More recently we have been exposed to calendula's culinary virtues, as its edible flower heads are increasingly used in cooking – the chefs in many fashionable restaurants find their vivid yellow and orange colour irresistible and add them to salads. I wholeheartedly recommend using the flower heads in my biscuit recipes (*see Chapter 2*). Calendula-infused sunflower oil is adored by dogs, cats and humans alike as it has a wonderful nutty taste and is highly nutritious; I like to make a salad dressing with it.

❧ Make your own ☙

Calendula biscuits
See recipe page 41.

Calendula-infused sunflower oil
See recipe page 50. Use this on any skin condition in dogs and cats, or for an animal with a poor coat and dull eyes in need of a nourishing spring tonic. On an emotional level, the oil helps with emotional trauma and self-confidence, and raises self-esteem.

Note: when making the oil use English marigolds (*Calendula officinalis*). The French marigold (*Tagetes patula*) is a member of the daisy family *Asteraceae* and does not contain the properties of calendula.

Calendula ointment
This is excellent for post-operative scars and contact dermatitis *(where the skin is intact)*; it also benefits furless, dry skin areas of the body. Follow the recipe for the comfrey ointment below, replacing the comfrey oil with calendula oil.

🌿 ❀ CATNIP *(Nepeta cataria)*
Parts used: aerial parts – leaves, stems and flowers.

Common uses and properties
Catnip is a member of the same plant family as mint, and is loved by cats and dogs alike as it works on the nervous system and stomach. It is a calming agent and an anti-spasmodic, easing tummy upsets and acting as a sedative. And for our feline friends it is a feline euphoric at the same time – the plant contains a chemical called nepetalactone, which has an extraordinary effect on many cats when they inhale it.

Some cats become so intoxicated by the smell of catnip that they rub themselves against the plant, roll in it and look completely happy – appearing to be in an almost trance-like state. Catnip forms part of my main practice: many of the cats I treat at rescue centres, on home visits and in private practice self-select catnip as it helps calm the nerves when there is restlessness or anxiety.

Top tip ✍

Over the years I have been a guardian to many rescued long-haired cats and I have found catnip to be most useful for cats with fur balls. Place a little catnip-infused sunflower oil on a clean saucer and let your cat self-select as and when they choose.

Oliver, my RSPCA cat, was almost classified as unsuitable for rehoming as he was a difficult animal to handle. He would extend his talons and lash out at anyone who came too close. He would spray everywhere and mark his scent and he permanently looked worried and anxious. When Oliver came to live with us we gave him all the time he needed to settle in, build up trust and unwind.

One of the many things we did was to place a tray of dried catnip near one of his beds. We left it down for days and he played with it for hours, tossing and turning and rolling in it. He would then seize one of my home-made catnip toys *(see below)* as if it were prey and purr with delight. *(To see Oliver and other cats in action with catnip, visit www.animalchoices.co.uk.)*

Oliver's confidence grew, and so did his stature. My students and graduates from the Diploma in Animal Healing course could not get over the change in him. If your cat is not always interested in catnip, do not dismiss this as a sign not to offer it anymore. I always offer this herb on an ad hoc basis.

⚘ Make your own ⚘

Buy a catnip plant from a garden centre

Ask for the *Nepeta cataria* variety as cats prefer this, and it grows well in the garden. Harvest the aerial parts in summer and leave till crispy dry. Or alternatively, buy good quality dried catnip. See *Resources section (page 296) for a list of retailers.*

Catnip cat toy

Cats will play with these for hours. Some shop-bought catnip toys have very little aroma, as the herb has passed its shelf life, and as a consequence cats ignore them. So it is best to make your own – here's how:

Sew together two 100 per cent cotton squares (each 15 × 15cm/6 × 6in), leaving a small entrance on one side. Stuff full with dried catnip and then sew up the entrance. Alternatively, take a clean 100 per cent wool sock and stuff it full of dried catnip before sewing up the entrance.

Catnip cat tray

Sprinkle generous handfuls of loose dried catnip into a clean, deep tray, at least 35cm (14in) wide, 50cm (20in) long and 10cm (4in) high. Cats can explore the scents and roll in ecstasy, releasing all those wonderful endorphins – the happy hormones – for a purrfect feelgood factor.

Catnip-infused sunflower oil

See recipe page 50. This is great for cats and dogs with anxiety, nervousness and tension because it is calming and acts as a mild sedative.

Catnip Feline biscuits

See recipe page 41.

🌿 ❀ CHAMOMILE, GERMAN *(Matricaria recutita)*

Parts used: aerial parts – leaves and flowers.

Common uses and key properties

Chamomile is a safe and gentle herb for both internal and external use. German chamomile, and its relative, Roman chamomile (*Chamaemelum nobile*), are among the most respected and widely used medicinal herbs in the world because of their calming and relaxing qualities.

German and Roman chamomile are practically identical in action and both are made into loose tea or teabags that are readily available in supermarkets as chamomile or (camomile) tea. The beautiful pollen heads and petals are used for the tea. I use chamomile tea when I am working in Sri Lanka on outreach projects where many dogs have tick infestations. After we have removed the ticks I sometimes make a chamomile wash (using the tea) to soothe their itchy, hot skin. It is useful for other skin problems, too, such as fleabites, stings, allergies and minor wounds (*see recipe below*).

Chamomile is useful for animals suffering from nervous tension and anxiety, restlessness and stress as it contains sedative properties. The plant has been shown to have significant anti-inflammatory and analgesic actions, too, so it is also useful for easing aches and pains.

Top tip ✍

When identifying a chamomile plant at a garden centre or on a foraging trip, note that the German variety has slightly larger flower heads and no scent, while the Roman variety has smaller heads and gives off a wonderful aromatic apple scent when you rub the stems with your fingers. This is the scent we sometimes smell when drinking chamomile tea, whose delicate aromas waft from the cup!

Chamomile tea is helpful for indigestion, colic, nausea, bloat (build-up of gas) and vomiting. Research from animal and human studies shows that compounds such as apigenenin, chamazulene and matricin, and other volatile oil constituents of the flower, act as strong anti-spasmodic agents in the digestive tract, which can improve the production of bile to stimulate the appetite.

✿ Make your own ✿

Chamomile soothing wash
Hot, swollen or inflamed skin, including that caused by insect bites, contact allergies and hot weather, can benefit from this simple, water-based topical wash. Add two chamomile teabags to 550ml (1 pint) of boiled water, steep for 2 hours until cool and then apply the liquid to the skin with a clean sponge, avoiding the eyes, mouth and genitals.

Chamomile eye infusion
A cool compress made with chamomile will be soothing and gentle for conditions such as mild conjunctivitis. To prepare, follow the instructions for the soothing wash above. Using a clean cotton cloth gently dab around the eye area, making sure you do not get any of the liquid in the eye itself. *Note: any eye condition must first be seen by a veterinarian.*

Chamomile and lavender pillow
This will help deter insects, ease anxiety, create a calm outdoor aroma and help eliminate pet odours. Here's how to make one:

Take an old 100 per cent cotton sheet and cut into two 25 × 25cm (10 × 10 in) pieces. Sew these together and then turn them inside out, leaving one side open. Fill with 115g (4oz) dried chamomile and 115g (4oz) dried lavender. Sew remaining side. Place pillow on top of your pet's bedding, so he or she can choose to sniff it, lie on it or ignore it.

Chamomile Tea & Honey biscuits
See recipe page 42.

Chamomile-infused honey
See recipe page 49.

🌿 ❀ CHICKWEED *(Stellaria media)*

Parts used: aerial parts – leaves, flowers, and stems.

Common uses and properties

Chickweed is a wonderful year-round herb that grows in fields, gardens and hedgerows. It is safe, delicious and very palatable – I use it raw in salads and make a pesto sauce with it. The plant is very recognizable: it has delicate pale green leaves and tiny, white, star-like flowers.

Taken internally, chickweed acts to soothe, protect and mildly lubricate the upper digestive tract. It is packed full of vitamins A and C, and minerals including magnesium, copper, silicon, zinc and iron. It is a gentle restorative that helps animals with anaemia, skin problems and disorders of the digestive tract, lymphatic system and upper respiratory tract. Chickweed is available to pick from March until November everywhere, and I pick small clumps from meadows and footpaths.

🌾 Make your own 🌱

Chickweed-infused sunflower oil

See recipe page 50. This is dog- and cat-friendly, supports the immune and lymphatic systems and helps itchy skin. Many long-coated cats self-select this oil to help with hairballs and soothe any minor irritation.

Chickweed ice cubes

This recipe is particularly useful for senior dogs that may be restless, need to keep cool and require a steady stream of small and nutritious snacks.

A large handful of fresh chickweed
1 teaspoon unset (runny) honey

1. Place the chickweed in a blender and add the honey and 2 tablespoons of water. Blitz until smooth.

2. Freeze the chickweed juice in ice-cube trays. Take out one cube at a time and allow your dog to lick it. This activates the salivary glands, helping to release tension in the lower jaw.

🌿 COMFREY *(Symphytum officinale)*

Parts used: aerial parts – leaves (topical use only).

Common uses

This plant is used to heal wounds and treat burns, skin ulcerations, abrasions, lacerations, flea and other insect bites, bruises, arthritis, tendons, ligaments and simple fractures. Although we are dealing only with cats and dogs in this book, I would like to bring to your attention how effective comfrey was for treating my horse, Betty, who at the age of 19 ruptured her left hind suspensory ligament.

My vet warned me that the injury might take up to a year to repair itself, if at all, as it was severe. He was more than happy for me to nurse her with my complementary treatments, healing and herbs, so I made up a comfrey ointment and applied it liberally, massaging it into the lower leg several times a week.

Betty was on box rest for six months, with regular visits from my vet, who monitored her progress. At the end of that period the vet was delighted – Betty had made a full recovery. Today, at the age of 25, she still enjoys a gentle hack around the countryside. I am convinced the comfrey ointment contributed to her recovery.

Key properties

Comfrey contains allantoin, which helps speed cell reproduction, both inside and outside the body. It also contains rose-marinic acid and several other compounds that exhibit anti-inflammatory, analgesic and astringent qualities. The comfrey ointment I use has been a useful aid in chronic cases of arthritis, and cruciate ligament and joint problems in dogs.

⚘ Make your own ⚘

Over the years clients have picked some of the English comfrey growing in my herb gardens and have made the ointment themselves, using the following recipe.

Comfrey ointment

500ml (18 fl oz) comfrey-infused sunflower oil (*see recipe page 000*)
20g (¾oz) high-quality beeswax
15 drops lavender essential oil

1. Heat the comfrey infused in sunflower oil in a large glass bowl over a bain-marie until it is warm to the touch.

2. Grate or chop the beeswax and add to the oil; stir until the beeswax has dissolved. Add the lavender essential oil (this acts as a preservative).

3. Transfer the mixture into sterilized jars. Allow to cool and harden, and then label the jars. Ointments made this way can last for up to a year.

To use the ointment, gently massage a little of it between your fingers and apply to the skin. Inevitably you may have some fur in the way, but continue to work in and around the hair follicles.

Unlike the aloe vera gel, which is water based and quickly absorbed into the skin, the comfrey ointment can clog up the fur (due to the beeswax and the oil), so be mindful of how much you are using. The aim is to get to the skin. Think of the Chinese saying, 'where tissue grows energy goes' – gentle massage stimulates blood circulation and brings blood to the surface.

⚘ GARLIC *(Allium sativum)*
Parts used: bulb.

Common uses

Throughout history garlic has been revered for its culinary and medicinal properties. There is a great deal of anecdotal and scientific evidence supporting the benefits of using this plant internally and externally in both humans and animals – garlic's credentials are pretty impressive and wide-ranging.

Key properties

Garlic can be used as a powerful broad-spectrum antibiotic, an antiseptic, an antifungal, an anti-parasitic, an insecticide, an antiviral and a nutritive. It is also good for fungal infections, worms, upper respiratory tract infections, for strengthening the immune system, the blood, the cardiovascular system... the list is endless.

Garlic is packed with nutritious compounds such as calcium, iron, phosphorus, sodium and copper. It is rich in potassium and contains an impressive array of vitamins – B6, B1 (thiamine) and C – plus niacin, taurine, zinc and riboflavin. The pungent, sometimes overwhelming, smell of garlic is due to the vast amounts of sulphur in each clove. Insects tend to steer clear of anything that smells like garlic, which is why we use it in the neem insect repellent (*see recipe under neem cold-pressed oil below*).

I plant garlic every year in my herb gardens as I use it externally for ringworm, lice and tick bites in animals; it is also included in some of the food recipes I create for dogs. Taken internally, garlic cleanses the blood, supports the natural gut flora to aid digestion and is one of the best ways to support the immune system. For centuries now garlic has been used as a blood tonic. Overall, it is one of the most impressive broad-spectrum antimicrobial substances available in the natural world.

Garlic has the ability to help regulate blood sugar and it reduces cholesterol and triglycerides while purifying the liver by helping with detoxification. It also contains selenium, a powerful antioxidant which activates enzymes that protect against cancer. Cancer is the leading cause of non-accidental deaths in dogs. The National Cancer Institute has found garlic to be effective in slowing the growth of cancer cells. And at least 30 other compounds contained in garlic have been shown to be useful for conditions ranging from skin disorders to tumours.

There have been reports that feeding dogs a lot of garlic can cause a condition called hemolytic anemia. However, you would need to feed 50 cloves at one time to reach that level of toxicity. Feeding one or two cloves a few times a week is perfectly safe. The AAFCO (American Association of Feed Control Officials) has acknowledged that garlic is safe; this body gathers information from US toxicologists and is responsible for monitoring the safety of animal feed products.

Caution: many cats do not like garlic and prefer the milder herb chives (see opposite).

⚘ Make your own ⚘

Garlic-infused honey
See recipe page 49.

Garlic K9 biscuits
See recipe page 46.

Ear mite garlic oil remedy
Garlic oil helps get rid of ear mites and wards off re-infestation.

1 large clove garlic, minced
Olive oil

1. Place the garlic in a saucepan and cover with oil to a depth of about 1cm (½in).

2. Warm gently over a low heat for 1 hour. Strain the oil and allow to cool. Bottle, label and keep in the fridge.

3. To use, dip a cotton-wool bud into the oil and apply to ears.

🌿 CHIVES *(Allium Schoenoprasum)*
Parts used: aerial parts – leaves only.

Common uses and key properties
I have chive plants dotted about my herb gardens to deter the aphids from gorging themselves on my rose bushes, and I sometimes substitute chives for garlic when making healthy recipes for cats (who generally prefer chives to garlic) as the herb has a milder taste and action, yet similar properties to garlic. Chives are rich in vitamin A and C, iron, calcium and sulphur. They have antibacterial and antifungal qualities and help to boost the immune system.

Wild garlic, or *Ramsons Allium ursinumis,* is just as important medicinally as shop-bought garlic bulbs. I have located a woodland glade within the national park where I live that is awash with wild garlic during May and early June. Wild garlic has lush green leaves and round, white flower heads. There is always a familiar pungent smell wafting through the air in this glade, so there is no mistaking I am in garlic territory! This aroma is more to do with the wild garlic leaves, which ooze the garlic smell; in some instances these are more palatable than garlic cloves.

ꙭ Make your own ꙭ

Wild garlic leaf-infused oil for dogs

Pick a handful of wild garlic leaves on a sunny afternoon (so they remain dry). Roll them individually into thin tubes and pop them into a glass bottle of mild olive oil. Label and keep in the fridge. Leave for a couple of weeks to infuse and then offer a teaspoon of oil a few times a week on a self-selection basis.

Chive Feline treats

See recipe page 46.

ꙭ GINGER *(Zingiber officinale)*

Parts used: root.

Common uses

Ginger is one of the most versatile herbs – it is used in culinary dishes all around the world, and is helpful as a digestive aid for animals and humans suffering from nausea, colic, flatulence, vomiting and lethargy.

Quite often I see dogs and cats at my clinic who are suffering from travel sickness, or are undergoing chemo- or radiotherapy treatment for cancer, and I have found ginger to be most useful in dealing with symptoms of nausea. Although none of my animal clients have self-selected raw ginger root, I have perfected a couple of recipes in which ginger is one of the prime ingredients and animals happily self-select my ginger-infused honey and/or my ginger biscuits as part of their rehabilitation programme.

Top tip ✍

It is best to use fresh ginger root, which can be bought from the supermarket. Keep in the fridge to retain freshness and improve longevity.

Key properties

Ginger contains anti-inflammatory compounds called gingerols, which help with circulation. This is particularly useful for senior animals that are a little unsteady and worried about their mobility. Ginger has a stimulating and warming effect on the body, and as we are dealing with the root of the plant, I tend to think anything used from beneath the soil has real earthy and grounding qualities.

This is certainly the case with ginger, as it works quite quickly. In winter I particularly like to drink ginger-infused tea to help combat a circulatory condition I suffer from called Raynaud's, which affects my fingers in cold weather. The ginger helps to increase circulation to the peripheral parts of the body (hands and feet) and within minutes of drinking the infused tea I can feel the warmth spreading to my hands and fingers. Amazingly, the swelling and redness that is a characteristic feature of Raynaud's disappears.

⅍ Make your own ⅍

Ginger-infused honey
See recipe page 49.

Ginger K9 biscuits
See recipe page 46.

❀ 🌿 LAVENDER *(Lavandula angustifolia)*
Parts used: flowers and leaves.

Common uses and key properties
Lavender is loved and respected all over the world for its aromatic fragrance, pretty indigo flowers, and calming and relaxing qualities. As early as Roman times this common herb was added to bath water to help soothe aches and pains and minor irritations. Its Latin name, *lavere,* means 'to wash'.

A lavender tea, made by infusing a handful of fresh or dried flowers in 550ml (1 pint) of water, can be a useful topical wash to soothe and relieve animals from itchy and irritating skin ailments, especially when they are stressed and need calming.

Lavender also works well as an insect repellent: I often use the recipe below on my own dogs as a preventative measure as it deters insects from biting them and using them as a host on which to feed and multiply. If you suspect or already have an insect problem, though, you must visit your veterinarian immediately.

ᵗ❧ Make your own ☙

Lavender is added to the insect repellent recipe below as a topical application as it soothes the skin and has antibacterial and astringent qualities and calms a nervous animal. Plus, most insects dislike lavender. This repellent has been really useful when I treat stray and abandoned sick animals in animal outreach projects in countries such as South Africa, Sri Lanka, Portugal and Egypt, where mange, ticks and fleas are rife.

Insect repellent for dogs and cats

1 handful fresh lavender flowers
3 fresh sage leaves
3 sprigs fresh rosemary
1 handful fresh lemon balm
2 garlic gloves, peeled
4 drops warm neem oil (see *Neem* entry below)

1. Put the lavender, sage, rosemary and lemon balm in a blender and add 500ml (18 fl oz) water. Blend the ingredients on a high speed for 1 minute.

2. Pour the mixture into a glass bottle with a tight-fitting lid and leave on the windowsill to infuse for 1 day.

3. Sieve the liquid and discard the herbs. With a pestle and mortar grind the garlic cloves to a very fine pulp and add this to the liquid. Pour the liquid back into the bottle and then add the warm neem oil.

4. Place remedy in a glass jar, label and keep in the fridge for up to a week. Shake the jar from time to time to help infuse the garlic.

5. When applying the insect repellent use a soft new sponge. Gently sponge down the back and flanks only, keeping clear of the face and genitals.

Chamomile and lavender pillow

See *Chamomile*, above.

❦ LEMON BALM *(Melissa Officinalis)*

Parts used: leaves.

This plant is related to mint and its leaves have a gentle lemon scent. It is often used in insect repellents (*see recipe above*) because of its high (24 per cent) citronella content.

✧ LINSEED *(Linum usitatissimum)*
Parts used: seeds.

Common uses

Throughout history, linseed has been consumed by humans and animals for its health benefits, and as a food source. While linseed is rich in protein, research suggests that its health benefits are probably down to its fatty acid and fibre profile. Approximately 42 per cent of linseed is oil, of which nearly three-quarters is polyunsaturated fat – a healthy fat.

Linseed plant oil is cold-pressed from unprocessed flaxseeds/linseeds (same name), and contains a unique balance of omega-3 and omega-6 essential fatty acids. Omega-3 accounts for one quarter of all cell membranes in the body and enables the body to absorb important nutrients. It strengthens the membranes around the body's 700 million million cells. Linseed oil contains a host of amino acids, antioxidants and phyto-nutrients.

Flaxseed is the richest plant source of alpha-linolenic acid (ALA), an omega-3 fatty acid that is also found in some green vegetables, such as kale, spinach and salad greens. It has many important functions. It is mainly used for energy and converts to long-chain omega-3 fat such as eicosapentaenoic acid (EPA) and docosahexaenoic acid (DHA). Like humans, animals cannot manufacture these themselves and cannot survive without them, so it is important to offer your pets a nutritious supplement like cold-pressed linseed oil on a self-selection basis.

Key properties

ALA helps prevent heart disease and stroke; it also reduces inflammation and helps in autoimmune diseases such as arthritis. Due to its high alpha-linoleic content, linseed can help eliminate dull, dry coats in animals and the itching and scratching that can accompany them. It promotes healthy skin and a shiny coat, and also encourages strong, healthy nails.

Recent research shows that it is helpful with some cancers as it is rich in lignans – components that researchers believe assist in the prevention of stomach and colon cancer – and antioxidants, which help reduce the activity of cell-damaging free radicals.

- **Milled linseed meal** – when the seeds are ground to a part powder they contain high quantities of both soluble and insoluble dietary fibre and plant lignans (phytoestrogens). These components play a role in the maintenance and improvement of general animal health and digestion. Soluble fibre reduces blood cholesterol levels, while insoluble fibre helps create good bowel movements. Keep milled linseed in an airtight food storage box in the fridge and use within seven weeks of purchase. Milled linseed meal provides up to 800 times more lignans than any other plant. (Note, however, that linseed oil contains virtually no lignans.)

Pregnant animals benefit from taking linseed meal/oil as it helps them produce more milk and reduces the likelihood of mastitis. Many pet food manufacturers include milled linseed as a source of essential fatty acids in their premium pet foods. Linseed oil should be kept cool and in dark bottles, making the refrigerator a good storage location.

Top tip ✍

Linseed oil can become rancid very quickly and has a short shelf life. Buy freshly cold-pressed oil that has at least three months' shelf life. Keep it in the fridge at all times. Taste the oil before use – it should have a lovely nutty taste. Steer clear of chemically extracted linseed, which uses harmful solvents, additives and heat.

- **Pure, cold-pressed linseed oil** – an exceptional plant source of omega-3, -6 and -9 fatty acids, and packed full of goodness for improved energy and healthy circulation, skin and coat. It is highly nutritious, has anti-inflammatory properties and is beneficial against autoimmune diseases.

⚘ Make your own ⚘

Linseed K9/Feline biscuits
See recipe page 52.

✧ MILK THISTLE *(Silybum marianum)*

Parts used: seeds.

Common uses

Milk thistle is a dog- and cat-friendly herb that is used to help with all manner of liver conditions in both animals. It helps protect the liver cells from contaminants and toxins and helps activate liver repair by boosting protein synthesis. This is particularly useful when animals are receiving chemotherapy or a number of conventional drugs at the same time as it aids getting rid of the unwanted side effects.

Key properties

Milk thistle contains a chemical compound called silymarin, which enhances liver function, especially when the liver is in crisis. Together with other compounds this antioxidant creates a powerful barrier to unwanted poisons. Vets have used milk thistle to help treat jaundice, hepatitis, kidney damage and vaccination complications, and in the recovery stages of parvovirus. Milk thistle powder is best used for conditions in which the liver is under stress – these need to be diagnosed by a veterinarian – it is not necessary to use it as a daily supplement.

Top tip ✍

With milk thistle powder freshness is paramount, so make sure what you buy is 100 per cent pure and within date. Alternatively, you can grind a small quantity of seeds to a powder yourself, using a coffee grinder. To keep the powder fresh, store it in an airtight jar and use within three months.

❀ MINT *(Mentha piperita)*

Parts used: aerial parts – leaves.

Common uses and key properties

Mint, best known as the peppermint variety *Mentha piperita,* is one of the best digestive aids available and helps soothe and relax the digestive tract. Many human and animal prescription drugs contain mint because it helps with all manner of digestive complaints, including indigestion, flatulence, nausea, colitis, bloat and colic; it has antispasmodic and calming qualities that help settle the stomach.

The 'mintiness' we smell and taste when we drink mint tea comes from aromatic oils in the plant which contain chemical compounds such as menthol and volatile oils that help to stimulate the liver, increasing the flow of bile. Mint also has anti-inflammatory properties and can be added to my aloe vera basic gel (*see recipe above*) and used as a topical application to help with aches and pains.

When I work at Animal Care Egypt in Luxor, I harvest fresh peppermint, which is cultivated nearby, in fields bordering the River Nile. It is an important crop – many Egyptians drink mint tea as it is refreshing and cooling in the long, hot summers. It is also used in many local dishes, not just to flavour food but also for medicinal purposes as it has a dual action – it calms stomach tension (as in Irritable Bowel Syndrome) and has rejuvenating qualities that relieve mental anxiety and help maintain focus.

I use mint in a topical wash (infuse two mint tea bags in 1 litre (1¾ pints) of cold water for 30 minutes and gently sponge over the back and flanks) to help keep animals cool when it is hot, and I use fresh mint in the biscuits I make for the local dogs suffering from an unsettled stomach. Mint's culinary virtues are well known and it is a very easy herb to grow. In fact, it can seed itself everywhere and dominate the garden, so in my herb gardens I grow peppermint (*Mentha piperita*) and applemint (*Mentha rotundifolia*) in large tubs to help keep the plants' growth in check.

⚘ Make your own ⚘

Mint-infused sunflower oil
See recipe page 50. This is dog-friendly, but cats are not so interested in it. It assists dogs with aches and sprains, calms the stomach, is nourishing and cleansing, and opens up the airways. It is fresh and mentally clearing, helping keep dogs alert yet grounded, and alleviating boredom.

Mint K9 biscuits
See recipe page 53. Many dogs love these, and they help with bad breath, travel sickness, anxiety and depression.

🌿 NEEM *(Azadirachta indica)*

Parts used: fruit, bark, leaves and seeds. Caution: topical application only.

Common uses

The neem tree, which is native to India and Southeast Asia, is very versatile, with all parts being used in traditional medicine. The tree has been used for thousands of years to treat a variety conditions in both humans and animals. I work with an international rescue centre in Sri Lanka, helping to rehome and rehabilitate stray animals, and have seen how the locals regard the neem tree as the village dispensary for many of their ailments.

Unfortunately, most do not think to extend this help to the stray dogs that roam the streets, covered from head to toe in ticks and fleas. It is heartbreaking to see how anxious and distressed they are. Desperate to remove these parasites, many dogs gnaw at their own flesh, some causing a secondary infection to take hold and creating an even bigger problem to solve.

✧ NEEM COLD-PRESSED OIL

The cold-pressed oil made from the fruit and seeds of the neem tree is a valuable ingredient in the topical insect spray I make to help combat ticks and fleas *(see recipe below)*. I have to make sure I buy the very best cold-pressed oil and not a cheap, chemically extracted version which, through the extraction process, removes some of the powerful plant compounds that actually deter the insects in the first place.

Top tip ✍

Always buy good-quality cold-pressed neem oil. Avoid solvent, extracted or cheap diluted versions, which are lower in quality and not robust enough to deter insects.

Key properties

Neem is widely respected because it kills and repels insects, including mosquitoes and fleas. It deters them from laying their eggs on animals and humans. Research has found a compound in neem called azadirachtin, which apparently prevents young insects from growing properly and the adults from reproducing and laying eggs. It also appears to stop insects from feeding on the host animal.

The cold-pressed oil also has antifungal, antibacterial and antiviral qualities. It should only be used externally on the skin as part of a topical treatment and not taken internally. It helps with many skin conditions, including ringworm, eczema, fleas, ticks, mange and mites.

⚘ Make your own ⚘

Neem insect repellent for dogs

Good-quality cold-pressed neem oil has a thick and sticky consistency and is difficult to use. Making this recipe therefore requires patience and trust, as the neem oil and the base ingredient, water, do not really mix. However, with a bit of determination, and a little magic with some washing-up liquid to help bring it together, hey presto we have a remedy!

1 tablespoon neem oil*
500ml (18 fl oz) warm water
1 drop of washing-up liquid

1. Heat the neem oil in a glass bowl over a bain-marie until it is warm to the touch and thinner in consistency.

2. Add the water and the washing-up liquid and beat together vigorously with a whisk for a few minutes, until the mixture comes together. Place the liquid in a glass bottle, label it and keep in the fridge. Use within two months.

3. When applying the neem insect repellent use a clean cloth. Gently sponge down the back and flanks, keeping clear of the face and genitals.

If you do not use all of the bottled neem repellent at once, when you come to use it later you will notice that the neem oil has separated from the water – forming fat globules – and appears to be unstable. Do not be alarmed, though – place the bottle over a bain-marie again to warm it, shake the bottle well and try a little on your arm, to test the temperature. Apply as above.

* See Resources section (page 296) for stockists.

Treating cats with neem

The amazing pest control qualities of the neem tree are not only found in the oil pressed from its fruits and seeds, they are also found in its bark and leaves, both of which have antimicrobial compounds. Cats, I find, are more willing and interested in my neem-leaf tea and powdered bark recipes *(see below)*. The leaf and bark are safe to use, even if a cat has self-groomed and ingested some, as there are no known adverse side effects.

When I am working overseas on outreach cat programmes I make up both recipes. Short-haired cats fare better with the powdered neem bark recipe, as I can reach the skin more easily, and long-haired cats do well with the neem-leaf tea version as it penetrates the hair shaft. Both are safe and help as a preventative measure. Every cat is individual so it is important to try different ways to achieve the desired outcome.

⟿ Make your own ⟾

Neem-leaf tea insect repellent for cats
4 tablespoons fresh or dried neem leaf*

1. Place the neem leaf in a cup, then fill the cup to the brim with just-boiled water. Steep overnight until cool.

2. Strain the liquid and place in a glass jar; label, and keep in the fridge for up to a week.

3. Take a clean cloth or sponge and apply to the back and flanks; avoid the face and genitals.

* See Resources section (page 296) for stockists.

Neem bark powder insect repellent for cats
4 tablespoons neem bark powder*
4 tablespoons internal green clay*

1. Place the bark powder and green clay in a glass jar with a screw-on lid. Shake the jar to mix both ingredients together and then label it.

2. Take a small handful of the powdered mixture and rub through the back and flanks; avoid the face and genitals.

* See Resources section (page 296) for stockists.

🌿 NETTLE *(Urtica dioica)*
Parts used: aerial parts – leaves and stems.

Common uses
Nettles are a rich source of vitamins A and C, iron, sodium, chlorophyll, zinc, silica, protein and dietary fibre (the high vitamin C content enables the iron to be absorbed more efficiently by the body). Nettles are an excellent tonic and a general blood cleanser and conditioner.

They also stimulate the circulation, which makes them ideal for conditions such as rheumatism and arthritis, and are one of nature's best nutraceuticals. They also have antihistamine properties, which makes them excellent for animals that have sensitivities and allergies to pollen and tree bark and therefore have compromised immune systems.

Top tip ✍

When harvesting nettles, wear gloves and a long-sleeved top – to avoid being stung! Harvested nettles will wilt after being exposed to air, heat and cooking and this neutralizes the antigenic proteins that are responsible for the plant's sting. These compounds break down quickly and when correctly prepared (see Chapter 4: *Harvesting Nature's Bounty*) the green leaves of young nettle plants are delicious.

Key properties

Nettles contain a vast array of nutrients. In fact, 100g (3½oz) of dried nettle plant contains up to 30g (1½oz) of crude protein (30 per cent by weight), 2,970mg of calcium, 680mg of phosphorus, 32.2mg of iron, 650mg of magnesium, 20.2mg of beta-carotene and 3,450mg of potassium, along with vitamins A, C, D and B-complex – all in a highly palatable form that can be effectively assimilated into the body without creating excess stress upon the liver, kidneys or digestive tract.

One of the graduates of my Diploma in Animal Healing course, Kajsa, comes from Stockholm in Sweden and she told me how important nettles are as part of a balanced diet in her home country. For six months of the year most parts of Sweden are covered in snow and many people and animals are starved of vital green nutrients, as the problem of producing nutrient-rich food is compounded by a short growing season.

Many Swedes forage for the winter-hardy nettles that are sometimes cultivated as a fodder crop and a vegetable source and make them into herbal teas. Nettle also makes an excellent additional food source for animals needing extra trace minerals and vitamins in their diet.

⁓ **Make your own** ⁓

Nettle seeds
These are a useful support to the adrenal glands. In the summer months strip the seeds from the stems, dry them for five days and then gently bruise using a pestle and mortar. Keep in a labelled glass jar and sprinkle a little on your pet's food.

Nettle K9 biscuits
See recipe page 53.

Nettle-infused sunflower oil
See recipe page 50. This cat- and dog-friendly oil is a nutritious tonic that aids those with anaemia and improves circulation. It is also a nourishing food for pets in convalescence and recuperation.

Nettle-leaf K9 rinse
This is an excellent skin and coat rinse that nourishes a pet's fur and provides symptomatic relief for itchy skin and fleabites. The nettle's sting is removed by cooking. Use young nettle tops, as they are more flavoursome than the older leaves at the bottom of the plant.

4 tablespoons fresh nettle tops

1. Place the nettles in a cup, then fill the cup to the brim with just-boiled water. Steep overnight until cool.

2. Strain the liquid and pour into a labelled glass jar.

🌿 **PARSLEY** *(Petroselinum crispum)*
Parts used: aerial parts – fresh leaves.

Common uses and key properties
Parsley is one of the most nutritious common garden herbs around and is very easy to grow. It can happily be nurtured and grown in tubs, window boxes and vegetable plots. It is packed full of minerals and protein and rich in vitamins A and C, iron and copper, chlorophyll, magnesium and beta-carotene, which makes it ideal as a general blood tonic, a digestive aid and a wonderful supplement for anaemia. It is a lovely addition to home-made treats for cats and dogs.

Top tip ✍

You can add very finely chopped fresh flat or curly leaf parsley to most of my dog and cat recipes. This not only creates a fabulous green colour, it also adds fibre to the diet. Alternatively, place a couple of handfuls of parsley in a blender, add 2 tablespoons of water, blend until a soup consistency is achieved and add to the pet treats, biscuits and casseroles in Chapter 2.

✧ ROSEHIP *(Rosa canina)*

Parts used: fresh or dried hips.

Common uses and key properties

When August comes around I cannot wait to harvest the ruby-red rosehips that grow freely throughout hedgerows, scrubland and woods. The hips are a rich source of vitamins A, C, K, B1 (thiamine), plus niacin, riboflavin, and volatile oils. When used in my rosehip-infused sunflower oil (*see below*), rosehips make an excellent spring tonic and serve as a tasty and nutritious snack for animals.

In fact, my three dogs are often found in the hedgerow when we are out on a foraging trip, self-selecting rosehips and ripe blackberries. The whole hip can be fed, either fresh or dried. Dried hips can be ground in an electric grinder and added to my Hedgerow Hip Bites treats (*see recipe page 47*).

❧ Make your own ❧

Rosehip-infused sunflower oil

See recipe page 50. This dog- and cat-friendly oil is highly nutritious and supports the immune system.

Rose petal water for cats

All parts of the rose are edible and usable; however we are concentrating on the petals for this recipe. You can use any rose species. Personally, I like to use the dog rose, which can be found growing in hedgerows – it flowers in June and July.

1. Collect as many scented rose petals as you can find (enough to fill 3–4 cups) and place in a large saucepan.

2. Pour boiling water over the petals, until completely covered. Stir for a few minutes and then let the water cool completely. Leave in the fridge overnight.

3. Strain the rose liquid into a clean glass jar and label.

4. Pour a little rose water onto a clean plate and allow your cat to sniff the aromatic aromas.

Some cats may wish to lick some rose water, too – this is perfectly safe. Do not mix it with your cat's drinking water, though, and always have plenty of fresh water available in a separate bowl.

Top tip ✍

Excess rose water can be frozen in ice-cube trays and used one at a time, melted onto a saucer. They are beautifully scented and some cats adore the smell as it helps with behavioural, loss and abandonment issues.

🌿 🏵 ROSEMARY *(Rosmarinus officinalis)*

Parts used: leaves, stems, and flowers.

Common uses

I mentioned earlier that any plant with *officinalis* in its Latin name is known for its medicinal virtues and rosemary has been used for thousands of years in cooking and in pharmacy. It is a popular herb as it can be harvested all year round. An attractive, woody shrub, rosemary has pretty lilac-blue flowers and a wonderful aromatic smell, especially when you rub your fingers in between the leaves to release some of the precious oils.

On my trips to rescue centres in the Mediterranean I forage locally for rosemary as it is native to southern Europe and it grows well everywhere. I like to use local herbs in my remedies and share the recipes with the local rescue centres, so they in turn can use them. Many of the centres I work with have very little funding and are totally reliant on donations to help with feeding and medicines.

Key properties

Rosemary is a useful addition to the insect repellent recipe on page 74, as it has excellent antimicrobial, antibacterial and antifungal properties and studies have shown that it is also active against infections such as staphylococcus albus, staphylococcus aureus and E coli. On more than one occasion when overseas I have witnessed stray dogs rolling in rosemary bushes to help deter insects from biting them.

When I am treating senior dogs with arthritis, stiffness and muscular aches I sometimes make up a rosemary acupressure massage oil *(see recipe below)* as rosemary also has proven anti-inflammatory properties. I pour a little on my fingers and thumbs and gently apply it topically to specific points on the animal's body. See *Fingers and Thumbs* chapter for more on acupressure.

Rosemary also has calming and soothing qualities that help with anxiety, nervous exhaustion and long-term stress. This is particularly useful for rescue animals that are waiting for a new home and have been in a shelter for a long time.

As for its culinary properties, I like to add a pinch of rosemary to the tasty treats I bake at home for my dogs, cats, animal guests and myself. Rosemary has anti-spasmodic qualities and helps with digestive problems; researchers have also confirmed that it is an effective antioxidant and helps to slow down cell damage.

✥ Make your own ✥

Rosemary acupressure massage oil
Note: this oil is for topical use only

150ml (5 fl oz) sunflower oil
6 sprigs dried rosemary

1. Heat the sunflower oil gently in a saucepan – taking care not to let it boil – and then add the rosemary sprigs.

2. Remove from the heat and stir the mixture with a wooden spoon.

3. Allow to cool and infuse for 48 hours. Strain the oil, pour into a dark bottle and label. Use within six months.

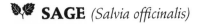 SAGE *(Salvia officinalis)*
Parts used: leaves

Common uses and key properties
Sage is an effective remedy for mouth, skin or digestive problems in dogs and cats. It is great for keeping teeth clean and preventing gingivitis as it contains thujone, a powerfully volatile oil that has antiseptic, antibiotic and antimicrobial qualities.

I like to plant sage because I use it in cooking and make a sage tea for myself. I place a handful of fresh leaves in a mug and add boiling water. I let this infuse for 10 minutes and sip it throughout the day. Sage tea is an excellent remedy for mouth ulcers and for when you are generally feeling run down. When the tea has cooled I sometimes use it to clean my dogs' teeth to maintain healthy gums (see 'make your own' below).

Sage is an important culinary herb, having been used in cooking for the last 2,000 years. My dogs and cats love small amounts of it chopped up very finely and added to home-baked treats; it also adds fibre to their diet. As with all culinary herbs a little goes a long way.

⟨ Make your own ⟩

Sage toothpaste

A couple of times a year, take a small children's toothbrush, dip it in some cooled sage tea (see instructions above) and then gently brush around the teeth and gums of your dog or cat. This is a wonderful opportunity to have a closer inspection of your pet's mouth. If there is excess tartar or gum disease you will need to have your pet's teeth looked at by your veterinarian.

Add to dog and cat treats

Add a small handful of very finely chopped sage to any of the biscuit recipes in Chapter 2.

🌿 SPIRULINA *(Spirulina platensis)*

Parts used: whole plant, ground to a powder.

Common uses and key properties

Spirulina is a species of algae that has inhabited the planet for more than 3 billion years. It grows wild and abundantly around the world in very alkaline, mineral-rich, largely pollution-free waters, and also thrives in very warm soda lakes. It has the most remarkable concentration of nutrients: 60 per cent vegetable protein, a complete and digestible source of vitamin B-complex, beta-carotene, phyto-nutrients and antioxidants and a wide variety of minerals.

Spirulina is an excellent all-round nutritional supplement for dogs and cats and a good source of essential fatty acids to help promote a healthy skin and coat. It is helpful for senior animals as it encourages appetite and strengthens and boosts the immune system. In return dogs and cats will receive vital nutrients for body repair.

Spirulina powder is a vivid blue-green in colour and is expensive to buy, but as it is rich in nutrients, only small amounts are needed. My dogs and cats enjoy eating my pet treats containing spirulina, rather than licking the powder from a plate. Add 1 teaspoon of spirulina to any of the biscuit recipes in Chapter 2.

❀ 🌿 THYME *(Thyme vulgaris)*
Parts used: aerial parts – flowers and leaves.

Common uses and key properties
This wonderful kitchen garden herb is easy to grow and adapts well to most soil types. I have a number of plants in my herb gardens and decorative tubs outside the back door. I often pick a few sprigs of thyme and make a small bouquet to add to my chicken broth *(page 15)*.

Like many culinary herbs thyme has a pleasing taste, and it helps aid digestion and boost the immune system. Thyme owes some of its success to a wonderful chemical compound called thymol, which has powerful antiseptic, antibacterial and antifungal qualities. Thyme is a good antiseptic for the mouth and throat and is useful for fighting gingivitis in dogs and cats.

⚘ Make your own ⚘

Mouth infections/gingivitis prevention
A strong thyme tea can be directly applied to the gum lines or infected sites with a swab. See instructions under *Sage toothpaste* above, substituting the sage for thyme.

Add to dog treats
To help the digestive tract of dogs with conditions such as an upset stomach and colitis, add 1 teaspoon of finely chopped thyme to any of the dog treat recipes in Chapter 2.

Thyme-infused honey
See recipe page 49.

᚛ VALERIAN *(Valeriana officinalis)*
Parts used: root.

Common uses and key properties

Valerian is valued medicinally as a sedative and is a gentle, safe, relaxing herb for dogs and cats. However it is interesting to observe how valerian affects some of our feline friends compared to our dogs. It contains a chemical compound called valerinone, which acts as a stimulant in cats and is similar to catnip *(Nepeta cataria)* in as much as it can drive some cats into a frenzy.

On one occasion I was sewing a valerian-filled cat toy at the kitchen table for an animal charity fundraising event when my rescue cat Oliver raised his nose, sniffed the air and suddenly pounced at the toy, grabbing it from me with his front paws and holding it to his chest, purring loudly as he head-butted it. He then flipped over and writhed, snake-like, on his back, his tail thumping the table and an expression of pure ecstasy on his face. Needless to say I did not get the cat toy back!

A valerian cat toy (see 'make your own' below) can help in a variety of situations, including rehabilitation after surgery; when cats are bored, or are stressing about other cats in the neighbourhood or their cat housemates; when cats are anxious or nervous, or are suffering from emotional trauma. It also helps cats that are settling into a new home, or are lethargic or depressed, or are needing mental stimulation or pure amusement.

I have often placed valerian cat toys in my dogs' day beds to observe their reaction. There is never a sniff or nose twitch or funny five minutes from any of them. However, preparations made with valerian root taken internally can help calm a dog with anxiety, and your veterinarian can advise you accordingly. Many holistic veterinarians are also using valerian to help with epilepsy and to reduce the frequency of seizures in dogs.

⚘ Make your own ⚘

Valerian cat toy

Cats will play with these for hours. Sew together two 100 per cent cotton squares (15 × 15cm/6 × 6in), leaving a small entrance. Stuff full with dried valerian root and then sew up the entrance. Alternatively, take a clean 100 per cent wool sock and stuff full with dried valerian root before sewing up the entrance.

🌿 WHEATGRASS *(Triticum aestivum)*

Parts used: whole plant.

Common uses

How can anyone fail to notice the psychedelic green colour that screams wheatgrass? The bright green shoots and leaves of this wheat plant radiate goodness and ooze with nutrient-rich chlorophyll. Wheatgrass has become very popular for use in energy drinks and as a food source, and dogs and many cats like to chew on the young green tips and self-select the whole plant!

Key properties

Wheatgrass contains an impressive number of antioxidants and nutrients, including vitamins A, C, E and K, plus iron, zinc, folic acid, copper, selenium, potassium and calcium. It is a wonderful companion plant for dogs and cats to self-select as it helps to improve digestion, adds fibre to the diet, and helps to alkalize the blood and stimulate cell rejuvenation and enzyme activity.

Wheatgrass is cleansing and as it grows all year round it is an excellent 'pick me up' tonic during the dark winter months – especially for housebound cats in need of extra nutrients. It also helps cats with fur balls, feline immunodeficiency virus (FIV), bladder and urinary conditions and an overactive thyroid.

Some cats will chew on wheatgrass, ingest it, and then regurgitate it. This is somewhat reminiscent of the way in which their cousin, the cheetah, chews on the long savannah grasses in the wild – for fibre and to help in regurgitating parts of their prey. Do not be surprised if your cat eats the wheatgrass it has regurgitated – it is perfectly safe.

You can buy wheatgrass plants from garden centres or purchase seeds online and sow them year round. Alternatively you can buy organic wheatgrass powder and offer it on a self-selection basis or add it to dog and cat treats. (*See Resources section for stockists of seeds, plants and powder.*)

⚕ Make your own ⚘

Grow your own wheatgrass

If you decide to grow wheatgrass from seed, keep several small seed trays on the go. Sow seeds 12cm (5in) deep in a good compost and water well. When sprouted keep on a deep window ledge indoors, where cats can self-select and eat the tips of the lush green grass, which contain the most chlorophyll. Indoor cats especially will welcome this tasty snack, so be aware that you could be replacing the seed trays regularly!

Add to cat and dog treats

Add 1 teaspoon of wheatgrass powder to any of the biscuit recipes in Chapter 2.

 **YARROW** *(Achillea millefolium)*

Parts used: aerial parts – leaves and flowers.

Common uses and key properties

This is one of my favourite herbs and it travels with me all over the world when I am treating animals at rescue centres; I also use it at my animal clinic in the UK. It is particularly beneficial for urinary infections such as cystitis, when a simple topical remedy is required for application to the lower abdomen. It also encourages the healing of wounds and burst blood vessels and helps improve the blood supply and circulation to peripheral blood vessels.

Yarrow can be grown at home *(see Resources section for stockists of seeds and plants)* or harvested from the countryside. Yarrow forms part of the water-based gel I make for dogs with aches and sprains. It complements the basic aloe vera gel beautifully, as together they are soothing and readily absorbed into the body. Both have analgesic and anti-inflammatory properties and contain small amounts of the painkiller salicylic acid.

✿ Make your own ✿

The topical remedy below is particularly useful for chronic conditions such as arthritis, joint problems, and torn ligaments that are taking a long time to heal.

Aloe and yarrow gel

Note: for external use only

115g (4oz) yarrow leaves and flowers
6 tablespoons aloe vera basic gel (*see recipe above*)
½ teaspoon xanthan gum*

1. Place the yarrow leaves and flowers in a pestle and mortar and bruise them to release some of the precious oils. Place in a cup, add boiling water and steep overnight until cool.

2. Strain the liquid and pour into a blender with the aloe vera gel and the xanthan gum. Blend until a smooth gel is formed. Pour into an airtight glass jar and label. Store in the fridge for up to one month.

3. Apply topically and massage gently to affected areas, avoiding the face and genitals.

* Xanthan gum is a natural thickener you can buy online. *See Resources section (page 296) for stockists.*

Chapter 4

⁓

Harvesting Nature's Bounty
for Your Pet – Gathering
and Preparing Herbs

Herbs and plant extracts have been used for their healing and culinary properties for thousands of years. The ancient Egyptians, the ancient cultures of the Far East and the Romans used herbs in cooking and in medicines, both for themselves and the animals in their care, and throughout the ages there has been much documentation of the herbal treatments used on domesticated animals.

Folklore tells of the generations of families and farmers who relied heavily on foraging for herbs in the hedgerows, meadows, forests and wilderness areas to feed their livestock, dogs and horses. Many people observed their animals self-selecting local plant material and it became second nature for humans and animals to share alike in the goodness of these healing plants – a vital resource for keeping the body healthy.

No one could afford to lose a working animal and with no professional veterinary advice available until a few hundred years ago, many a lay person used his or her own simple herb and culinary recipes to resolve a problem. Over millennia, and for millions of people, foraging for herbs and plant material became a way of supplementing the diet.

EXPLORING NATURE'S MEDICINE CABINET

I have identified at least 30 herbs growing within a 6.5-km (4-mile) radius of my home in Sussex, England, in the heart of the South Downs National Park. I feel very blessed that I share my home with such a great variety of culinary and healing plants, which include nettle, mint and wild garlic.

I harvest these plants at certain times of the year – mainly late spring, summer and autumn. June, July and August are the busiest months for harvesting catnip, calendula (marigold), yarrow, chamomile, rose petals, cleavers, lavender, red and white clover, lemon balm, chickweed, sage and chamomile, among others. All of these herbs play a very useful role in the food recipes and topical remedies I make for myself and my pets.

Late summer and early autumn herald a new burst of colour, as rich ruby red and deep purple berries such as rosehips, elderberries and blackberries make themselves available. These are packed full of beta-carotene, vitamins and trace minerals that take care of wild animals during the long winter months when they find it hard to forage for food. Autumn is a great time for them to stock up on vital nutrients when times are hard.

I never have any particular expectation of which herbs I am going to source on my foraging trips, and I am always pleasantly surprised by a new find. Every single outing is like finding a treasure chest full of gold, except in this case it is an array of healing, nutritious herbs. Most days I take my dogs for a walk in the meadows near my house. It is a wonderful opportunity to spend quality time with them and to observe them delicately picking off the fresh young shoots of grass, packed with chlorophyll – an important trace mineral for animals. Over the years I have identified most of the herbs growing in these meadows, and I have a rough idea of where and when they will appear.

Top tip ✍
Take note of where herbs and plants grow in your area. Carry a small notepad with you when foraging for herbs and jot down the location, date and plant species.

However, sometimes nature has a funny way of catching us out. One day I spotted a small clump of chickweed in a new location. A delicate, tiny white flower had caught my eye – it was nestled in a damp, shallow ditch among a carpet of grasses. I took note and marked it on my Ordnance Survey map. The next day I returned and harvested a small amount of it. I was delighted that the chickweed had taken root and found a new home.

Foraging kit

I always wear trousers on my foraging trips – in case I find myself in the thick of a hedge or in knee-high grass: thorny stems are unforgiving! Most harvesting takes place on warm, sunny days, so a wide-brimmed hat is a must to protect my skin from the glare of the sun. I carry a pair of scissors, secateurs, and a trowel in a hip/bum bag or a small haversack, along with a notepad and pen and a couple of small brown paper bags to keep herbs dry and clean. (I try not to use plastic bags, as plants tend to sweat in them.)

I recommend carrying a small herbal reference book, with colour pictures of leaves and flowers, so you can identify plant species easily and quickly. Do not forget to pack a bottle of water, too, to stay hydrated: you may find yourself in the middle of nowhere, a long way from a shop.

Top tip ✍

Some flower heads look very similar to each other in colour, shape, location and flowering times. Always look at the shape and colour of the leaves and stems to identify accurately plants you are unsure about.

Harvesting rules

Be mindful when harvesting herbs. Only take what you need and never uproot an entire family of plants. If the remedy does not require the roots of the plant, carefully dig down and around the main tubers and gently prise away an offshoot of the rooted plant. Carefully replace any remaining soil.

If the herb you are using requires the aerial parts of the plant (those that grow above ground) take cuttings from about 5cm (2in) above the ground. When you are harvesting berries it is important to pick them when they are ripe and luscious.

Top tip ✍

When harvesting fruits and berries gently squeeze a berry/fruit between your thumb and forefinger – if it feels slightly soft, has a vivid colour and you can taste the flavour without bitterness – PICK! I never harvest fruits or berries without tasting them first, and interestingly you rarely see animals eating unripe berries and fruits either. Like us they appreciate the natural sweet flavours, colours and energy values as a food reserve to help them survive.

Harvesting equipment

The beauty of working with herbs is that you do not need to invest in expensive equipment. Below I have listed the items I use on a daily basis:

- Earthenware and Pyrex glass mixing bowls – 2 and 4 litre (3½ and 7 pint) capacity

- Glass jars with screw-on lids – 225g and 450g (8oz and 1lb) capacity

- Glass measuring jug – 1 litre (1¾ pint) capacity

- Stainless-steel saucepans – 18cm/7in (2 litre/3½ pint capacity) and 20cm/8in (3 litre/5¼ pint capacity)

- Stainless-steel straining funnels (in an assortment of sizes)

- Stainless-steel sieves (in an assortment of sizes)

- Brown glass bottles – in an assortment of sizes, from 50ml (2 fl oz), 100ml (3½ fl oz) and 200ml (7 fl oz) up to 500ml (18 fl oz)

- Three-tier stainless-steel cooling rack (on which to dry herbs)

- A plastic tray measuring 600 × 400 × 120mm (24 × 16 × 5in) with small holes in it – for harvesting herbs

- A blender with a glass measuring jug is essential. I strongly advise against using plastic measuring jugs, as some of the herbs are quite pungent and their odour may stay on the plastic and taint recipes.

- A large pestle and mortar – I have a granite one because it is robust and deep enough for mixing an assortment of herbs together

- Weighing scales – digital or manual. When buying scales, look for one with a large basin – at least 5kg (10lb) capacity – in which to place herbs for weighing.

Top tip ✐
All the above, and other good quality cooking equipment, can be purchased at www.lakeland.co.uk and in the USA at www.cookware.com and www.starwest-botanicals.com.

Other useful equipment includes pure cotton muslin, labels and a notebook for recipes. When you need to clean glass bottles or jam jars for reuse, a nylon brush cleaner is invaluable for reaching inside difficult areas – these are available in a variety of sizes from any good cook shop or wine-making store. Save glass jam jars and their lids.

Top tip ✐
When I am bottling and I need special jars and dark brown glass jars and lids I use Wains of Tunbridge (www.wains.co.uk) and www.baldwins.co.uk, who will sell small quantities of bottles and lids. US readers can try www.specialtybottle.com.

When to harvest
I harvest herbs after midday, as this allows any dew or dampness to be absorbed by the plant. Also, if the sun is out more rays are absorbed and goodness captured. Use a good pair of scissors and a flat tray with holes in the bottom (*see above*) to keep air circulating to the plants; do not overload the tray. If you are harvesting a plant like calendula, pick the very best flower heads; when picking mint take the whole stem, leaving approximately 5cm (2in) at the base so as to cultivate another crop later on in the harvest. Keep herbs separate from each other.

USING FRESH AND DRIED HERBS
As much as I love working with fresh herbs in the summer months it becomes a problem when working out of season. Many fresh herbs are at their best only in the summer and so a very good way of preserving them for the rest of the year is to dry them.

This is achieved by selecting and picking the very best herbs on a warm day – preferably when there have been at least five days of sunshine beforehand. I have lost an entire crop in the past due to damp conditions, with mildew forming on the plants. Do not leave herbs outside to perish in the cold.

There are two methods for drying herbs, depending on which part of the plant is being used. Calendula (marigold) and other flower heads can be spread out evenly on a tray with holes in it, creating a single layer. A three-tier stainless steel cooling rack does the trick; use the second and third tier as the first is too close to the base and air cannot circulate properly, leaving the flower heads damp.

Do not cover the herbs with another layer, as this will prevent them from drying properly. Place the stainless-steel cooling rack in an airing cupboard, or in a room which is not damp, and leave to dry for up to two weeks.

Another way of drying, suitable for long-stemmed herbs, is to tie a small bunch of the same herb together – i.e. nettles – and hang them up in an airing cupboard or tie them to a clothes horse in a dry room. Try to keep them out of direct sunlight. Make a note of the date you prepared the bunches for drying – in the past I have left herbs to dry and forgotten about them, only to find that damp conditions and sunlight have ruined them.

Storing dried herbs

When the herbs are crispy dry it is time to store them. When storing herbs find a suitable *dry* place, away from direct sunlight, where you can keep them all together. I used to have dried herbs all over my house and inevitably I forgot where some of the key ingredients for my remedies were located! I am now in the fortunate position of having my own apothecary, where all my dried herbs are stored.

With long-stemmed herbs such as mint and nettle you can discard any tough stalks – have a clean tray ready to catch the leaves as you strip the plant. When you have a sufficient quantity of dried leaves, scrunch them up in your hands, especially larger leaves, so they take less space. Dried flower heads such as marigolds do not need to be stripped.

Top tip ✍

Always label your herbs: note the name of the herb, the parts used, the date of harvest, the year and the weight.

Dried herbs can be stored in brown paper bags or in airtight glass jars (preferably dark in colour, to prevent the herbs from fading in the light). I do not recommend plastic tubs or plastic bags. Weigh the dried herb before storing. Dried flower heads and leaves can be stored for up to a year, while roots and barks will last for up to 18 months.

When using dried herbs in any of the recipes in this book remember that much of the moisture will have evaporated during the drying process and so they will be lighter in weight than fresh herbage.

Part II

HEALING
AND INTEGRATED
VET CARE

Chapter 5

Chapter 5

How to Give Healing to Your
Pet – Everything Is Possible
for Those Who Believe

These days, many people are interested in how animals can be healed through the use of simple relaxation techniques. My clients often ask me if they, too, can do these techniques. Well, the answer is *yes*! Everybody has the ability to intentionally send loving thoughts to animals, whether they have healing experience or not.

My dogs, cats and horses love to have a healing session as it is deeply relaxing and allows them to rebalance their natural energy. Healing and prayer work have been very well received and documented in many scientific and medical papers, and this type of healing is complementary to orthodox medicine.

Animal healing can enhance the bonds of love between you and your pet; it can enrich your animal's life and have many benefits for you, too. At my animal clinic, and in the healing circle I run (*see below*), cats and dogs find the sessions very relaxing and grounding. Guardians come away feeling positive, more relaxed and focused and with a greater awareness of the present moment. One of my clients has a favourite saying: 'Yesterday has gone, tomorrow has not arrived and today is the gift – nothing else matters and let us enjoy the Now.'

FROM WILD ANIMAL TO MAN'S BEST FRIEND

But before I share these healing techniques with you, we need to look back in time to see how the incredible relationship between cats/dogs and humans came about. How did these two predator species infiltrate the human world and win our hearts and minds? Today dogs and cats are content to live with us as companions, and they have many similarities with us, including the illnesses we suffer from. Underneath the fur, whiskers, paws and a waggy tail their souls are the same as ours.

Let us look first at our canine friends. It took a major evolutionary change for a wild animal like the wolf to become what we know now as a dog. The wolf had to adapt to a new habitat and adjust to a human environment. Dogs were man's first domesticated companions – the remains of dogs have been found buried alongside humans in graves that are at least 12,000 years old.

Dogs are completely unrelated to humans but they can often understand and relate to us more than we understand and relate to each other. In a 2013 trial conducted at the University of Lincoln in the UK 17 dogs were shown photographs of human, dog and monkey faces as well as inanimate objects. The scientists observed that the dogs' eye and head movements focused on the right-hand side of the human faces – the side that best expresses our emotional state.

This did not occur with the other images the dogs viewed, so it seems that during the thousands of years of interaction between dogs and humans, an incredibly special bond has developed. Like us, canines are predators with eyes set to the front of the head, so they can absorb our every expression and energy change; they can read our body language and are in tune with our emotions.

Domestic cats have undergone a fairly similar transition from their wild ancestors. The first felids, or cats, emerged some 10–15 million years ago, and the basic structure of the *Felidae* family we see today – which includes panthers, leopards and the house cat – has changed very little. They are all predators with incredible eyesight, especially night vision, which is six times more sensitive than our own. They are agile and have a broad face and a short jaw that allows for a more powerful bite.

According to the latest scientific research, the domesticated cat turned up around 10,000 years ago. While I was working at Animal Care Egypt in Luxor

I met up with an Egyptologist at Karnak Temple because I was very keen to learn more about the hundreds of mummified cats found buried in and around the temples on the banks of the River Nile, and the felines depicted on the hieroglyphics that adorn the temple walls.

I was told that the bronze cat sculptures I saw in museums were of the Egyptian goddess Bastet, who apparently began her life as a lioness but morphed into a house cat around the time that cats were domesticated in Egypt – some 4,000 years ago.

The Egyptians used cats as part of their arsenal for controlling the rat infestations that affected the harvested crops around the mighty River Nile, and cats soon earned the right to live and stay in Egyptian homes. It was not long before the cat courted favour with the royal household, too, which found them to be good companions. Royal architects, painters and sculptors became so mesmerized by the luxurious body shape of the feline, and amazed by its social ability, that they immortalized the cat in images of the Sphinx.

When I am in South Africa treating large cats such as cheetahs, the similarities between them and my own cat never cease to amaze me. I love how the big cats purr and groom themselves in the same way my cat does; they love dried catmint just as much as he does, too – they roll in it and appear to be in a state of ecstasy. In fact, big cats and house cats are only a cousin away from each other.

An unbreakable bond

Let us fast-forward to the last 2,000 years, during which time cats and dogs adjusted to a variety of circumstances in order to survive and flourish with us as we populated most parts of the globe. We formed a close-knit bond with our feline and canine friends, who started out working for us – catching rodents, guarding livestock, hunting, and herding prey.

We rewarded them with scraps of food and shelter and they began to feel at ease around us. Children of all ages have always adored puppies and kittens, which are cute and irresistible to the touch; they were also capable of mesmerizing the most hardened parents, who began to melt a little and convince themselves that these animals could earn their keep and offer companionship at the same time.

Today, cats and dogs are very much part of our family lives and play a major role as our friends and companions. Some are even seen to be more important than human family members. Numerous studies have shown that having a cat or a dog can make us happy and healthy and help increase our life expectancy.

The affection and love we shower on our four-legged friends is returned a hundredfold – and it is unconditional, with no strings attached. This bond we share is infectious, as dogs and cats are instinctively in tune with our emotions. They never judge us and simply love us for who we are, whether we are happy or sad. It does not even matter to them what we look like when we get out of bed in the morning – they are always there for us.

Our pets have an incredible ability to empathize with us too, and that can help us to heal. They can sense our anxieties and worries, especially the mental and emotional stress we put ourselves through every day. They live every moment with us. In fact, they can read us like a book. When I observe my dogs playing together, sleeping when they are tired, eating when they are hungry, they are so focused on the 'now'.

If only *we* could be like this; instead we are preoccupied with the next thing on our 'to do' list and sometimes even forget to breathe properly. So what better way to be 'in the moment' than to bond and connect with your animal friends at an even deeper level, relaxing together and healing together.

MINDFUL MEDITATION FOR PET GUARDIANS

I am now going to show you how you can minimize your own stress and how you and your pets can achieve this together through a practice called mindful meditation. If you are feeling calm and relaxed your pet will pick up on this and react accordingly. Animals live in the moment and they can teach us how to do that too! As Ernest Hemingway said: 'A cat has absolute emotional honesty: human beings, for one reason or another, may hide their feelings. But a cat does not.'

Today, mindful meditation is becoming very popular, as people around the world increasingly seek a more spiritual kind of wellbeing. Originally, mindful meditation was a Buddhist practice that promoted an awareness of the moment: it allowed an opportunity not to think about unpleasant memories from the past, or to think ahead to impending tasks that must be achieved. All these thoughts whirring around the headspace culminate in a sense of despair, depression and unhappiness.

Mindful meditation teaches you how to just *observe* your thoughts and feelings, and not to over-analyze, or react to, or get in the way of them. When I am on a walk with my dogs in the countryside, I sometimes do an outdoor meditation exercise that helps me train my brain to work in a more methodical, peaceful way.

I simply observe a cloud in the sky. I momentarily stand still and breathe down through my body into my feet. I simply observe the cloud, without over-analyzing it, and then watch it quietly drifting away. When I do this, I automatically feel I am adapting to the forces of nature – the elements and the huge expanse of sky above my head – which I am witnessing with my own eyes. Suddenly those niggling thoughts and the mental chatter evaporate – simply by observing the awesome beauty of a big white fluffy cloud wandering across the sky.

There is a significant body of scientific evidence showing that mindful meditation is effective. For example, a 2014 report analyzing data from 47 clinical trials involving 3,000 people showed that mindful meditation improved symptoms of stress and anxiety by up to 20 per cent and helped enhance quality of life. The UK's National Institute for Health and Care Excellence have approved the practice for clinical use in depression and British GPs are increasingly recommending meditation for anxiety and stress. Even Google has a mindfulness training camp in California.

ELIZABETH'S GUIDE TO HEALING YOUR PET

Healing happens the moment you intentionally send unconditional feelings of love to your pet. A healing session may last for just five minutes or for as long as 40 minutes. If at any stage your animal moves away and makes it very clear it has had sufficient healing, respect these wishes, gently give thanks to your pet and offer a prayer or thoughts that they may continue receiving healing for their highest good and remain fit, well and healthy.

Preparing for a healing session

One of the best ways to prepare yourself for giving healing to animals is through mindful meditation. This can be a relaxing time for both you and your pet. The aim of mindful meditation is to create a state of relaxed awareness – it is quite different from sleeping or dozing. In meditation you direct your attention inwards to become an observer of yourself – your thoughts, feelings and sensations. Meditation aims to quieten the mind.

Mindful meditation does not require hours and hours of sitting still – you can start off slowly with a few minutes at a time. I book an appointment with myself – in my diary I find a time when I know I will not be disturbed and stick to that allocated slot. First, I switch all phones over to voicemail or answering machine and tell anyone who needs to know that I am unavailable. I have a small, quiet travel alarm clock that I set for 40 minutes or so ahead. This allows me not to worry about going over time.

⇨ *Getting comfortable*

I invite the dogs to come with me and we find a comfortable, quiet space in my lounge. I play some soft instrumental music at a low volume and light an unscented candle (I prefer not to use scented candles or to burn incense as an animal's sense of smell is hundreds of times more heightened than ours and we want this to be a pleasurable experience).

I like to get really comfy before I begin. For me, this usually means sitting on the floor, cross-legged in the lotus position. Sometimes I sit on the sofa or on a stool; anywhere is fine as long as my feet can touch the floor, and the lit candle is in my view. My dogs know the routine and settle down beside me.

My back is straight, but not rigid and I am able to relax and release any tension in the body. My feet are firmly on the floor and I am able to mentally ground my energies. For me it is a connection to the Earth beneath me, and it also helps me to ground my dogs' energies.

⇨ *Focusing on the breath*

I always begin with positive, intentional thoughts. I give thanks for this wonderful opportunity to be with my dogs and myself. I extend feelings of love, peace and harmony between us all. I then focus on my breath: I inhale slowly through the nose and exhale slowly through the mouth.

I then imagine I am standing in a shaft of pure, golden sunlight – absorbing the sun's rays, feeding all my senses and nourishing my body with the goodness, the glow and the warmth of this bright, pure energy. I instantly feel nurtured and good to be alive.

I take another long, deep breath, oxygenating my whole body. I hold my breath for two seconds and then exhale slowly until every last bit of it has left my abdomen. I repeat this sequence for four breaths. Then I intentionally breathe down through my body, legs and feet, purposefully feeling heavier, as if I have magnets in my feet.

⇨ *Visualization*

On the next in-breath I visualize the tree analogy: I imagine I am a large oak tree with roots spreading deeper into the ground. My body is the trunk of the tree, solid and strong, and my arms are the branches, with my fingers gently resting on my thighs.

My eyes are half open. I take steady, deep, rhythmical breaths. I relax a little bit more deeply, but I am not going to sleep as I surrender to the inner silence of my mind. The moment my mind wanders I look at the flame of the candle, flickeringly softly, and I let go of any distracting thoughts.

I repeat to myself the words: 'I am grounded, I am centred, I am present.' I take my thoughts to my heart space and take another deep, loving in-breath. On the out-breath I send thoughts of unconditional love to my dearly beloved animal friends. For me it is important to acknowledge my animal friends by their names and also to thank them for being a part of this session.

This sequence is my way of attuning myself to being in the moment and fully present. It enables me to be fully in tune, and to create a calm, relaxing environment that my animal friends can adapt to. It works for me and I hope you can find the same peace and tranquility for your preparation for a healing session.

⇨ *Asking your pet to join you*

After you have spent some quiet time in preparation, you can invite your animal friend(s) to join you in a healing session. Whenever I am conducting a face-to-face animal healing session I always seek permission from the pet(s). Gaining permission is a polite and endearing way of entering into this two-way healing.

Often, animals will draw nearer to you to be in your energy field. Some will look up approvingly as your eyes meet and gaze at each other lovingly. Some pets may be almost asleep following your initial preparation and barely move, yet you instinctively know it is right to continue. Others may wander around the room, taking in the smells and atmosphere, and as you catch sight of each other there is a knowing look or a nod that indicates it is okay and they decide to stand or lie down at a distance.

Some animals have had a rough start in life and can be nervous, shy and timid – they may hide behind furniture or under beds. If this is the case with your pet, sit quietly at a distance and offer distant healing (*see below*). Never chase an animal or demand he or she sit with you.

Do not take it personally: this is about building up trust between you both. It is like peeling an onion – there are many layers. Like humans, animals have a history. We do not always know what has happened to them in the past and they might need time to trust again. It is important not to force our own emotions or needs onto a pet. Both parties are going to get a great deal out of this healing session.

Conducting a healing session

First read 'preparing for a healing session' (*above*) and then follow this step-by-step guide to giving hands-on healing to your pet:

1. If your pet is lying by your side or is stood close by, gently allow the love to pulsate from you to them. Find a comfortable seated position, and keeping your hands relaxed, gently stroke your pet. Keep holding thoughts of unconditional love for you and your loved one. Sit still and gently allow the love to pulsate from you to them. Keeping your hands relaxed, slowly and gently stroke your pet with both hands for several minutes.

2. Experiment with raising your hands about 5cm (2in) away from the stomach area, and just sense what you are feeling. Intentionally breathe down through both arms, into your hands, through your fingers – just projecting loving thoughts. You may feel a tingling sensation in your hands as you connect to the energy field surrounding your animal friend.

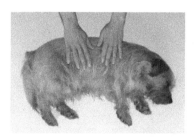

3. Keeping your hands relaxed and still, use them as sensors to find the distance you feel comfortable with. Try not to make sudden hand movements that could scare your pet. Do not put your face or hands directly near or in front of an animal's face and always keep your eyes open, yet soft and unstaring, so you can observe your pet's body language, movements, emotions and feelings. Keep holding thoughts of unconditional love for you and your loved one. From time to time softly caress your pet's shoulder. Slowly and quietly move your hands back towards the rump and lower back.

4. Gently and slowly move both hands to the pelvis. Keeping hands soft and open, quietly hover them over the hip – about 5cm (2in) away. Then sense and feel the energy at the sacrum, which is situated between the two hip bones. Be aware of what you are feeling and scan the area. You may feel hot, cold, tingling, pulsating, or you may feel nothing at all. Healing is

taking place when you have an open heart and positive intentions. Note the different sensations being picked up. Do not panic or worry if you feel nothing, as this will block the energy. Feel the energy flowing between you and your animal friend. Sense the vibrations of each area of the body.

5. Holding your hands a little distance away from the body, scan the heart centre and throat, breathing nice and fully and feeling relaxed and comfortable in your own seated position. Never let yourself get uncomfortable: if you feel an ache in your arms from holding them up – or if you are stooping over, causing backache – try mindfully to adjust your position. The more relaxed you are in your body the more relaxed your animal friend will feel and the better they will adapt to the positive environment you have created – internally and externally.

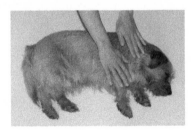

6. With one hand hovering over the lower back and hip area and the other hand hovering over the neck and shoulder area we commence the spinal flush. Breathe down through your arms and hands, sensing and feeling the energy at these two very important junction points. You may feel that one of your hands feels cooler than the other: if so try to stay here for a little while to bring about a feeling of warmth in both hands. Our aim is to balance the spinal energy in both areas together.

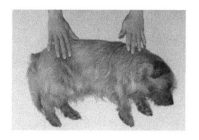
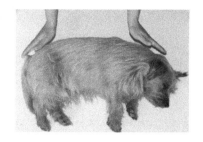

7. Keeping the hands soft and open, continue to radiate loving thoughts to your loved one. Towards the end of a healing session gently place your hands near or on the paws of your animal friend; this brings about a sense of grounding your energies and those of your pet. *If your pet is in a wonderful deep sleep, or may not appreciate you touching the paws, then do not!* In your mind's eye intentionally see yourself and your animal friend grounded, and then follow the procedure described in 'ending the healing session', below.

Giving healing to cats

When you are giving healing to cats it is sometimes a good idea to be seated on a comfy sofa or chair. Sit with your legs uncrossed, feet planted on the floor, back straight, but not rigid, so you are able to relax and release any tension in your body.

Several of the cats to whom I give healing love to jump up onto my lap, purring and head-butting my hands before I have even started. They rub their face into my hands, ushering me to commence the healing. Then the whole body moves into my hands, softening and relaxing as the purring increases, and they knead me with their claws/paws. Most of the time they will then settle down, closing their eyes and nestling into my lap. As they surrender to my touch I feel their muscles relax even further.

⇨ *What to look out for during a session*

To be thoroughly in the moment you cannot be in your mind, and the mental chatter that goes with it. Keep coming back to the breath and keep the focus and intention on purely loving thoughts. You may even find yourself yawning and releasing stress as the parasympathetic nervous system is activated.

There is a flow of energy synchronized between you and your pet during a healing session, so keep your eyes open to the signs. These might be licks, sighs, yawns or a sleepy, contented look. Also be aware when animals roll over to present a part of their body they wish healing to be given to. Respond by quietly moving your hand to scan over that area, sending loving thoughts. Some animals may reverse themselves right into your lap, seeking out your hands for healing.

By being in the moment you are fully aware of your animal's needs. This becomes a very rewarding session, as it is not about your own thoughts, emotions or reactions – it is your animal friend who is guiding the way. You and your pet are working together as one, like a perfect music ensemble.

At any stage of a healing session an animal may get up and wander off. Remain seated and continue to send healing from a distance (*see below*). Your pet may need time to process the session thus far, and have some space. Some animals settle down a little distance away. Respect this and observe some of the processing – such as a sigh, a vacant look, licking and chewing, self-grooming or falling asleep. These are vital signs that the body is relaxing. After a period of time your pet may come back and settle down beside you again and you can continue with hands-on healing.

At some point during the healing, you may find that your animal friend has had enough for one session. They may have a really good stretch, yawn and look alert and energized. They may become distracted by something else that is happening in the room or outside, or retire to their bed and settle down to sleep. Or they may become hungry or thirsty and seek out the food or water bowl.

You may intuitively feel the session has come to an end, or as you are re-scanning the body you no longer feel any particular sensations in your hands. Remember: it is not the time spent but the quality of the healing that counts. Do not worry if the session has lasted only a few minutes – the more you can perfect your healing skills the more you and your loved one will benefit.

⇨ *Ending a healing session*

The end of the healing is as important as the start. This is a wonderful opportunity to offer a prayer of thanks to your pet for joining you in this session. In your mind's eye, see them in good health. We always want the best for our animals, friends and family and this point is a wonderful time to continue that. Good intentions are paramount. Energy follows thought and our thoughts create our actions.

We started with the tree analogy and I would like you to end with it – for yourself and your pet. You may wish gently to touch your pet's feet and quietly sense them grounded, although some animals do not like to have their feet touched.

Continue to use creative imagery and see that lovely deep-rooted tree in your mind's eye, solid and strong for yourself and your pet. Take a long, deep in breath and imagine drawing your energy field in and around you. Then say to yourself: 'I am grounded, I am centred, I am in the present moment.'

Have a really good stretch, and then gently stand up and feel your feet firmly on the ground. Usually animals notice this change of energy and join in with you. They wake up, have a good yawn and stretch the body too.

Hopefully by now you should feel as relaxed as your pet. By giving healing love you are receiving love and also rewarding yourself with some well-deserved quiet time for *you*. By taking a little time out for yourself and your animals for meditation and healing you can create a more methodical way of approaching impending tasks, instead of worrying about which one to tackle first. You will feel positive and content.

Healing works!

During healing, the more you are able to remain relaxed and surrender to the silence within yourself, the more you are able to sense the same silence in others and to let go of everything in your mind. You are then able to have the discipline to do a methodical practice – to perfect and craft your healing skills.

When I have finished a healing session, I bring my focus back into the room. I glance around at the dogs, all snoring peacefully, blissed out and totally relaxed. This is no placebo affect and it gives me a warm feeling of oneness.

My dogs are responding to the energy I have created in the room – it is a truly beautiful experience. I find peace within myself and in any situation that may have upset me. In that moment my animals are happy and contented because I am happy and calm.

Practise giving healing to your pets as often as you can. If you would like to train in a professional Diploma in Animal Healing or enlist the help of a professional animal healer, visit www.healinganimals.org for more information.

DISTANT HEALING

Sometimes it is not possible to conduct hands-on (or contact) healing, as your pet may be away from you – perhaps in kennels, or recovering from surgery at the vets. Or you may be travelling or working away from home. In these cases, you can conduct distant healing – in which you send healing from a distance – which offers a wonderful opportunity for you to practise your healing skills.

There have been many studies conducted on the power of prayer work and intentionally sending loving, healing thoughts to our loved ones. This unconditional love is directed to all life, with no strings attached. And you can enlist the support of some friends: creating group energy is very effective for distant healing, as you are like-minded souls with one aim – to see healing being directed to named animal friends and pets, endangered species and planet Earth and all its inhabitants, including humankind.

We all share this planet and the more we can hold loving thoughts and stay positive the more we will be able to create the change we wish to see. My motto is 'one for all and all for one'. See below for more information on conducting distant healing in a group.

The animal healing circle

I run a monthly animal healing circle in Sussex, England, and people come from all over the UK to join us, armed with photographs of animals they love and cherish, including endangered species. This sacred, tranquil space is a Mecca for animal lovers – one in which everyone can drink up the peace and unconditional love for all life. During the evening we conduct both distant and hands-on healing; here is what happens:

- Everyone takes a seat in the circle. In the centre of the circle are lit candles and the animal photographs the circle members have brought along; soft, ambient music plays in the background. I lead us into a guided meditation to attune with the natural world. We all focus on the flames of the candles, warm and bright, as we find the inner focus, positive intentions and deep relaxation to be fully present in the moment.

- With our palms facing upwards on our thighs and the soles of our feet sinking into the carpet we take it in turns to say out loud the names of the animals and people we would like to send healing to. For my turn, I read from a written list of about a dozen animal clients from around the globe. I speak slowly and rhythmically, saying: 'I place into the healing light Milly, Jake, Storm, John Smith (Storm's guardian)', and so on. At the end of my dedicated list I like to include planet Earth and all its inhabitants. Finally I say 'thank you'.

- The next person then recites the names of the recipients on their list; they do so in almost a whisper, yet we can still recognize them as we breathe unconditional love from our hearts down our arms and our hands and into the healing circle, creating an electrifying energy that is positive yet calm and unified.

- All our hearts and minds are united in peace, unconditional love and harmony. The energy of the room is like a vast ocean. It is contagious because, like the sea, it gains momentum and strength – it is never ending, like the ebb and flow of the waves. That continuity is like the cycle of life on Earth.

- When each person has read out his or her list we sit in silence for a few minutes. I then like to engage visually with some of the animal photographs – to cement my feelings of unconditional love and to continue to send healing for the highest good of all.

- When it is time to bring the healing circle to a close I give thanks to all the healers present and to those beautiful animals we have been privileged to work with. Our intention is to see our loved ones – two- and four-legged – safe, well and healed.

- Because energy follows thought, energy travels at the level of the thought. If we create doubt, anxiety and a negative attitude, this will not only create fear for us but also for the recipient. A motto I stand by time and time again is: 'Everything is possible for those who believe.' Healing works on many layers of the body, re-balancing the subtle energy levels. Vets refer to this as the 'homeostatis balance' in the body.

- It is important that at the end of the healing circle everybody is feeling fully present. Towards the end of the closing meditation I ask the group to take some long, deep breaths and breathe down through their bodies – taking the awareness to the soles of their feet. This strengthens our connection to the Earth beneath us.

- Then I say out loud: 'I am grounded, I am centred, I am present.' I ask the group to very slowly bring their awareness back into the room, then have a good stretch and drink a glass of water – this is important when you may be feeling very relaxed or a little spaced out.

After the session, some members of the healing circle are keen to share their experiences, and this is a wonderful opportunity to express feelings and insights. Many say that they feel such warmth and camaraderie from the healing group; they remark that it is as if they have come home. Some are amazed to discover that we have been in meditation and distant healing for over an hour. People also have an opportunity to give feedback from the previous month's distant healing group.

Top tip ✍

When conducting distant healing write down the names of pets, their guardians and endangered species, so you have a list you can refer to and add to. I have a beautiful embroidered A5 notebook in which I record the names of animals, their carers, rescue centres and their staff.

A healing circle is also a self-development group where you can perfect your healing skills, self-awareness and mindful meditation. Animals join us in the second part of the healing evening and receive healing, which is a wonderful opportunity for members of the circle to gain more experience in healing their own pets. To find an animal healing circle near you, please visit www.healinganimals.org.

Chapter 6

~~~

Fingers and Thumbs – You
Can Do It Acupressure

Hippocrates, the father of modern therapeutic science, is believed to have said: 'It is nature that heals, not the physician.' For centuries people believed that there was a Vital Force, or regulatory agency, in the body that protected it against disease or brought about healing. Naturopaths also believed that 'it is the body that acts upon the drugs, and not the drugs upon the body'.

In modern Western medicine, our approach is predominantly minimalistic and focuses so much on the minute parts of an individual that in the process we lose sight of the whole. In the words of Dr William Gutman of New York Medical School: 'This system treats each symptom in isolation, prescribing analgesics for pain, antipyretics for fever, laxatives for constipation, etc.'

In contrast to this, Traditional Chinese Medicine (TCM) – along with many other centuries-old systems of medicine like Ayurveda and homeopathy – adopts a more holistic approach. Acupuncture is a 3,500-year-old component of TCM that is based on the principle that 'Qi' (pronounced *chee*), or energy, flows throughout the body along specific pathways. These pathways are commonly known as 'meridians'.

Over hundreds of years practitioners have located and mapped certain external pressure points along these meridians, which are referred to as 'acupoints'. By stimulating these acupoints one can regulate 'Qi'. It is also believed that disease or illness is a consequence of the imbalance or disturbance in Qi. The food we eat, the air we breathe, the oxygen content of the air and air pollution can all affect the quality of Qi.

Acupuncture professes that this energy flow can be improved and balanced by the insertion of very fine metallic needles into these specific points on the meridians. The fundamental promise of acupuncture is that it is possible to heal the body by using its own natural healing mechanism.

Using the same principle, you can stimulate the flow of Qi by applying pressure at the acupoints using just your fingers and thumbs, a technique known as acupressure. According to the *Sushrut Samhita*, an ancient Sanskrit text on medicine, acupressure therapy was popular in India 5,000 years ago. It then spread to Sri Lanka and from there, Buddhist monks took it to China, where it was further developed as acupuncture.

WHY TRY ACUPRESSURE?

But why should you bother with acupressure when there are so many drugs available to help heal your pet, among them NSAIDs, steroids and opiates? Well, as I explain in Chapter 8: *Which Drugs and Why*, all drugs have side effects. In elderly animals, those with other concurrent illnesses or those who have chronic disease, you can reduce the use of these drugs by using acupressure or acupuncture. They are another tool in your tool box, and they are free from side effects, safe and holistic.

Both acupuncture and acupressure are accepted by the Royal College of Veterinary Surgeons (RCVS) and the American Veterinary Medical Association (AVMA). There is good, solid science behind them, and a lot of evidence showing that they work. Moreover, they can beautifully complement and integrate with conventional medicine. In one episode of the recently broadcast BBC series *Trust Me, I'm A Doctor*, acupuncture was tested and proven to work.

Like many practitioners, I too believe that by sending our own loving Qi through our fingertips into our pets we can further enhance the acupressure treatment. In the UK, and in most other countries, acupuncture using needles can only be practised by a qualified veterinarian, but acupressure can be used by you to heal your pet.

Acupressure can relieve many painful conditions (see *A–Z Common Conditions* chapter), prevent illness and quicken your pet's recovery. Research has shown that stimulation of acupressure points releases endorphins, which relieve pain. Moreover, I have seen it work, and so have people all over the world.

Acupressure points (or acupoints) are identified by one or more letters and numbers. Going into more detail is beyond the scope of this book, but simply put, the letters are an abbreviation for the organ that rules the particular meridian. For example, ST stands for stomach meridian and BL for bladder meridian. There are 12 major meridians and if we connect the dots of the acupuncture points on the body's surface, we will end up following each of these 12 channels or pathways.

Every time I show a pet guardian the acupoints on their pet's body, they ask, 'What if I press the wrong acupoint?' But there is no need to worry or panic about doing this, because it is not dangerous to press on any other point. You may not be solving the current issue, but no harm will be done. So if you are unsure, even pressing *near* the correct acupoint will help.

However, there are certain situations in which you should *avoid* giving acupressure to your pet, and these are given below:

- If your pet has cancer, or has wounds or abscesses, as you can make matters worse.

- If your pet has just had strenuous exercise – allow at least an hour for them to become calm and relaxed.

- If your pet has just eaten – wait 1–2 hours after a meal.

- If your pet is pregnant, as you may apply unwanted pressure on the foetus.

Preparing for an acupressure session

First of all, choose the perfect location for your acupressure session. This place should be peaceful, have minimal distractions and most importantly, be somewhere your pet feels safe and relaxed. Read Chapter 5: *How To Give Healing To Your Pet*, and follow the procedure described in 'preparing for a healing session': this is really important.

The next step is to prepare yourself to give acupressure. As Elizabeth explains in Chapter 5, being calm, present, grounded and relaxed is essential for successful healing. If you or your pet are anxious or stressed, any treatment is unlikely to work. I have always grounded and calmed myself before giving acupuncture or acupressure.

Please note that as with healing, acupressure should not be forced on your pet. If your pet walks away, respect that. You must be patient and willing to wait and observe for signs or signals from your pet that indicate permission. For example, your pet may sit close to you, nudge your hand, lick your hand or even lie down quietly beside you. Once you are both settled, you can start the assessment process to ascertain problem areas:

- Begin by gently stroking your pet with the heel of your hand, mentally making a note of the areas of the body that your pet is uncomfortable with, or finds painful when touched. Avoid these for the moment and come back to them later.

- Start with your pet's head and gently stroke it. Then go down to the neck, back, sides, belly and finally legs (many pets hate their feet being touched, so leave these till last). Lightly pet the sensitive parts and then quickly move to the less sensitive ones, so your cat or dog gets used to it (it is best to start doing this early on with a new pup or kitten, so they become desensitized and will not resent you touching them anywhere). You will also be able to sense hot and cold areas, which can be useful when you become more experienced.

Opening an acupressure session

Start your session with an opening massage. Use your fingers or thumbs, or the heel of your hand (whichever is easy for you), and feel free to gently squeeze the muscles – provided your pet is okay with it.

Start at the base of the skull, with your hands on either side of the head, then travel down the spine, working your way to the base of the tail. Do this twice. During the third time, start from the skull base as before, but stop where the ribs end and follow the ribs round until both your hands meet underneath the belly.

Acupoint work

Now you are ready to focus on the acupoints. You can work on as many or as few points as your pet will permit. There are acupressure point charts available which show all the points one can use for a particular condition or illness *(see the further reading section for books and other sources).*

You can follow these charts and stimulate every point depicted in them, or just pick the points detailed under the individual conditions listed in Chapter 7: *A–Z Common Conditions in Cats and Dogs*, and in the 'acupoints for beginners' list below.

- **First, identify your acupoint**. This is always in a valley or dent, usually between muscles and the bones. If possible try to treat points on both sides, left and right, along major meridians. You can use your thumb or one finger (your pointer) or two fingers (middle finger pressing on your pointer, almost as if you are crossing your fingers). This technique is described nicely in the book *Acu-dog: A Guide to Canine Acupressure*, by Amy Snow.

- **Apply light pressure if your pet is small and more if your pet is large**. You can either use light, sustained pressure or try gentle, rhythmic pulsing, depending on your pet's response; press for between 15 seconds and a maximum of three minutes.

- **Make sure you observe your pet's response**. This will help you decide if you have released or shifted the energy at the point, so you can then move on to the next point. Your pet may lick his lips or yawn or stretch or shiver, or even pass wind. Some pets just snore away! All of these signs can be indicators of unblocked, released Qi, circulating freely again.

- **Move on to the next point**, or if your pet has had enough, bring your session to an end with a closing massage (see below).

Closing an acupressure session

Finish the session with a closing massage, repeating the procedure described for the opening massage: the only difference is in your intention. You can make a silent wish that your gift of acupressure should be beneficial to your pet and help him heal. As massage ensures a good flow of Qi, you can use this massage technique weekly or even daily, as it is a useful way of balancing Qi and therefore preventing illness.

Tips for enhancing a session

Many experts believe that the secret to a good massage lies in the application of even pressure, rather than the intensity. So please listen to your pet and pay attention to their response. If they seem to be uncomfortable, you may be applying too much pressure. Stroking their neck and ears can help calm them. Try massaging the Bai hui or GV 20 (*see below*), as this can also help relax your pet if they are agitated.

You can use Elizabeth's rosemary massage oil (*see recipe page 86*) on your fingertips to enhance a treatment, especially for pain relief. Remember that excess fat on your pet's body will inhibit the flow of Qi so you may need to apply a bit more pressure or give more than two treatments per day for ailments.

Finally, after a treatment, do avoid sudden temperature changes, hectic exercise or feeding – at least for an hour. The frequency of treatments will depend on the circumstances. It is sensible to allow a gap of 3–5 days between full acupressure sessions so that your pet can adjust to the energy changes.

You can do the treatments twice daily if necessary for specific ailments. A wellness or maintenance treatment to ensure healthy Qi flow can be given weekly. There are wellness charts with acupoints in the books listed in the further reading section at the back of the book.

KEY ACUPOINTS FOR BEGINNERS

I have listed below some important and easy-to-locate acupoints that you can use when your pet exhibits the particular symptom or condition mentioned under each point. Two important *emergency* acupoints and eight easy-to-use ones are described here, and the accompanying illustrations show me pointing to these points on dear Morris (Elizabeth's pet), who was very cooperative.

You can familiarize yourself with these acupoints to start with. If you find them effective, and your pet is cooperative, you can buy the books recommended in the further reading section and try more points. There are also acupressure courses available, which you can take if you wish to raise your knowledge to the next level. *See Resources section (page 296) for details.*

*Please note that what follows is **not** a sequence of points; instead, each point helps with a specific problem.*

Acupoint 1: GV 26

Emergency point in heart attack or breath-holding. GV 26 or 'Governing Vessel 26' is located at the centre, just below the nose and above the upper lip. If your pet ever stops breathing or is in shock and unconscious, you need to jab repeatedly at this point with the tip of a pen, your fingernail or a needle. Usually this will get your pet breathing. I have often used it in anaesthetized animals, who can sometimes breath-hold, and it worked every time. DO NOT try this on a conscious animal – you will get bitten!

Acupoint 2: LU 7

Emergency point for asthma or wheezing – especially in cats. 'Lung 7' is located immediately above the wrist bone in a tiny depression on the inside aspect of the front paw. By just massaging this point, it is possible to help your pet breathe more easily and prevent an asthma attack. Of course, if their breathing is severely laboured, you must make sure they are seen by a vet and use appropriate prescribed drugs. However, if you are stuck or there is a delay before you can get to the vet, this could be very useful.

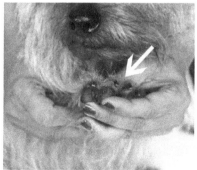

Acupoint 3: BL 60

Aspirin point – useful point for pain relief. 'Bladder 60' is located on the outside of the back (or hind) leg, in the Achilles depression behind the leg bone (above the calcaneous), where it meets with the ankle. When your pet is in pain, applying constant pressure for 1–2 minutes on this point twice daily can help relieve it.

Acupoint 4: GV 20

Bai Hui – Hundred convergences. 'Governing Vessel 20' is known as the point of hundred convergences, or summit of the bodily mountain. It is located pretty much at the top of the head, or the crown, in a depression that is in line with the ears. In dogs and cats it is also the name for the acupoint in the dip between the spinal vertebrae on the back, where there is a flat area between the hips.

It is considered a traditional point for animals and is beneficial for balancing liver Qi and stabilizing or calming the emotions. Most pets love being massaged at this point, with either the thumb or two fingers. GV 24 is another point that is located on the head, along the central line, but more in line with the back of the eye; this can be massaged in epileptics and in those with emotional disorders.

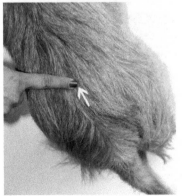

Acupoint 5: ST 36

Powerful point for energizing and enhancing. 'Stomach 36' is located behind or lateral to the tibial crest, on the outer aspect of the back leg, just below the knee in a depression where the lower leg (tibia) joins the knee. Stimulating this point can help with stomach or gastrointestinal upset. ST 36 is known to relieve exhaustion and it energizes a tired dog so much that he can walk a further 3 miles (5km) – which is why it is known as the 'three mile point'. It can also help improve the appetite if your pet is anorexic.

Acupoint 6: LI 4

Longevity point for maintaining good health. 'Large Intestine 4' is located on the front paw, in the depression of the dewclaw webbing, or where the thumb and forefinger meet. Massaging it increases protective Qi circulation and can contribute to a long, healthy life.

It is also useful for reducing aggression and for relieving allergies, aching neck, shoulder pain, a blocked nose or even sinus problems. Take care with this point as not all pets like their feet being touched. Morris is quite hairy, so in the photograph I have just pointed to the location of the point.

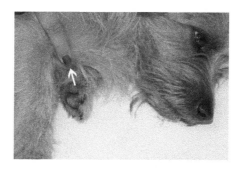

Acupoint 7: BL 10

Local neck and ear point. 'Bladder 10' is located below and behind the ear, between the first and second cervical vertebrae, just off the centre of the spine. There is one on either side, bilaterally symmetrical, so you can stimulate them simultaneously. Most pets love having these points massaged. This massage can help with ear disorders like smelly ears, otitis and ear infections. It can also relieve neck pain.

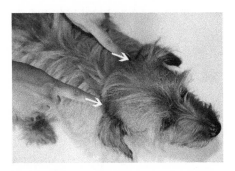

Acupoint 8: HT 7

Key heart point. 'Heart 7' or 'Spirit is Door' is located on the outer aspect of the front leg, at the wrist, in a triangular depression formed by the tendon and the wrist bone. After flexing the wrist gently while lifting the paw, you may massage this point in a circular fashion for a couple of minutes. This helps reduce heart palpitations and stabilizes the emotions. Cats have a natural instinct to lick themselves here while grooming, which may be calming to them.

Acupoints 9, 10 & 11: BL 54, GB 29 & GB 30

Hip triangle. 'Bladder 54' is located in front of the femur, or thigh bone, below the hip joint; 'Gall Bladder 29' is located on the hip bone, in front of the hip joint; and 'Gall Bladder 30' is located on the back side of the pelvis, below and also behind the hip joint.

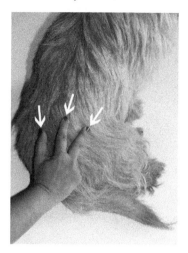

By making a three-finger tripod using the thumb, index finger and middle finger, where the index finger is at the top of the bone and the thumb and middle fingers on either side, you can gently apply pressure for about a minute to relieve any pain in the hip joint and the area around it. It is very useful in dogs with hip dysplasia or arthritis of the hip.

Acupoints 12, 13 & 14: BL 13, 14 & 15

Balance points for organs in the chest. 'Urinary Bladder (BL) 13, 14 and 15' are located on either side of the spine, starting from the shoulder blades, and then the 3rd, 4th and 5th intercostals or rib spaces. They help balance energy in the lungs and the heart and can also help relax the diaphragm. Massaging them in a back-and-forth motion for a couple of minutes is beneficial for restoring proper balance.

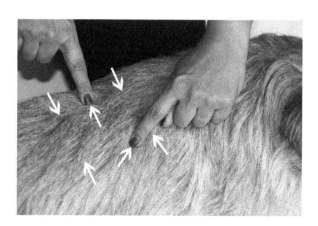

Quick acu-checklist

Unlike many other complementary modalities – including acupuncture, where you may cause damage if you have no training – acupressure is quite forgiving. So go ahead and try it. Here is a useful checklist to remind you of the key points and get you started.

- Select a quiet location where you and your pet can feel safe and undisturbed.

- Ground, calm and focus yourself.

- Set your intention – to relieve pain, balance emotion and energize.

- Perform the opening massage as described above.

- Select your acupoint, which is always in a valley or dent, usually between muscles and the bones.

- Try to treat points on both sides – left and right – along major meridians.

- Apply light pressure if your pet is small and more if they are large.

- Use steady pressure or slow, rhythmic pulses, depending on your pet's response; press for between 15 seconds and a maximum of three minutes.

- Stimulate specific points twice daily if needed for ailments, but allow a 3–5 day gap between full treatments.

- Give weekly wellness treatments if you can, to maintain balance.

- STOP if your pet walks away or will not allow it. Respect your pet's wish.

- Remain relaxed and calm throughout, and breathe easy.

- Finish with a closing massage and a positive intention for your pet's wellbeing.

Remember: acupressure is a very useful tool, available at the tips of your fingers, but it is not a substitute for veterinary care, so please use it as a complement rather than an alternative.

Chapter 7

∼͡

A–Z Common Conditions in Cats and Dogs – Easy Reference with Treatment Options

In the previous chapters, Elizabeth and I explained how we can all provide holistic care to our pets. It would be wonderful if both we and our pets could be healthy always – by eating the right food and following a holistic, stress-free lifestyle. Unfortunately, though, because of a number of reasons and predisposing factors, illness does occur.

Conventional medicine teaches us that disease is primarily caused by pathogens such as bacteria, fungi, viruses and other microorganisms. We all know that these can only cause disease if the conditions for them to thrive are conducive. Over the years, we have identified many new diseases – some are caused by our genes, others by lifestyle, or the wrong diet or eating too much; some are caused by germs, by environmental pollutants and toxins, or by genetically modified foods and additives. And there are still many diseases for which the cause remains a mystery.

As a holistic integrative veterinarian I also believe that emotions (both our own and those of our pets) are an important cause of ill health. My job is difficult because many a time I have had to treat animals, or at least alleviate their symptoms, even if the actual cause is unknown. In my experience complete cures *can* be achieved, but only if the root cause of the disease is identified and eliminated. Correct diagnosis is therefore very important, and a systematic approach to disease is key to successful outcomes.

Obtaining a thorough history from the pet guardian is priceless for enabling a correct diagnosis. My humble request to pet guardians worldwide is that they should be honest with their vet and mindful of their pet. It is vital to look out for any abnormal behaviour in your pet and contact your vet quickly if you are in doubt. An incorrect history can waste valuable time, as we will all end up barking up the wrong tree. Just your honest version of events can help immensely in ensuring a correct diagnosis and the right treatment.

HOW TO USE THE A–Z

In this chapter, I have listed the most common conditions or diseases that I see in cats and dogs. Each condition is described briefly and followed by a summary of the probable cause, the key clinical signs, the conventional methods of diagnosis and then both the conventional and holistic treatment options available, including special home-made diets, healing, herbs and acupressure where applicable.

As a vet I regard your support in treatment as crucial, which is why under each condition there is information under the heading 'you' which describes *your* role. I sincerely hope you will find this helpful and follow it when the need arises. Remember: only a qualified vet can make a diagnosis, but you can help them arrive at it quickly by recognizing an emergency, taking your pet to the clinic in time, providing the right information, complying with the medication regime, keeping follow-up or revisit appointments and feeding the right diet.

The list of conditions is lengthy, but you need not read it in one sitting. It is designed as a quick, user-friendly reference section that you can consult when your pet shows any of the symptoms listed. Please note that the same symptoms may be present in different conditions, so always check with your vet if you are confused. The aim here is to educate you so you can make an informed decision and be there for your pets when they need you most. Remember: your pet depends on you. So let us get started.

ABSCESS

An abscess is a localized collection of pus that has built up within the tissue of the body and is usually contained within a cavity.

Causes

In both dogs and cats the single most common cause of an abscess is a bite from another animal. Dogs are often seen fighting with each other and if the skin is punctured and heals quickly an abscess may follow in 2–3 days. Cats are seldom observed fighting – the awful noises that accompany most cat fights may be the only clue.

The teeth of cats and dogs resemble sharp little needles and can inflict deep punctures in the skin and underlying muscles. These small wounds heal quickly but damage may have been done because the teeth carry infection (bacteria), which is injected into the tissue at the time of the bite and forms an abscess 2–3 days later. Other organs that can develop abscesses are the tooth roots, the prostate gland in male dogs, the anal glands, the eye, the pancreas and the liver, but these are less obvious and can only be diagnosed by a veterinarian.

Symptoms

In dogs, a swelling or lump, at the place where he or she was bitten, is the classic symptom that an abscess may be forming. In cats it is not that obvious. Cat bites are commonly seen on the tail, the top of the head or on any of the limbs, or sometimes on the side or the back. So any sudden onset of lameness, swelling on the head, hissing when stroked, tail held low or just not eating after being out the night before may be symptoms that warrant a trip to your veterinarian.

Diagnosis

Pus oozing from a swelling on the skin is a clear indication of an abscess and can be easily diagnosed by a watchful pet owner. However, as mentioned above, in cats especially, a thorough physical examination by the vet or the owner is needed to identify an abscess on the skin, because the abscess is well hidden in the fur or long hair.

Pain and vocalizing when the pet is touched or stroked can also reveal the site of an abscess. Abscesses inside the body are trickier. Fever, if the abscess has not ruptured, and sepsis if the abscess ruptures internally will alert your vet to the possibility. They may then perform appropriate blood tests and/or an ultrasound examination, depending on the organ involved.

Treatment

⇨ *Your vet*

Most vets tend to prescribe a 7–14 day course of antibiotics for a bite wound, along with a course of painkillers or anti-inflammatory drugs. If the abscess is very large, extensive, or your pet is too fractious or aggressive, then the vet will have to anaesthetize/sedate them and surgically lance and drain the abscess, flush out the pus and then place drains for continuous drainage. Some medium-to-large bite wounds may need to be sutured or stitched up.

⇨ *You*

Your vet will also advise you to clean the abscess at home with an antiseptic, usually dilute chlorhexidine. Further infection can be prevented by keeping the wound clean, and preferably keeping the pet indoors till the wound has closed over. You can complement this with healing and herbs, as detailed below.

⇨ *Healing & herbs*

Animal healing is a fantastic complement to veterinary care and can be safely given by you to your pet. Read Chapter 5: *How to Give Healing to Your Pet*, for instructions.

⚘ Make your own ⚘

Elizabeth recommends feeding garlic-infused honey (*see page 49*) and calendula-infused sunflower oil (*page 50*).

ACCIDENTS

Unfortunately, the most common accident seen nowadays in small animal veterinary practice, in both dogs and cats, is the RTA (road traffic accident). RTAs are emergencies and it is extremely important that your pet is rushed to the vet as quickly as possible.

Causes

Cats seem to be involved in RTAs more than dogs, especially at night. The headlight glare from fast-moving vehicles seems to make them freeze on the spot and they tend to get hit mainly while crossing the road. Most cats tend to have poor road sense. Puppies and young, excitable dogs tend to get hit when they run out of their homes and straight across the road in front of oncoming traffic. Male dogs that have not been neutered are also more likely to be hit when they chase after bitches in heat.

Symptoms

If your cat has been out all night, do check that it has returned for breakfast. A cat walking slowly, limping or dragging itself into the house, or breathing rapidly after a night out, should be taken straight to the vet. RTAs involving dogs are usually witnessed by their owners, or the driver who hits the animal.

Diagnosis

It is very important that an accurate history of the cat's whereabouts is provided to the vet, as this is crucial for an accurate diagnosis. In cats scuffed nails will alert the vet to the possibility that the animal may have been involved in a RTA.

A complete and thorough clinical examination will be carried out by the vet, in order to identify which organs or body systems have been affected by the accident. Pelvic fractures, mandibular fractures, bladder rupture, fractured limbs, diaphragmatic hernias, kidney damage and head injuries are common post-RTA. Based on the injuries it might be necessary to take radiographs, MRIs and blood tests to check their extent.

Treatment

⇨ Your vet

Emergency treatment to stabilize the shocked animal is the first priority. Treatment will involve immediate pain relief, starting an intravenous drip to combat fluid loss, blood transfusions, and antibiotic treatment if there are open wounds. In some cases immediate surgery may be necessary if there is a ruptured bladder or a complicated diaphragmatic hernia.

If there are fractures, these will be confirmed by X-rays and then, depending on the urgency, type of fracture and the vet's expertise, they will be repaired immediately or at a later date. Treatment of RTAs can be expensive and prolonged. Some animals involved in serious RTAs who suffer multiple severe injures will carry a poor prognosis and the vet may advise euthanasia.

⇨ *You*

Take your pet to your vet as soon as possible following an RTA, because almost every accident could be an emergency. I understand that this can be an incredibly stressful time for you and your pet, but you need to be calm and collected. I recommend using the relaxation technique outlined by Elizabeth in *How to Give Healing to Your Pet*. You can practise this on your way to your vet and you will find that it prevents both you and your pet from panicking. After the visit, and once your pet has been stabilized, you can carry on using complementary care to hasten the healing process as advised below.

⇨ *Healing & herbs*

Animal healing is a fantastic complement to veterinary care and can be safely given by you to your pet. Read Chapter 5: *How to Give Healing to Your Pet* for instructions.

⋌ Make your own ⋋

Elizabeth recommends catnip-infused sunflower oil (*see page 50*) and dried catnip (*page 64*) for cats. Also, chamomile-infused honey (*page 49*) and calendula-infused sunflower oil (*page 50*).

AGGRESSION

The joy of owning a pet is replaced by fear and worry when the pet in question, be it a cat or a dog, is aggressive. While cat aggression is usually a problem to the guardian or to the veterinary fraternity, dog aggression has huge social implications, especially in the current climate. Needless to say, 70 per cent of dogs that present to veterinary behaviourists have a diagnosis of aggression.

Aggression is also one of the top reasons for the euthanasia of healthy dogs. The societal effects of aggression are also quite significant. There are implications for both the human–animal bond and also on public safety.

The majority of the dogs, and frequently cats, given up to rescue centres and shelters are reported to have some type of aggression-related problem.

I have decided to address this topic in as much detail as the scope of this book will permit, because I believe that this is one area where *you*, the guardian, can really make a huge difference to the outcome.

Common causes of aggression in dogs
⇨ *Dog-related*
It is not always possible to wholly understand the reason for aggressive behaviour in a dog. Knowledge of when the behaviour started can help in identifying the motivation for it, but this is not always possible, especially if you got the dog when it was already an adult. It is therefore important to ascertain not only when the problem behaviour first became a concern, but also when the dog first displayed this behaviour – be it fear or aggression. This is not only important to plan the treatment but also to give a prognosis.

⇨ *Owner-related*
Owners and other humans can play a very key role in an aggressive dog's behaviour, for better or worse. Harsh training techniques, abuse, miscommunication between human handler and dog, and inconsistent reward and punishment can all confuse a dog big-time. It is difficult for a dog to differentiate between a thief, a window cleaner or a postman, so if you want your dog to guard your property, then it is more likely that he or she will become aggressive.

⇨ *Diet-related*
An important biological relationship seems to exist between aggressive behaviour and serotonin levels in the brain. A study looking at the serum levels of this neurotransmitter found that aggressive dogs had lower serotonin levels compared to non-aggressive ones (Cakiroglu et al, 2007). See Chapter 1: *Food Is Medicine*, for advice.

⇨ *Home environment*
Kennel-raised pups tend to show aggressive behaviour towards unfamiliar people, especially vets!

Risk factors for aggression

There are several identified and well-documented risk factors for canine aggression, both dog-related and human-related.

⇨ *Breed*

Certain dog breeds, among them Rottweiler, Chow Chow and German Shepherd Dog, rank higher for territorial aggression as they were historically bred for this behaviour. However, caution should be exercised, as there are large variations between individuals within breeds – your pet need not be aggressive just because of its breed.

⇨ *Gender*

Male dogs tend to be over-represented, compared to bitches. This is where castration is usually recommended. It may not get rid of the aggression entirely but it will decrease it. Also, research has shown that there is no correlation between age at castration and the outcome of decreased aggression post-castration.

⇨ *Management*

The dog's housing, training and management have a definite effect on its behaviour towards unfamiliar people. It has been proven that poor socialization of puppies between 3–14 weeks of age can make them more aggressive or fearful. Similarly, fatal attacks on humans have been documented as those in which dogs were left unrestrained on the owner's property. Pit Bull Terriers, Rottweilers and German Shepherd Dogs, in that order, have been most commonly involved in such attacks, which suggests a breed predisposition.

Common signs of canine aggression

Most people can easily identify aggressive behaviour in dogs. The following are classic signs, although not all dogs will show all of them.

• Staring down.

• Growling at you or a stranger.

• Standing in the doorway like an obstruction and daring you to get past.

- Rough play with you and other members of the family that gets out of hand easily and turns into an angry battle.

- Territorial aggression – which is displayed by chasing people or other animals out of the garden or house, barking incessantly when strangers or other animals approach your home and, worst-case scenario, attacking and/or biting people or other animals.

Diagnosis

Your vet should be the first port of call. It is important that a veterinarian examines your dog and rules out obvious and not so obvious medical conditions that may cause him or her to be aggressive. Painful orthopaedic conditions, gastrointestinal disorders, sensory deficits and neurological abnormalities can all predispose a dog to display aggression. Sometimes, blood tests may also be required to eliminate metabolic causes.

The vet will then usually refer your pet to either a vet colleague who specializes in behaviour, a behaviourist, or a trainer, who can then start the process of diagnosis. It is important to have an accurate diagnosis so that an appropriate prognosis and treatment plan can be formulated. If a primary diagnosis cannot be made then you should at least have a list of differential diagnoses to work with.

NB: Be very careful when deciding on a dog trainer, as some of them can make matters worse. Not all behaviourists are the same and not all their techniques will be suitable for your pet. So please shop around!

Risk evaluation

The vet or the behaviourist who is dealing with a case of aggression needs to make a risk assessment. Not only does this evaluation deal with the dog in question, but it also has to determine what risks are present when considering other dogs and people who might be affected by this dog's behaviour. Physical injury to this dog and others (dogs and people), emotional injury and potential liability must all be evaluated. Once this is done, treatment can be initiated.

Treatment

No assurance can be given that aggression will be 'cured', since this is a normal part of the behavioural repertoire of a dog. Treatment only focuses on managing the dog and changing the underlying motivation sufficiently. Hopefully there will be a significant reduction in the frequency and intensity of the aggressive behaviour, and the associated risk will be substantially minimized to an acceptable level.

⇨ *Your vet and you*

One or a combination of the following strategies may be advised by your vet, behaviourist or dog trainer, but only *your* compliance and strict adherence to their advice can bring about a reasonable change in your dog's behaviour. It is vital that you remain centred, stable, calm, present and relaxed. This is the foundation for the preparation work that will enable your dog to understand what you wish to change.

- **Avoidance** – simply avoiding the situation that triggers the aggression is one of the most commonly used methods. Confining your dog is part of this, but it may not always work for you and your pet. Blocking your dog's view can be useful too, especially in dogs that watch out for animals trespassing on what they deem to be *their* territory. Use your own body to block the line of vision between your dog and the other animal.

- **Reinforcement and reassurance** – this involves keeping the dog on a proper lead when outside. You may also have to be trained to change the way you interact with your dog.

- **Use of control and restraint aids** – head collars, muzzles that allow your dog to pant, drink and safely vomit may need to be used. Halties also fall in this category and can be extremely effective.

- **Desensitizing and counter-conditioning** – these strategies are the main techniques used to change your dog's response to strangers. The main goal here is to replace unwanted behaviour with positive behaviour – for example, from being aggressive to being calm and focused. I have found them very successful.

- **Pheromone therapy** – Dog Appeasing Pheromone (DAP) is supposed to be beneficial in decreasing anxiety, and consequently aggression. It is available as a slow-release collar, a plug-in electric diffuser for use within the house, and as a spray to use on bandanas, furniture, etc. Pheromone therapy is potentially safe, but its efficacy in reducing aggression is yet to be proven and I have not had great feedback about it from pet owners.

- **Medication** – I strongly believe that this should *never* be the first line of treatment. In my experience, most guardians tend to rely on medication rather heavily and do not take the behaviour-modification training programmes advised seriously enough. Also there is the problem of disinhibition – as the drugs alleviate anxiety, your dog may actually show more aggression as he or she starts feeling less fear.

  Then there is the usual problem of drug side effects. These can range from anorexia to anxiety, hallucinations and many others, depending on the drug used. The most commonly used medications for aggression are SSRIs like Prozac, tricyclic antidepressants like amitriptyline and clomipramine, and finally benzodiazepines like alprozalam and diazepam, which may reduce anxiety. It usually takes at least four to six weeks before their full effects are seen.

- **Surgery** – castration of male dogs is the main procedure recommended. There is evidence that a 50 per cent reduction is seen in dogs exhibiting territorial aggression. It is not a cure-all, but it may help to show that the owner is proactive. Some behaviourists now advise that dogs who exhibit nervous aggression, as compared to those that are dominant aggressive, should not be castrated, as they need their testosterone confidence to deal with stressful situations.

- **Acupressure** – energy imbalances can contribute to aggression, so alongside training and behaviour modification, I recommend stimulating acupressure points L 14 and LIV 2. L 14 is an acupoint that is located on the front paw, where the thumb and the index finger meet. LIV 2 is located in a dip on the rear leg, toe 2 on the inside at the 2nd joint.

  Just stroking these points for half a minute once a day can be beneficial. Warning: some pets hate their feet being touched so please start off by just touching the feet before proceeding to acupressure. See Chapter 6: *Fingers and Thumbs* for instructions.

- **Exercise** – tiring your dog out by increasing the amount of exercise it has can be effective. Play therapy is also good for distracting a dog from showing negative aggressive behaviour, as the mood changes straight away.

- **Diet** – feeding an aggressive dog natural, chemical-free foods can really help. I recommend that you read Chapter 1: *Food Is Medicine*, and cook Elizabeth's wholesome recipes (*see Chapter 2*). It has been documented that commercial pet foods may contain chemical preservatives such as ethoxyquin, which can make dogs irritable and cranky.

⇨ *Healing & herbs*

Animal healing is a fantastic complement to veterinary care and can be safely given by you to your pet. Read Chapter 5: *How to Give Healing to Your Pet*, for instructions. Hands-on healing can be given by you to your own dog or by an experienced animal healer after the dog has accepted him or her. Elizabeth strongly advises that distant healing is best for dangerous dogs that are people-aggressive; see Chapter 5.

᎓ Make your own ᎓

Elizabeth recommends offering calendula-infused sunflower oil by self-selection (*see page 50*), the chamomile and lavender pillow (*page 66*) and feeding Chamomile Tea & Honey biscuits (*page 42*).

Canine aggression is a very common problem but one that can be prevented in most cases. Prevention is always much better than cure. Proper selection of the right dog for the particular family or person is therefore very important. Vets should discuss prevention and identify early signs of aggression to stop it escalating into a major public health risk.

I believe that with an integrated approach that combines humane behaviour-modification techniques, Elizabeth's relaxation techniques to help you build trust, and feeding the right diet, it should be possible in most cases to improve the dog's behaviour and reduce the aggression significantly.

Aggression in cats

Top behaviourists consider feline aggression to be an outward manifestation of the internal emotional state of the cat. They believe that cats may direct aggression towards people due to fear, anxiety, frustration (seen in rescued cats who may have been outdoor cats but are now stuck indoors) or even misdirection of their predatory instincts. Lactating and nursing queens may be more aggressive in order to defend their kittens.

Similarly, fearful cats learn that their aggression helps keep people away, so they may start becoming more pre-emptively aggressive. Kittens that were not handled properly between the ages of two and seven weeks may become reclusive and show defensive aggression. Some feline aggression can be a result of inappropriate play behaviour, but inter-cat aggression is usually due to competition for food/water/mating, or even just space.

Symptoms

Cats tend to hiss, hide, make low-throated growls or high-pitched vocalizations when they are angry. Your cat may try to attack your feet suddenly when you are walking past. Some cats will suddenly grab the owner's hand and bite or scratch aggressively without letting go. Inter-cat aggression is characterized by fighting and chasing, or just staring from a distance for hours. If cornered, cats may actually launch themselves at the perceived threat and bite. Aggressive cats tend to be reclusive and may not like petting or stroking.

Diagnosis

If your cat is aggressive he or she will be confirmed as being aggressive towards people and/or aggressive towards other cats and animals by your vet, or by a behaviourist if your pet is referred to one. They will then carry out a risk assessment and formulate a treatment plan.

Treatment

⇨ *Your vet and you*

Cat attacks and bites can cause serious injury, so no matter how much you love your cat you must try and avoid situations that may cause your pet to turn on you. As a behavioural first aid, your vet may advise you to separate an aggressive cat from you or other cats, depending on who is the usual target for its attacks. If your cat attacks neighbouring cats, you will have to keep your cat indoors, at least temporarily.

It is absolutely crucial to provide an aggressive cat with coping strategies in the form of high or low hiding places, cat flaps to escape, playing stations, scratching posts, etc. I tend to focus on behaviour-modification techniques initially, but in extreme cases, especially if it has become obvious that the aggression stems from anxiety, I have prescribed certain calming medications.

Pheromone therapy with Feline Facial Pheromone (FFP) has been found to be effective in relaxing and relieving anxiety caused by social tension among cats. These come in the form of plug-ins or sprays. You can also try herb-infused toys, as described below, in order to encourage natural play and predatory behaviour, as this can also be beneficial. I strongly recommend that you read the section on mental and emotional wellbeing for cats in Chapter 1: *Food Is Medicine.*

⇨ *Healing & herbs*

Animal healing is a fantastic complement to veterinary care and can be safely given by you to your pet. Read Chapter 5: *How to Give Healing to Your Pet* for instructions.

⛬ **Make your own** ⛬

Elizabeth recommends fresh catnip, dried catnip, catnip toys and catnip-infused sunflower oil offered on a self-selection basis (see *pages 50 and 64*) and the chamomile and lavender pillow (*page 66*).

ALLERGIES

An allergy is a damaging immune response by the body to a substance, especially a particular food, pollen, fur or dust, to which it has become hypersensitive.

Causes

Flea allergic dermatitis is one of the most common allergies seen in veterinary practice. In most pets, grass, food, cleaning products, washing powder used to clean bedding, dust mites, pollen, mould and insect bites/stings can trigger an allergic reaction. Over-vaccinating has also been known to trigger allergies so it is worth discussing this if your pet's symptoms appear to be related to their boosters.

Pyotraumatic dermatitis, commonly known as wet eczema or hot spot, may be caused by self-trauma, licking and scratching that is a response to an allergy or even clipper rash from a dog groomer's clipper. It is more frequent in hot and humid weather.

Symptoms

These will depend on the allergen and can range from itchy skin, biting or licking the feet or skin, rubbing the face on the floor or against furniture excessively, restlessness, rashes, runny nose or eyes, sudden swellings like hives, and even recurrent ear infections. Hot spots – a well-demarcated, moist, red, sore, hairless patch on the skin – may be seen.

Diagnosis

Most of the time, a diagnosis can be made from the history and presenting clinical signs. In some severe cases where the cause is unknown, Intra-dermal Allergy testing or blood tests for specific sources of allergens may be recommended. In my experience these are quite useful.

Treatment

⇨ Your vet

As a responsible pet guardian it is your duty to notice symptoms quickly and then look for a possible cause before you take your animal to your vet. This will help the vet make an accurate and prompt diagnosis. Once your vet has examined your pet he or she may prescribe flea treatment if a flea allergy is found, advise a steroid injection to reduce hives and alleviate itching, prescribe creams or eye drops and recommend dietary changes, depending on your pet's diagnosis.

If the allergy is recurrent and it has not been possible to identify the cause, then the vet may advise blood testing to identify the allergen, after which immunotherapy vaccines may be needed.

Food elimination trials can be useful where food allergy is suspected (see Chapter 1: *Food Is Medicine*). Topical antibiotic and steroid gels may be prescribed for patches of acute moist dermatitis and the area will need to be clipped and cleansed with dilute chlorhexidine. Systemic antibiotics may be needed in certain breeds and when there is secondary bacterial infection.

Your pet may be prescribed special shampoos for itchy skin, antihistamines, and in chronic cases long-term steroids may also be necessary (although this is not ideal, and should be avoided where possible). Please read carefully Chapter 8: *Which Drugs and Why*, which describes the side effects of steroids.

I try my best to avoid treating pets with long-term steroids but in some cases I have to relent to pressure from the pet owners, either because they are not willing to be patient or they do not have the funds to investigate the skin condition. In cases where the pet concerned is itching so badly that it is literally ripping itself apart, steroids may have to be used.

⇨ *You*

Please insist on a proper diagnosis, rather than choosing temporary fixes like steroids. Consult your vet and spend time, money and energy on ascertaining the cause of the problem.

⇨ *Healing & herbs*

Animal healing is a fantastic complement to veterinary care and can be safely given by you to your pet. Read Chapter 5: *How to Give Healing to Your Pet* for instructions. You can give acupressure too, using acupoint L 14, as shown in Chapter 6: *Fingers and Thumbs*. Garlic is great for skin problems so try the garlic recipes in Chapter 2.

⤷ **Make your own** ⤶

For mild cases of wet eczema, Elizabeth recommends the aloe vera basic gel (*see page 59*) – try the seaweed version if it looks particularly sore – and feeding calendula- bladderwrack- or mint-infused sunflower oil (*page 50*) by self-selection. In cases of mild flea allergic dermatitis, Elizabeth has had great success in cats with the neem-leaf tea insect repellent and/or the neem bark powder insect repellent (*page 81*). For dogs she recommends neem insect repellent (*page 80*) and garlic-infused honey (*page 49*).

ANAL GLAND PROBLEMS

These two glands are situated each side of the anus at the 4 o'clock position on the right side and the seven o'clock position on the left. The duct that empties each gland opens into the rectum just inside the anal ring. Anal glands can be very troublesome in some dogs. The gland secretes a pungent-smelling, brownish discharge that is very distinctive and often smells of dead, decaying fish.

Causes

The anal sacs normally empty and refill every day. They empty when the dog or cat has a bowel movement and the smell of this fluid is unique to the pet. When the stools are not firm enough, the act of defecation fails to exert enough pressure to squeeze the glands, and as a result the fluid accumulates in the sacs over time, causing discomfort, itchiness and sometimes anal gland abscesses. This problem is extremely rare in cats.

Symptoms

Most people who observe their dog rubbing its bottom on the floor assume that he or she has worms. I have heard this particular symptom described variously as skating, scooting, dragging bottom on the floor, etc., all of which suggest possible anal gland involvement as the poor dog is trying to apply pressure on these sacs to empty them.

Some dogs will lick at their rear end excessively and make it sore. It is very important to examine your pet's rear end at least once a week, to check if there is any abnormal redness or swelling. Anal gland abscesses are very painful and need veterinary intervention.

Treatment
⇨ *Your vet*

If you think your dog is showing the above symptom you can try and massage the region around the anus with a warm flannel. This may cause the glands to empty. Small dogs can be placed in a warm bath and gently dragged across on their bottoms to empty the glands. If neither of these work then make an appointment with your vet to have your pet's glands emptied.

If the pet has an anal gland abscess then the vet will prescribe a course of antibiotics and some anti-inflammatory drugs. In severe cases your pet may need to be sedated and the gland lanced, drained and flushed with antibiotics. If your pet suffers anal gland problems recurrently, despite treatment, the vet may advise their surgical removal as a last resort. In my experience, it is not a good idea to manually empty the glands frequently as this is unnatural – it can increase inflammation and impaction and even stop them from emptying naturally at defecation.

⇨ *You*

An anal gland problem is best treated by you, as it can be prevented with the right diet. Elizabeth and I recommend feeding your dog a high-fibre diet with added vegetables like broccoli and carrots, as this can help the stools become harder and firmer, and as a consequence, the glands should hopefully empty naturally; see Chapter 1: *Food Is Medicine*.

⇨ *Healing & herbs*

Animal healing is a fantastic complement to veterinary care and can be safely given by you to your pet. Read Chapter 5: *How to Give Healing to Your Pet* for instructions.

✥ Make your own ✥

Elizabeth recommends garlic-infused honey (*see page 49*) and allowing your pet to self-select linseed cold-pressed oil (*page 76*); you can also try Linseed K9/Feline biscuits and Garlic K9 biscuits (*pages 52 and 46*) and the chicken broth recipe on page 15.

ANXIETY

Separation anxiety encompasses a range of separation-related behaviour problems that take place when the pet guardian is partially or completely absent. This condition may exist on its own, or pets that exhibit this condition may simultaneously display fears and phobias of new/novel situations, fear of strangers, heightened sensitivity and fear of loud noises, cars, fireworks, etc.

Causes

As domestic dogs consider their human family as their pack, they can bond excessively to certain family members and this over-attachment can be a cause of separation anxiety in some dogs. It may make you feel special that your dog loves you more than other family members, but for your pet's sake ensure it is not excessive. Not much has been documented about this condition in cats, but I have had many feline patients who have exhibited what appeared to be separation distress behaviour.

Fear of fireworks and thunderstorms is common, and may be down to the fact that your pet was not habituated, or exposed, to noises within the first three to six months of its life. Your dog may have had a traumatic experience or may have learned it from another pet or even from you – if you are scared of loud noises, your pet is more likely to be the same. There is some evidence that suggests that neutering animals before six months of age or earlier can make them more fearful of noise.

Symptoms

Dogs may bark constantly, destroy furniture or objects, urinate or defecate inappropriately and lick or groom themselves excessively. Cats may show stress over grooming and lick themselves raw; some may scratch furniture and show marking behaviour by house soiling. They may also hide a lot or turn aggressive or reclusive.

Diagnosis

A behaviourist or your veterinarian will arrive at a diagnosis of separation anxiety or phobias based on key findings in your pet's behavioural history. This can be quite a long consultation or may need several consultations. As these problems can have multiple and varied underlying motivations – including fear, over- or under-stimulation, territorial behaviour and hyper-attachment – a definitive diagnosis and a single treatment option may not always be possible.

Treatment

⇨ *Your vet*

During my TV talk shows, most of the calls I received were from worried pet guardians about their pet's abnormal behaviour. Unfortunately, this is one area where there are no quick fixes and no guarantees. Animal behaviour is complex and even the most experienced behaviourist can completely cure only some cases.

As a veterinarian, I deal with each pet on an individual basis and then try a combination of medication, management and coping strategies. As phobias and fears can potentially severely impact the health and welfare of a pet, the focus should be on treatment rather than just management.

Only after performing a complete physical exam and carrying out any routine blood tests to ensure vital organ function, will I start an animal on medication. Benzodiazepines are very effective, especially in acute episodes of noise phobia such as fireworks, and there are individual variations in response. In my experience they seem to work really well in some animals but not in others.

I start the animal off on the medication and when the management protocols are in place, I wean them off the drugs or ask that they be used sporadically. I have found that complementing drugs with appropriate behaviour and environmental modifications seems to have the best results in the long term.

In contrast, while dealing with separation anxiety problems, the focus should be on acute management protocols and behaviour training. Medications such as clomipramine hydrochloride or fluoxetine can be an add-on, but are unlikely to provide any long-term benefit on their own. In some cases Selegiline can also be tried as it does seem to benefit emotional disorders. Dog Appeasing Pheromones (DAP) are a useful adjunct to therapy as most medication can take several weeks to actually make a difference.

⇨ *You*

As a pet guardian your role is *key* when dealing with emotional disorders and phobias. Following the vet or behaviourist's advice with regards to management protocols is vital for ensuring a quicker and more long-term solution to your pet's problem without making them drug-dependent. As your state of mind plays a crucial role, I advise that you follow the grounding techniques described in Chapter 5: *How to Give Healing to Your Pet*, and become less anxious and worried, as this will be picked up by your pet.

Treating separation anxiety

Once your pet is diagnosed by a vet as having separation anxiety, you will be provided with tailor-made instructions on how to interact with your pet differently so he or she can stay 'home alone' eventually. You may be asked to play more with your pet, or exercise them more, as increased exercise tends to make pets calmer and decrease anxiety. In the short-term, you may be required to avoid leaving your pet alone and may have to take your pet to work, arrange a pet sitter or use a doggy day care service.

Dealing with a pet who has separation anxiety is not too different from leaving a toddler behind. You might have to eliminate your departure cues if this is a trigger – for example, you could pack your bag without your pet noticing or dress in casual clothes and change at work, or distract your pet with a chew, etc. Over time you may have to pretend you are leaving the house but actually not go anywhere. The aim here is to disassociate the cues from the actual departure.

Planned, graduated training departures are advocated by many behaviourists, and you will need specialist training with your dog to achieve this. Increasing your pet's independence and decreasing hyper-attachment is very important. You will have to ignore your pet's attention-seeking behaviour – such as pawing, leaning, nudging and barking – but attend to him when he is calm and quiet. Please note: do not ignore your pet – just ignore his attention-seeking behaviour.

Take your pet on more walks, play with him more, and go training together. I have recommended combined healing sessions for you and your pet using the Animal Whispers Sound Therapy music CD and have had great feedback from pet guardians. See Resources section for details. You can leave this music playing for your pet while you are out and he or she will find it very calming and therapeutic.

Sometimes, avoiding close contact with your pet may be necessary to reduce dependence and clingy behavior on demand. So do not encourage your pet to come and sit on you when he or she wishes to. It does not mean you should ignore your pet completely. Instead, you should be the one to initiate contact, once in a while.

You could spread a towel on your lap, which is a cue for your pet to sit there, or pat or call them to sit by you. Eating often decreases anxiety in a dog so giving them something tasty to chew while you are leaving the house can really help.

⇨ *Healing & herbs*

Animal healing is a fantastic complement to veterinary care and can be safely given by you to your pet. Read Chapter 5: *How to Give Healing to Your Pet* for instructions.

⨂ Make your own ⨂

For cats, Elizabeth recommends catnip-infused sunflower oil (*see page 50*), Catnip Feline biscuits (*page 41*), the chamomile and lavender pillow (*page 66*), rose petal water for cats (*page 84*), the valerian cat toy (*page 89*) and wheatgrass plants (*page 91*). For dogs, you can try Chamomile Tea & Honey biscuits (*page 42*), chamomile-infused honey (*page 49*), Prairie Woof Jacks (*page 53*) and calendula-infused sunflower oil for self-selection (*page 50*).

Treating fears and phobias

Your pets are not being stupid when they become scared. They have no control over their fears or phobias so realizing this is a first step to helping them get over them. It is very difficult to ascertain how noise sensitivities or fears have developed in each case, but there are two main types of theory, based on human research:

- Associative processes like social learning, as seen in monkeys.

- Non-associative processes, like poor habituation (exposure) to noises or fears in early life, sensitization to thunderstorms and chronic stress due to inadequate environment or lifestyle.

Desensitization and counter-conditioning (DSCC) using a noise recording is the standard treatment. By gradually increasing the exposure to a certain noise (fireworks or thunder, say) by using a CD with a recording of it, it is possible to habituate your dog to the sound. The hope is that your pet will basically get used to the noise and not show problem behaviour unless it is too loud. These recordings are readily available from your vet or behaviourist, or online.

Apart from this, for reducing the effects of thunderstorms, lightning or fireworks on dogs that are afraid of them, environmental modifications are recommended. Using blackout blinds and curtains can be effective. There is an antistatic cape called a Storm Defender that seems to be effective in some dogs.

White noise machines like fans, and providing dogs and cats with safe places to hide during fireworks and storms, along with medicating them, can help.

Pheromone therapy using Dog Appeasing Pheromone (DAP) diffusers, T-touch and acupressure-based massage therapy, and also using aids like the Thundershirt or Anxiety Wrap, have been known to help. While the Storm Defender has a thin metallic lining that claims to repel ionic charges, the Anxiety Wrap uses acupressure points all over and the Thundershirt mainly covers the girth.

Research conducted at Tufts University in the USA did not prove convincingly that the antistatic mechanism used in the Storm Defender was beneficial. More research is necessary so I cannot recommend any particular product. Unlike the Storm Defender, which is specifically designed for thunder-related fear, the other two products claim to help with other anxieties as well. I have had mixed reports about all of them so the best way is to try each one out.

You should try and ignore your pet's fearful behaviour and avoid cuddling or reassuring them, as this can reinforce the anxiety. Just distract them by starting a game, dancing to loud music or doing obedience training – all of which can be very useful. Punishing or shouting at your pet is definitely a big no, and can make matters worse.

Calming sound therapy, lavender and chamomile preparations (as described above under *Anxiety*) and giving healing can be beneficial. Increased serotonin levels, caused by feeding more carbohydrates, can also help, as they alter the mood. Feeding pasta or rice half an hour after a main, protein-rich meal is advisable.

Prevention is always better than cure so it is highly recommended that you expose your pet to various kinds of noise from when they are 12 weeks old, and do it gradually. Fears and phobias can be inherited so do enquire about the demeanour and responses towards noise, etc., of your prospective pet's parents. Finally, unless it is for medical reasons, do not get your pet neutered at an early age.

APPETITE LOSS

Any animal in good health will usually be ready for food – just like us. In the case of animals, though, it is the pattern of eating that is important. We all know a fussy pet that only picks at its food and may not eat even once a day, but after a couple of days suddenly eats a good meal. The old adage 'a healthy pet is a hungry pet' is for the most part very true.

Causes

Stress, changes in the family, depression, pain, fever, poor-quality or boring food, weather changes, parasites, oral lesions, infections, constipation and cancer can all cause loss of appetite. If the cause is simple then just changing the pet's food or giving them more attention may solve the issue. Severe gingivitis or dental disease can also cause an animal to go off its food. See the case study of Boris the Labradoodle on pages 13–17 of Chapter 1: *Food Is Medicine.*

Symptoms

Appetite loss (or inappetence) is usually a symptom of some underlying disease. If appetite loss is accompanied by other signs of ill health, these should be taken into account and the appropriate remedy given; if in any doubt seek veterinary help. Most pets will just stop eating completely or pick at their food.

Cats with respiratory infections cannot smell their food so they may come close to their bowl and then walk away without eating. Dogs and cats with painful lesions in their mouth may try to eat and then yelp or howl and back off from their food. These behaviours must be observed carefully and reported to your vet. If your pet is refusing all food, including favourite treats, then there is definitely some underlying cause that needs veterinary help.

Diagnosis

After obtaining a full history and performing a thorough clinical examination your vet will arrive at a diagnosis. Blood tests and X-rays may be needed if the vet suspects infectious diseases, pancreatitis, constipation, obstructions (foreign bodies inside your pet) or cancer. Cats with ulcerative stomatitis will have ulcers in the mouth that prevent them from eating. Most cancers will also cause pets to lose weight and appetite. Dogs and cats that have eaten foreign objects may have a blockage that will make them stop eating. Appetite loss may also be due to liver and/or kidney failure.

Treatment

⇨ *Your vet*

This will vary, based on the diagnosis. Simple cases of inappetance triggered by mild infections and fever will respond to antibiotics and painkillers. Animals who have swallowed foreign objects will need emergency surgery to remove the foreign body and clear the obstruction. Severely constipated animals may need enemas.

Dental extractions may be necessary if bad teeth are causing inappetance. If your pet has pancreatitis it may need to be admitted and placed on a drip until its appetite returns (*see Pancreatitis*). Cancer cases will need to have special treatment and appetite stimulants. Kidney and liver failure cases will need to go on special diets, appetite stimulants and vitamin injections.

⇨ *You*

If your pet refuses food but seems to be itself in every other way – alert, active and interested – there is nothing to worry about. It is okay for a cat not to eat for 24 hours and for a dog, 48 hours, but a sudden change in eating habits is certainly noteworthy. If at all possible you should examine your pet's mouth to check if there is any soreness in the gums/tongue or teeth. This is much easier with dogs than with cats but if your pet turns aggressive then *stop* at once and take him or her to your vet as soon as possible.

You can try swapping your pet's usual food to some tasty human food or another make of pet food. If your pet gulps it down there is nothing to worry about. Serving him or her warm food (body temperature) can stimulate the appetite, too, and feeding in a quiet place may help if the household is noisy.

⇨ *Feeding tips for sick pets*

Elizabeth strongly recommends using the superfoods shopping checklist on page 18 and trying the following recipes: chicken broth (*page 15*), K9/Feline fishcakes (*page 51*), K9/Feline Nature's Own Hotpot (*page 15*), Liver Cake K9/Feline bake (*page 52*) and Hard-boiled Egg and Eggshell K9/Feline treats (*page 44–45*).

You can try acupressure massage on BL 20 and ST 36 to help stimulate the appetite. See Chapter 6: *Fingers and Thumbs*, for location and technique.

In addition, try the following:

- Avoid feeding snacks.

- Feed little and often.

- Tempt your pet with fresh, home-cooked food.

- Do not leave food down if your pet does not finish it.

- Offer fresh food each time.

- Pamper your pet by hand feeding or placing food in a little saucer.

⇨ *Healing & herbs*

Animal healing is a fantastic complement to veterinary care and can be safely given by you to your pet. Read Chapter 5: *How to Give Healing to Your Pet* for instructions.

⚚ Make your own ⚘

For cats offer on a self-selection basis catnip- or bladderwrack-infused sunflower oil (see *page 50*), as this can help stimulate the appetite. Allow dogs to self-select from bladderwrack-infused sunflower oil and linseed cold-pressed oil (*pages 50 and 76*).

ARTHRITIS (OSTEOARTHRITIS)

'Degenerative joint disease' is a more appropriate name for osteoarthritis (OA) in veterinary medicine and it is probably the most common skeletal disease seen in dogs. The term osteoarthritis was derived from three Greek words meaning bone, joint and inflammation and is defined as a progressive degeneration of joint cartilage and the underlying bone, resulting in the formation of bony spurs at the margins of the joints. These spurs are the main source of pain and it is this progressive remodelling of bone that makes arthritis a degenerative and chronic disease.

Causes

Wear and tear is probably the most common cause of arthritis. When an animal walks or plays or runs, quite a lot of stress is inflicted on the joints and when this happens repeatedly over the years, the joint cartilage breaks down and arthritis can develop. This is usually the case in older animals, but it can also happen in young ones who are overworked or those that already have conditions such as osteochondrosis (OCD) or developmental disorders like patellar luxation, elbow or hip dysplasia (see *hip dysplasia*).

If your pet has had some sort of joint trauma (fracture, ligament injury, dislocation) that joint can consequently develop arthritis. In my experience, those joints that have been operated on, like the knee joint in cruciate surgery or to correct patellar luxations, tend to develop arthritis eventually.

Overweight and obese pets have a much higher chance of acquiring osteoarthritis. Certain dog breeds, like German Shepherd Dog, Labrador or other large breeds, tend to suffer from it more, mainly because they are genetically more likely to have developmental disorders like hip dysplasia.

Symptoms

Most pets will exhibit some form of lameness or stiffened gait. Dogs will show reluctance to jump into cars and cats will stop jumping onto higher surfaces. Because the actual articular cartilage lacks nerves, your pets will not feel pain initially, so they will continue to be active. This can actually make matters worse, because the disease then progresses to the next stage.

Once a lot of cartilage has been destroyed, the cushioning effect in the joints is lost and therefore the surrounding joint tissues, the joint capsule, the ligaments and the bones become swollen and painful. This is when lameness is observed in arthritis. The lameness can be intermittent, it can affect more than one joint and it can be made worse by prolonged rest or by exercise. Cold weather can also make the symptoms worse. The affected joint may be swollen, hot and painful.

Diagnosis

Most of the time arthritis is diagnosed by observant pet guardians, who see the symptoms described above. Vets confirm the diagnosis based on the symptoms and by manipulating the affected joint to feel the swelling and/crepitus (popping/cracking sounds) or reduced range of movement. A history of pre-existing conditions like osteochondrosis or hip dysplasia will point towards a diagnosis of osteoarthritis. If your pet has had a previous episode of trauma that caused joint instability, this will also alert the vet.

Sometimes, the vet may need to X-ray the affected joint to rule out cancer and to ascertain the extent of disease. It may also be necessary to perform a joint tap and send it off for culture and sensitivity, if there is a suspicion of septic/immune-mediated infectious arthritis. Blood tests may be necessary in sick or elderly pets to ensure their vital organs, especially the kidney, are in good condition to metabolize the medication that may be prescribed.

Treatment

⇨ Your vet

Modern-day management of OA involves a three-pronged approach – adequate pain relief, maintaining the correct weight, and regular, moderate exercise at the same time and for the same length of time each day. NSAIDs (see Chapter 8: *Which Drugs and Why*) are the most popular medications used today for the management of OA as they bring down the inflammation of the joint rapidly and quite effectively in the short term. However, they can cause side effects when used long-term.

Other types of painkillers – like tramadol, gabapentin, codeine, etc.– may also be prescribed. Steroids are very rarely used these days to treat OA, but some vets may use an occasional depomedrone shot in cats that refuse to take oral NSAIDs.

In dogs, Pentosan polysulphate, given as a sub-cutaneous (into the skin) injection once weekly for four consecutive weeks, can be very useful as it actually helps the regeneration of cartilage. Joint supplements containing glucosamine hydrochloride and chondroitin sulphate with Dexahan, krill oil, antioxidants and omega-3 fatty acids are very effective. The vet may also refer your pet to a veterinary hydro- or physiotherapist.

⇨ You

A pet with arthritis can have an excellent quality of life if you can provide a good, balanced diet that supports the joint (see Chapter 1: *Food Is Medicine*) along with natural joint supplements. Elizabeth recommends the following recipes: Hedgerow Hip Bites and Ginger K9 biscuits (*page 47*), K9/Feline fishcakes and K9/Feline Nature's Own Hotpot (*page 51*) and Linseed K9/Feline biscuits (*page 52*).

If your pet is overweight, then strict weight loss measures should be put in place, as the already struggling joints cannot carry excess weight. You must always feed your pet the right amount and feed them for the weight you want them to be, rather than the weight that they are. Most vets have free weight clinics and will help you achieve this.

Acupuncture and acupressure can help with chronic pain (see Chapter 6: *Fingers and Thumbs*). Hydrotherapy with a professional, or taking your dog swimming on a regular basis, can be very helpful as the water takes the strain off the joints, encouraging your pet to move without pain. You can take your dog on regular lead walks, starting with a gentle five minutes and building up to half an hour maximum, twice a day. You must listen to your dog and not overdo it.

⇨ *Healing & herbs*

Animal healing is a fantastic complement to veterinary care and can be safely given by you to your pet. See Chapter 5: *How to Give Healing to Your Pet*, for instructions.

⁂ Make your own ⁂

Elizabeth recommends offering your cat calendula-infused sunflower oil (*page 50*), and your dog linseed cold-pressed oil (*page 76*) on a self-selection basis.

BLADDER PROBLEMS

Problems pertaining to the urinary bladder are quite commonly seen in veterinary practice. Infections of the bladder, inflammation of the bladder (cystitis), urolithiasis (bladder stones) and urinary incontinence are observed in both dogs and cats. Feline Lower Urinary Tract disease, or FLUTD, is a broad term used only in cats and covers all the above conditions and plugged-penis syndrome.

1. URINARY INCONTINENCE

Urinary incontinence is defined as the involuntary or unintentional leakage or passage of urine and therefore indicates the loss of voluntary control of urination.

Causes

Mixed or multiple causes of incontinence have been documented in humans and this is very likely the case in dogs and cats too. In most instances it may not be possible to ascertain all the causes. It is much more common in middle-aged to elderly pets, neutered female dogs and juvenile female dogs and seems to affect medium to larger breed dogs more than the toy or small breeds.

Acquired urethral incompetence caused by low estrogen levels in neutered female dogs is common and is an example of hormone-responsive urinary incontinence. Developmental disorders of the urinary tract, lesions in the cerebellum, spinal cord lesions, lumbosacral disc disease, UTIs (urinary tract infections) and bladder cancer are some of the causes of urinary incontinence. Overflow incontinence due to an over-distended bladder is seen in traumatic fractures of the spine or pelvis. Obesity can also be a contributing factor.

Symptoms

Excited puppies may urinate in excitement inside the house or when they are still training. A neutered female dog may have little accidents in the house or her bedding, and legs may be damp from urine leakage. Most owners find that their dog's bed is wet and smelly, as she has leaked involuntarily overnight. Elderly dogs or those with spinal injuries will dribble or leak while just standing.

Diagnosis

Only a veterinarian can make a diagnosis, by differentiating between similar signs. By examining your pet and taking a full history, your vet will decide whether your pet is exhibiting voluntary but inappropriate urination, has polyuria or is just urine spraying (cats). Palpating your pet's urinary bladder to check its size and ability to express urine, and checking your dog's prostate (males only) and genitals will enable your vet to arrive at the correct cause.

Blood tests may be needed if your pet is urinating a lot and drinking too much (polyuria and polydipsia), in order to check whether they have underlying diabetes, kidney or liver disease. Testing your pet's urine sample will provide clues to infections, stones, cancer, diabetes and kidney disease so it is a good idea to get a urine sample before you visit your vet. Radiographs/ultrasound scans may be necessary to rule out stones, congenital problems, cancer and kidney pathology. It may also be necessary to perform a neurological examination or catheterize your pet as required.

Treatment

It is not easy to treat incontinence. There is also quite a bit of variation in the response of each animal to the same treatment. Moreover, in many cases there are multiple causes, so it may not be possible to stop involuntary urination completely, although it is possible to reduce it. After ruling out temporary incontinence due to infections, estrus (bitch in season), or behaviour, your vet will commence treatment.

Incontinence in neutered female dogs is responsive to estrogen. I have had good success with estriol, which is a synthetic, short-acting estrogen, as it increases the muscle tone in the lower urogenital tract and improves urodynamic function. Phenypropanolamine is also very successful in treating incontinence secondary to urethral sphincter incompetence. Surgery may be required if anatomical disorders are diagnosed and your vet will then refer your pet to a specialist. Prosthetic sphincter implantation is now available.

2. CYSTITIS

Cystitis simply means 'inflammation of the bladder' and it seems to occur more commonly in females than males (except in cats).

Causes

The urinary bladder is a sterile organ. Ascending bladder infections usually occur as a consequence of bacteria travelling up into the bladder via the urethra. As female dogs tend to crouch quite low while urinating, they can pick up infections from the ground or grass, etc. Cystitis in male cats has been attributed to eating various dried cat foods. Feline Idiopathic cystitis (FIC) is very common in cats and is believed to be stress and diet induced, but there is evidence that these cats may also have spinal cord changes and altered bladder wall function. Persian cats seem to be more prone to FIC.

Symptoms

Dogs seem to present with frequent urination and/or blood in their urine (hematuria). Cat owners find that their cat is urinating in strange places, like the sink or bathtub or on kitchen tops, or just going in and out of the litter tray frequently. Some cats may vocalize more. Both cats and dogs may be observed to lick their genitals excessively.

Diagnosis

Your vet will usually request a urine sample from your pet so it will save time and money if you can take one with you. It is not too difficult to collect a urine sample: when your dog starts to urinate just hold a clean, wide-mouthed container in the stream and collect it; it need not be sterile. A sterile sample is only needed if your vet wants to culture your pet's urine sample, in which case, he or she will obtain one by performing a cystocentesis with or without an ultrasound.

It is challenging to get a urine sample from your cat; however, it can be done if you can keep your cat in and provide a litter tray with special cat litter called Katkor. This litter will not absorb any urine and will therefore enable you to get a clean sample. Most vets will give you this litter if they want a urine sample.

Your vet will send the urine sample off to a lab, where it will be tested for bacterial growth, and recommendations will then be made with regards to the correct antibiotic that will work against them. This is very useful as it ensures your pet gets the right treatment. Urine microscopy, X-rays and ultrasound, with or without catheterization, may be necessary to rule out bladder stones and blockage of the urethra or ureters.

Treatment
⇨ Your vet

Most vets will start your pet on a preliminary course of broad-spectrum antibiotics. In recurrent cases, after sending your pet's urine for culture and ascertaining the organisms involved in the infection, a different or longer course of antibiotics may be needed. Pain relief may also be necessary.

A nutritional supplement called Cystaid is also prescribed by many veterinarians. This contains N Acetyl D Glucosamine, which helps to protect the bladder lining and is usually necessary in recurrent chronic cystitis. Pets with recurrent bladder infections are more prone to developing bladder stones. Your vet may advise a prescription diet that will help maintain the correct urine pH and/or prescribe urinary acidifiers in order to prevent bladder-stone formation. See *Bladder stones* for more information.

⇨ *You*

Your pet's diet can make a huge difference. Wet food is preferable to dry. In my opinion it is better not to feed dry food as the sole diet, especially to male cats, but to use it in small amounts, giving a teaspoonful at a time once or twice daily, in addition to fresh, home-cooked food or canned food.

I recommend adding the home-cooked chicken broth (*see page 15*) to dry cat food, to increase the water intake. As some cats seem to love dry food and may not eat wet food at all, it may be necessary to feed both. You need to increase your pet's water intake if it is mainly on dry food (see tips below for doing this).

Urine infections are more common in alkaline urine (pH>7) so diets that help acidify the urine will help. In general, vegetarian and cereal-based diets tend to increase the likelihood of alkaline urine, whereas animal-based protein sources tend to acidify.

3. BLADDER STONES

Uroliths (commonly known as bladder stones) can be of different types, based on their composition. They form in the bladder as microscopic crystals, which then precipitate into larger macroscopic stones. While the majority of uroliths form in alkaline urine, some do form in acidic urine. Struvite urolithiasis is more common than other types, in both cats and dogs. Cats with FLUTD suffer with urethral plugs, which may be struvite crystals or just composed of sloughed tissue and blood. These plugs occlude the penile urethra and cause plugged-penis syndrome.

Causes

Certain dog breeds are more predisposed genetically to certain types of stones. There is a high incidence of struvite uroliths in Miniature Schnauzers, whereas Dalmatians are highly likely to suffer with urate urolithiasis. Any breed can suffer with bladder stones, although the above-named breeds, plus Shih Tzu, Lhasa Apso, Cocker Spaniel, Miniature Poodle and Bichon Frise, have a breed predilection.

Recurrent urinary tract infections by urease-producing microbes, a diet that makes the urine alkaline, and some other metabolic factors can contribute to struvite stones. Cats that are primarily on dry commercial foods high in cereals and vegetable materials tend to suffer more with urinary caliculi.

Symptoms

The symptoms of bladder stones are the same as those of cystitis, except when a stone or stones tries to pass the urethra (then it can be very painful). If the stone is large enough or there are many of them, they can block the urethra, in which case the dog or cat cannot urinate. This is an *emergency* and you must rush your dog/cat to the vet to have them unblocked.

Blocked male cats are very common in practice because they usually have underlying FLUTD and therefore the urethral plug occludes the penis, making it impossible or very difficult for them to urinate. I have palpated (felt with my hands) a large, grapefruit-sized, rock-solid bladder in some cats while examining their belly area, which indicates blockage.

Diagnosis

I have also palpated stones in the bladders of cats and dogs in the consulting room many times. Obviously the ease with which a vet can do this with your pet will depend on the size of the stones and the size of your pet. Examining a urine sample under the microscope will enable the lab or the vet to identify the type of stone, based on the crystals seen.

An ultrasound scan and/or X-rays may be necessary to confirm the position of the uroliths if more than one is suspected. It will also enable the vet to rule out kidney stones and hydronephrosis (engorgement of the kidney due to obstruction). If left for too long, renal failure is a possibility so blood tests may be required to check if kidney function has been affected.

Treatment

➪ *Your vet*

A blocked cat has to be admitted and dealt with as an emergency. It will need to be sedated and a urinary catheter placed and sewn externally, to enable it to pass urine. Any stones are flushed back into the bladder. If the stones look tiny on the X-ray, the cat may be discharged after a couple of days on a special prescription diet that will dissolve the stones. But if they are too large, and are repeatedly blocking the catheter, then it may be wise to perform a cystotomy (open the bladder) surgically and remove the stones.

The diet prescribed will depend on the type of uroliths identified, so it is very important that the stones are analyzed before a diet is changed. Your vet will also prescribe antibiotics if the diagnosis is infection-induced struvite urolithiasis. Anti-inflammatory medication for pain relief and to suppress the inflammation of the bladder wall and/or urethra may be prescribed.

➪ *You*

If you are the owner of a male cat who is predominantly on dry food, you have to be extra vigilant and observe him urinating if possible. If your cat looks quiet or lethargic and seems to be licking his penis excessively, please get him checked out immediately. Wherever and however possible, increase your pet's water consumption. Wet food and fresh, home-cooked diets contain plenty of water, so it is worth trying them. See Chapter 1: *Food Is Medicine*, and Chapter 2: *A–Z Food Recipes*, for ideas.

➪ *Tips for making your pet drink more*

- Buy a pet water fountain.
- Add tuna or chicken flavour to water.
- Add water or a low-salt broth to food.
- Cats love to drink from a tap, so let your tap trickle on and off.

Elizabeth recommends reading about home-cooked diets in Chapter 1: *Food Is Medicine*, and trying the following recipes: chicken broth (*page 15*) and K9/ Feline Nature's Own Hotpot (*page 51*). Adding chives to these recipes is also a good idea, especially for cats.

⇨ *Healing & herbs*

Animal healing is a fantastic complement to veterinary care and can be safely given by you to your pet. See Chapter 5: *How to Give Healing to Your Pet* for instructions.

⚕ Make your own ⚕

Elizabeth recommends applying aloe vera and yarrow gel to the abdomen to ease bladder discomfort (*see page 92*). For dogs, you can offer on a self-selection basis bladderwrack-infused sunflower oil, and for cats, catnip-infused sunflower oil (*page 50*).

BURNS AND SCALDS

Burns cause cell death and as a consequence they cause breakdown of the cell integrity. Burns and scalds are common in humans but relatively rare in animals, maybe because their instinct is so good that they escape or avoid getting hurt. Any burn or scald should be taken seriously. A burn may not immediately be apparent because of the animal's fur or hair, and the extent of the injury may not be easy to assess. If there is any doubt at all, it is best to consult your veterinary surgeon without delay. Burns are an *emergency*.

Causes

Burns may be caused by radiation therapy, microwave radiation, thermal or chemical sources. Fires, heating lamps/pads, hair dryers and faulty electrosurgical units can cause thermal burns in practice. Scalds are caused by boiling water or oil and are more common at home, when pets are in the kitchen.

Allowing cats to walk on kitchen worktops can lead to burns if the animal touches the hot surface of an electric hob. Chemical burns can occur from caustic or acid materials. I have seen burns on the tongues of cats and dogs that have tried to drink hot tea or coffee from their guardians' cups. Burns are classified as superficial, deep or full-thickness burns, depending on how much of the skin structure is damaged.

Symptoms

Some burns are obvious immediately, but most can take 2–5 days to be seen. Singeing of hair or fur is usually easily visible and can be the only symptom in some pets. Burns caused by hot metals and fires can be seen immediately, but it may take 24–48 hours for the full extent of the burn to become visible. Chemical burns tend to be erosive and necrotic in nature. Your pet licking itself at a particular spot/not eating/sore feet, etc., may all point to burns; if in doubt check with your vet.

Diagnosis

If you have actually witnessed the burn, then diagnosis is clear, but if not a superficial burn may be difficult to diagnose. Your vet will perform a full physical examination, including eyes, ears, mouth, respiratory tract, urogenital tract, anus and footpads, before arriving at a diagnosis. If there are extensive burns and concurrent shock, and/or breathing difficulties, this will be assessed by your vet. For a concrete diagnosis, a biopsy of the lesions, including their margins, may be necessary.

Treatment

⇨ *Your vet*

After a full exam, as detailed under diagnosis, your vet will decide on the course of treatment. Sedation may be necessary if your pet is fractious, and to evaluate and treat the burn accordingly. Hair will need to be clipped very carefully from the burned surface and if it epilates easily that may be indicative of a deep burn.

If the burn has just happened, your vet will aim to cool the burned area by lavaging with saline or water (at 3–17°C/37–63°F) for a minimum of 30 minutes in order to relieve pain and stop the burn from progressing deeper. If extensive burns are present, or your pet was in a fire and inhaled smoke, then treatment will be on a higher footing and will be expensive and extensive. Treatment for shock with fluid therapy, bandaging and surgical debridement, with or without reconstruction, may be needed.

Topical antibiotic therapy to prevent wound infection and silver sulfadiazine in dressings will be used. Superficial partial-thickness wounds may be left to heal as an open wound. Each burn is dealt with on a case-by-case basis, taking into consideration costs, the extent of the burn and, most importantly, your pet's welfare and long-term prognosis.

Note: your vet may refer your pet to a surgical specialist if he or she requires extensive reconstructive (plastic) surgery following a burn.

⇨ *You*

If you witnessed the burn and are sure it was caused by hot water or a chemical substance, the first thing to do is to rinse the area with cold tap water for 10 minutes. If your pet is agitated or tries to bite you or escape and will not allow you to do this, then it is best to take them to the vet immediately as he or she can sedate your pet safely to treat the wound.

⇨ *Healing & herbs*

Elizabeth recommends distant healing in the case of burns and scalds, as your own body heat radiating from your hands or close contact can be uncomfortable to your pet.

⁓ **Make your own** ⁓

For superficial burns, aloe vera basic gel (*see page 59*) can be applied quickly, as it has antiseptic and soothing properties. If you are unsure about the type of burn, please contact your vet. Use calendula ointment (*page 63*) when the skin is healing post-burn.

If your vet has diagnosed your pet's burn as superficial then you can try homeopathic burn ointments that contain hypericum. According to Francis Hunter, an expert in veterinary homeopathy, Cantharis (Remedy 6) is a very effective treatment for minor burns and scalds. Give one tablet every hour, up to four doses, then one tablet every two to four hours during the day for a few days, until your pet is obviously no longer distressed, is able to rest comfortably and, most important, not trying to lick the affected area continuously.

CANCER

Cancer is very common in small animal practice and is seen in both dogs and cats. It is the most feared and dreaded disease among both humans and pets. Cancer is responsible for the deaths of almost 50 per cent of older pets, especially those more than 10 years of age. However, it should also be noted that not all cancers result in death. If diagnosed early, some of them, like solid tumours, can be surgically fully removed and this is curative.

The word 'cancer' does not actually refer to a single disease but to a large group of them. Their two main features are uncontrolled cell division or growth in the body and the ability of these cells to travel from their original site to other parts of the body. Death occurs if this spread cannot be controlled. Cancers are given names based on the type of cell from which they originate or the body part affected. The table below provides a list of some common dog and cat cancers and the main organs they affect:

Common dog cancers	Common cat cancers
Lymphoma – blood and lymph nodes	Lymphosarcoma or lymphoma
Mast cell tumours – skin	Skin tumours
Mammary tumours – breast	Mammary tumours – breast
Osteosarcoma – bones	Leukemia – blood and organs
Haemangiosarcoma – spleen, heart, bone, skin	Haemangiosarcoma – bone, liver
Transitional cell carcinoma – bladder	Squamous cell carcinoma – skin, ear tips, nose, neck
Mouth or oral tumours	Mouth or oral tumours
Brain tumours	Thymoma – thymus gland
Anal sac tumours	Bile duct carcinoma
Prostate cancer – prostate gland in male dogs	Abdominal – pancreatic cancer, liver and kidney cancer
Melanoma	Lung cancer

Causes

Every time I report a confirmative diagnosis of cancer to an anxious pet guardian, I am always asked, 'What has caused my pet's cancer?' The answer is – I do not know. This is because it is impossible to pinpoint a single cause for cancer.

There is a huge list of possible causes though, and I am mentioning the most commonly implicated ones here. Bad genes or breeding, neutering too early or too late, carcinogens in the environment, using plastic feeding bowls, drugs or chemicals in the water, carcinogens in commercial pet foods, viruses, chronic inflammation, vaccines, stress due to owner stress and even an excess of sunlight can cause cancer.

Most of these causes are also true for us. As our pets share our environment, they are also exposed to everything that we face. There is also some evidence to suggest that dogs, and especially cats, can develop lung cancer due to passive smoking – inhaling because owners smoke around them.

Recent research suggests that our negative emotions also impact on our pets, as they look up to us and share deep bonds with us. In my experience, most stressed owners also have stressed pets and sick owners also have pets that fall sick more often. More research into this would be invaluable.

Symptoms

These tend to vary, depending on the location and the type of cancer, and in most cases they are very general. Most pets show at least one of the following signs – lethargy and exhaustion, vomiting, weight loss in spite of eating, appetite loss, struggling to swallow, lumps and bumps, non-healing sores or even bleeding. It is important that you consult your vet if any of these symptoms develop, especially if your pet is middle-aged or elderly.

Diagnosis

If your pet develops a growth, get it checked by your vet. You will be asked about how quickly the lump is growing and also how long it has actually been on your pet. Taking a series of photographs of the lump will be very useful. Your vet will usually be able to tell you if it is a tumour. Tumours can be benign or malignant: the benign ones have a low or zero potential to spread and are therefore not deemed dangerous, while the malignant ones are cancerous and very likely to spread.

To be sure if the tumour is benign or cancerous, your vet may perform a FNA (fine needle aspirate) of the tumour or insist on a biopsy of the tumour or a bone marrow biopsy in certain cases. FNAs can usually be performed without anaesthetizing your pet, whereas biopsies can only be obtained by sedating or giving a full general anaesthetic. These biopsies or FNAs are then sent to a histopathologist, who will report if it is cancerous, where it will spread to and how quickly, and also provide the grade and prognosis.

X-rays are necessary for bone tumours and ultrasound examination for abdominal tumours. MRI and CT scans help diagnose brain or spinal tumours. Blood tests are required to identify certain types of cancer, such as those caused by feline leukaemia virus (FeLV) or feline immunodeficiency virus (FIV) in cats. It is best to get advice from a veterinary oncologist before carrying out too many tests or surgical tumour removal. They can perform a proper diagnostic evaluation and advise on the best options after considering the type of tumour your pet has and the extent of disease.

Treatment
⇨ *Your vet*

Depending on the type of cancer, your vet or oncologist will advise chemotherapy, surgical excision or radiotherapy. In some cases your pet might need a combination of these treatment methods. In most cases, grading and staging the tumour will provide a guide to the appropriate treatment method.

For example, solid tumours will require surgical removal and then perhaps radiotherapy afterwards, especially if it has not been possible to get a clean margin (tissue around the tumour that is free of tumour cells) for various reasons.

An experienced oncologist and a radiation specialist will make this decision, as radiotherapy will not be effective against all cancers. Similarly, chemotherapy will work best in some cancers, especially in dogs, and can actually cure them. It is not really used in cats, as it can be more dangerous to them. Most people are scared of chemotherapy and its side effects, but in reality most dogs do very well on it compared to humans and have very mild side effects such as nausea, vomiting or diarrhoea.

Going into detail about each of these options is beyond the scope of this book, and I strongly advise enlisting the help of an oncologist. Although oncologists are expensive because they are specialists, their experience and knowledge is invaluable and if you find the right one, they can actually save you money by avoiding unnecessary tests.

⇨ *You*

I strongly recommend that you read Dr Demian Dressler's book, *The Dog Cancer Survival Guide*. In it he describes a full-spectrum treatment schedule in which you can play an active role to ensure your dog with cancer has both a good-quality and a long life. Dr Dressler advises using a combination of conventional vet treatment, nutraceuticals like Apocaps, immune-system boosters, the correct diet and finally brain chemistry modification as the backbone of cancer care, which I fully endorse.

Traditional Chinese medicine, Ayurvedic medicine and homeopathy can also be considered, but must only be performed by a veterinarian who has trained in these modalities. This may be the only choice left if your pet has advanced cancer with a poor prognosis with conventional therapies. An experienced complementary therapist and healer like Elizabeth or a holistic vet like myself can advise you on the use of herbs (especially if you cannot afford nutraceuticals), healing techniques and also natural diets that help support your pet through cancer.

Finally, please do not be scared of the statistics that provide the median survival time – how long your pet will live once diagnosed with cancer. Each pet is unique and the numbers may not necessarily apply to your pet. Be proactive, speak openly to your vet or oncologist and then decide on the right treatment plan – one that will suit you and your pet. The decision is yours, but try to educate yourself well so you can make the correct choice for your pet and provide the right support.

⇨ *Healing & herbs*

Animal healing is a fantastic complement to veterinary care and can be safely given by you to your pet. See Chapter 5: *How to Give Healing to Your Pet* for instructions.

ꙮ Make your own ꙮ

Diet is very important for pets with cancer. See Chapter 2: *A–Z Food Recipes* for the following cancer-fighting recipes: Combat Cancer Vegetable Combo, Combat Cancer Fruit Combo and Vegetable Harvest Bake (*page 43*), K9/Feline Nature's Own Hotpot (*page 51*), the Ginger K9 biscuits (to help with nausea) (*page 46*), the Hard-boiled Egg and Eggshell K9/Feline treats (*page 44–45*), Calendula biscuits (*page 41*) and Charcoal K9/Feline De-Tox biscuits (*page 42*). Elizabeth recommends that you offer on a self-selection basis calendula-infused sunflower oil (*page 50*) and cold-pressed linseed oil (*page 76*).

COLITIS

Colitis refers to inflammation of the colon that results in the reduced ability of the colon to absorb water and store faeces. It is a very common cause of diarrhoea in small animal practice and usually a recurring problem in the same animal.

Causes

Colitis can be caused by bacterial or protozoan infections or it can be dietary. If your pets are allergic to the protein in their food or have eaten abrasive material including bones or some foreign body, colitis can occur. Histiocytic ulcerative colitis is observed in Boxers and can usually start by the time the dog is two years old. Colitis can also occur in cats or dogs secondary to chronic pancreatitis.

Symptoms

Both cats and dogs present with semi-solid to liquid faeces. There is an increase in the frequency of bowel movements, but only a small amount of faeces is voided each time. Your pet may strain for a long time before or after defecating. Dogs may have chronic diarrhoea with mucus and blood, but cats tend to have solid but bloodstained faeces. Some dogs may also vomit.

Diagnosis

The symptoms above, combined with a history of dietary indiscretion (your pet eating something they are not supposed to eat, or scavenging), is usually enough for your vet to arrive at a diagnosis of colitis. Your vet will have to differentiate between colitis and the possibility of cancers like lymphoma and adenocarcinoma, which have similar symptoms. By performing a rectal examination, your vet will rule out recto-colonic polyps and by feeling your pet's abdomen they will check for intussusceptions.

If your pet strains frequently or vomits a lot, then one section of the intestine can telescope into another, which is known as intussusception. Blood tests may be necessary if there is a lot of bleeding. Faecal smear examinations are necessary if protozoan infection is suspected and abdominal ultrasound may be performed if cancer or foreign bodies are possible.

In recurrent colitis, or in Boxer dogs, colonoscopy with biopsy or an exploratory laparotomy followed by biopsies of the intestine may be indicated. X-rays are only needed if intussusceptions or bony foreign bodies are suspected.

Treatment
⇨ You
If your pet has mild colitis, then fasting him or her for 24–48 hours may be enough. You can also try a hypoallergenic prescription diet containing a protein that your pet has not been exposed to. Or if there is no likelihood of an allergy just feed home-cooked chicken and rice. Supplementing the fibre intake with bran or adding psyllium can help bulk the faeces up to bind faecal water and ensure formed faeces. See Chapter 1: *Food Is Medicine*.

In early colitis, start with chicken and rice, then move on to the chicken broth (*see page 15*), along with Charcoal K9/Feline D-Tox biscuits (*page 42*) and finally K9/Feline Nature's Own Hotpot (*page 51*). Feed the Hard-boiled Egg and Eggshell K9/Feline treats (*pages 44–45*) when your pet has almost recovered.

⇨ Your vet
Mild colitis cases will be treated as outpatients, but if your pet has bled a lot from his rectum or has become dehydrated then he may be admitted for blood tests and fluid therapy. Antimicrobial therapy may be initiated if faecal cultures reveal giardia, salmonella, histoplasma or campylobacter.

Anti-inflammatory drugs or steroids may be prescribed if your vet thinks the colitis is of inflammatory origin or immune-mediated. Motility modifiers may be added in to stop the diarrhoea and help the formation of normal faeces. Surgery is only needed if cancer, foreign body or intussusception is diagnosed on radiographs or ultrasound.

⇨ *Healing & herbs*

Animal healing is a fantastic complement to veterinary care and can be safely given by you to your pet. See Chapter 5: *How to Give Healing to Your Pet* for instructions.

ᕫ **Make your own** ᕬ

The Mint K9 biscuits are excellent and quick to make (*see page 53*) and so are the Chamomile Tea & Honey biscuits (*page 42*). Garlic-infused honey is good (*page 49*), but *avoid* feeding all herb-infused oils until the colitis has resolved fully.

CONSTIPATION

Constipation can be defined as difficult, incomplete or infrequent defecation accompanied by the passage of hard or dry faecal matter. This condition is not as common as diarrhoea in pet animals, but it does occur in older cats and occasionally in dogs. Although it appears to be a simple issue, it can be a symptom of serious health problems and therefore worth understanding.

Causes

In dogs the dietary causes of constipation are mainly eating cooked bones; in cats it is eating hair or fur balls or other foreign materials. If your pet does not exercise because it cannot move for some reason, or is just lazy, constipation is a possibility. Dirty litter boxes can make cats constipated and dogs that are hospitalized tend to become constipated because of the lack of familiar surroundings.

In dogs, constipation can be secondary to prostatic disease, pelvic fractures, spinal paralysis, megacolon, cancer and foreign bodies. If your pet has a painful condition near its anus, like anorectal disease (anal sac issues, anal gland abscess, rectal prolapse, perianal fistula or perineal hernias), he or she can become or appear constipated. Defecation becomes painful and is therefore avoided.

Bite wounds around the perianal area can also cause your pet to defecate less frequently or not at all. Debility or general muscle weakness, dehydration and conditions that impair the smooth muscle function can also cause constipation. Obesity can predispose your pet to constipation.

Symptoms

The symptoms are usually obvious to dog owners as their pets usually defecate while out on a walk, but they can be missed in cats, who tend to be secretive or do not use the litter tray. Straining to pass faeces, passing tiny, pebble-like or hard and dry faeces, or not passing faeces at all is usually observed in constipated pets. Passing blood or mucus may also be a symptom. Some pets may vomit or stop eating if the constipation is prolonged and has gone unnoticed.

Diagnosis

A rectal and perianal examination by your vet is necessary for a diagnosis. Hard faeces are usually found sitting in the colon and can also be palpated in the abdomen of thin dogs/cats. Sometimes a radiograph/ultrasound exam may be needed if there is a worry that it could be cancer-related, or down to prostate issues, accidents, megacolon or foreign bodies like bones.

Barium enemas may be necessary to identify a mass in the lumen of the intestines that could be causing an obstruction and thereby constipation. Painful urination in cystitis can be mistaken for constipation, as the pet is just observed straining, so that will need to be ruled out. Blood tests may be required if your vet suspects dehydration, kidney disease or hypothyroidism.

Treatment

⇨ *Your vet*

Treatment depends on the diagnosis of the cause of constipation. In mild and recent cases, a laxative like lactulose or liquid paraffin may be sufficient, but if your pet is dehydrated he or she will need to be an inpatient. After aggressive fluid therapy, your pet will need to be sedated and given an enema, with your vet manually removing the faeces. If investigations have revealed other causes of the constipation your vet may need to perform surgery or treat the primary cause of constipation.

⇨ *You*

Elizabeth recommends the chicken broth recipe with added vegetables (*page 15*). You can also try feeding roasted vegetables – for example squash, sweet potatoes and courgettes (zucchini) – plus bananas, fresh fig and grated apple. Try the following recipes: K9/Feline Nature's Own Hot Pot or K9/Feline fishcakes (*page 51*), Ginger K9 biscuits (*page 46*) and Linseed K9/Feline biscuits (*page 52*).

⇨ *Healing & herbs*

Animal healing is a fantastic complement to veterinary care and can be safely given by you to your pet. See Chapter 5: *How to Give Healing to Your Pet* for instructions.

⁀ Make your own ⁀

To cats, offer on a self-selection basis, catnip-infused sunflower oil (*page 50*) and to dogs, linseed cold-pressed oil (*page 76*).

COUGH

A cough is actually a clinical symptom of many conditions and not a condition per se. It is therefore not prudent to treat a cough without actually diagnosing the cause of the cough or the condition causing it. The cough reflex is one of the most powerful reflexes in the body and is actually a warning that something is not quite right with the pharynx or the respiratory system. Suppressing a cough without a diagnosis can be dangerous.

Causes

Diseases affecting the sinuses, tonsils, trachea, lungs and heart can all cause an animal to cough. The pattern of the cough, its frequency and characteristics can suggest the probable cause for the cough. For example, coughs caused by congestive heart failure and tracheal collapse tend to be more nocturnal whereas coughs that are exacerbated by exercise or excitement are usually due to irritation in the larynx or trachea or bronchi.

Diagnosis

Your vet will enquire about the duration, the timing and the type of cough before performing a full clinical exam. Pinching the throat of your pet to elicit a cough is helpful too. In my experience, most pets do not cough in the consulting room and start again at home so it is a good idea to video your pet's cough to enable a more accurate diagnosis. Blood tests may be required to rule out lungworm, heartworm or eosinophilia.

If your pet's cough is accompanied by bleeding from either the nose or mouth, then it may be necessary to perform a coagulation profile to rule out bleeding disorders. X-rays, thoracic ultrasound, bronchoscopy or laryngoscopy are other diagnostic tools that may be necessary, especially if foreign bodies or tumours are suspected. Feline asthma is quite a common condition and radiographs of the lung can help confirm it. CT scans are the best way to evaluate the sinuses.

A differential diagnosis of coughs is given below, so you can appreciate why diagnosis is crucial before treatment.

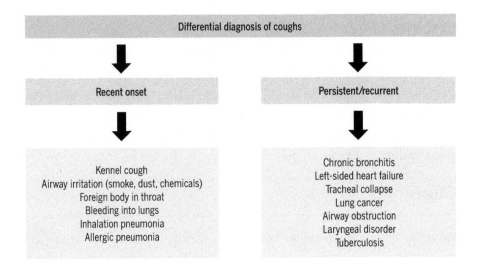

Differential diagnosis of coughs	
Recent onset	**Persistent/recurrent**
Kennel cough Airway irritation (smoke, dust, chemicals) Foreign body in throat Bleeding into lungs Inhalation pneumonia Allergic pneumonia	Chronic bronchitis Left-sided heart failure Tracheal collapse Lung cancer Airway obstruction Laryngeal disorder Tuberculosis

Treatment

⇨ *Your vet*

Coughs appear very disconcerting to the owner and the noise can be upsetting. Unfortunately, investigating a cough does require time and money. Most vets will try to treat a cough symptomatically with antibiotics, bronchodilators, cough suppressants, mucolytics, expectorants and sometimes steroids. Cardiac coughs will need diuretics and treatment for the heart condition. If the cough is non-responsive or persistent, then further diagnostic work is needed before an appropriate treatment can be chosen.

⇨ *You*

Try to avoid feeding dried kibble while your pet is coughing. If they seem to be having trouble swallowing and your vet has ruled out a foreign body in the throat, then try the following meals and treats: K9/Feline Nature's Own Hotpot (*page 51*), Hard-boiled Egg and Eggshell K9/Feline treats (*pages 44–45*), chicken broth ice cube (*page 16*), Woof Berry and Yoghurt dog treats (*page 54*).

⇨ *Healing & herbs*

Animal healing is a fantastic complement to veterinary care and can be safely given by you to your pet. See Chapter 5: *How to Give Healing to Your Pet* for instructions.

⸙ Make your own ⸙

Elizabeth recommends the K9 Bark Berry cough remedy (*page 48*), and to help soothe you can offer the herb-infused honey with sage, thyme or chamomile (*page 49*).

DENTAL DISEASE

Dental care and surgery are becoming much more common in modern-day veterinary practice, thanks to the advancement of veterinary dentistry and dental techniques. It is also important to mention here that the popularity of veterinary dental procedures is increasing because more domestic pets need them nowadays, compared to their wild ancestors, who had good teeth. Today, our dear pets are plagued by rotting teeth, abscesses and gingivitis, but it is up to *us* to change this.

Predisposing factors for dental disease
⇨ *Breeding*

We have been breeding all kinds of dogs over generations for all sorts of reasons. Some have been bred to hunt, some to show better and others merely to look cute. By doing this we have distorted the natural shape of a dog's jaws.

Today, most of the toy breeds have such tiny jaws that it is impossible for all the required teeth to be accommodated in the space. Overcrowding of teeth therefore results in impactions and misalignments, and predisposes the dog to gum disease. In practice, vets can vouch for the fact that Yorkshire Terriers are over-represented when it comes to dental disease – most of them have lost half their teeth by the time they are four years old, or even younger.

⇨ *Diet*

This is probably the *most important* reason for bad teeth in our domesticated pets today. Animals are meant to chew raw food that is chelated, rich in vitamins, minerals and enzymes. Contrary to what most pet food manufacturers would like us to believe, dry food and crunchy biscuits do not clean a carnivore's teeth.

In the wild, chewing through tough skin and bones scrubbed a dog's teeth like a toothbrush and thereby prevented the build up of tartar. Unfortunately, commercial pet foods do not require much teeth action at all. In fact, they form a kind of glue that adheres to the teeth, contributing to dental decay. Poor food also leads to halitosis (foul breath), as it festers in the gut and the offensive odour then backs up.

⇨ *Disease*

The presence of certain infectious diseases – like feline immunodeficiency virus (FIV), feline leukemia virus (FeLV), and feline calici virus in cats and metabolic disease such as diabetes mellitus in cats and dogs – increases the risk of acquiring periodontal disease.

Causes

In dogs, actual tooth decay only causes 10 per cent of dental problems. Periodontal or gum disease, which is the inflammation of the soft tissues surrounding the teeth, is actually much more common. Statistics show that more than two-thirds of dogs over three years of age suffer from some form of periodontal disease. The formation of plaque and tartar irritates the gums, resulting in gingivitis.

If left untreated, gingivitis results in periodontal disease, which is unfortunately irreversible. As I explained above, old age, genetics or bad breeding, tooth alignment, diet and chewing, general health, grooming habits, dental home care and finally the mouth environment all contribute to the development of dental problems in dogs.

In cats, dental disease is also very common and there are several contributing factors to its development. Tooth alignment, which is poor in breeds like Persian, Siamese, chinchillas and some other British breeds, is one factor. Diet, oral chemistry and poor dental care and grooming habits are also responsible.

Infectious diseases such as feline leukemia virus and feline calici virus cause severe gingivitis and periodontal disease. The most commonly observed dental diseases in cats are gingivitis, periodontitis, feline ulcerative stomatitis, feline odontoclastic resorptive lesions (FORL) and fractures of teeth due to trauma or jaw abnormalities.

Symptoms

Dogs with dental disease exhibit halitosis (bad breath), bleeding gums, pawing at the mouth, drooling, stained teeth, tartar and plaque on teeth, purulent exudates (pus) around teeth, general malaise, irritability, depression, loose teeth, sensitive teeth and difficulty in chewing or eating.

In cats, symptoms range from persistent bad breath or halitosis to bleeding gums, reluctance to eat and groom, approaching food then running away after tasting it, vocalizing, pawing at the mouth, drooling, swelling on face under the eye, teeth discolouration and tartar formation.

Diagnosis

Veterinarians should be the first port of call when dental problems are suspected. Most vets will check the teeth of domestic pets when they go in for their annual booster vaccination or health check. This is the time when subclinical or asymptomatic early dental disease is picked up. Obviously if a pet shows any of the symptoms listed above, the vet will suspect dental problems.

Clinical examination of the teeth is the first step. X-rays may be required if teeth root damage is suspected. Blood tests may be required if the pets are geriatric or there is suspicion of underlying infectious diseases causing the dental problem. A general anaesthetic may be required if the animal is fractious or if there is significant evidence that extractions are imminent.

Treatment

⇨ *Your vet (conventional veterinary dentistry)*

In dogs, treatment of periodontal disease is multi-faceted and depends on the stage of the disease. Prophylactic dental treatment is carried out by a veterinarian. The plaque and tartar are removed under a general anaesthetic using a professional ultrasonic scaler and the teeth are polished to remove microscopic scratches that predispose to tartar build-up. After descaling and polishing, the teeth are assessed visually, by probing and by radiography if necessary, and a decision is then made on the treatment options.

Depending on the condition of the teeth any one or a combination of procedures may be required. If your finances do not permit and there is advanced periodontal disease the veterinarian will have no choice but to perform tooth extractions, both by manual and drilling techniques. If you can afford a veterinary dentist they may be able to save the teeth by using advanced procedures. Specially selected antibiotics may also be prescribed.

In cats, early gingivitis and mild periodontal disease may be treated with just a simple descale and polish, as described in the dogs section above, under a general anaesthetic. Endodontic disease with pulpitis may need X-rays and then either root canal treatment or extraction.

Feline odontoclastic resorptive lesions (FORLs) are difficult to treat and the cost-effective option is to extract the affected teeth. Tooth root abscesses usually require tooth extraction and then flushing, followed by antibiotic cover. Lymphocytic plasmacytic stomatitis and feline ulcerative stomatitis are very resistant to treatment, and sometime drastic measures like extracting all teeth besides the canine teeth may be advised as a last resort.

⇨ *You*

Elizabeth recommends the Garlic K9 biscuits for dogs with gingivitis and the Chive Feline treats for cats (*see page 46*). If your pet has had extractions or is struggling to eat due to dental disease then feed them the following: K9/Feline

Nature's Own Hotpot (*page 51*), the chicken broth with added vegetables (*page 15*) and the Woof Berry and Yoghurt treats (*page 54*). Some cats will need their food pureed if they have severe gingivitis, stomatitis or FORLs.

Prevention

There is no doubt that with dental disease, 'an ounce of prevention is worth a pound of cure.' Unlike many health conditions, it can be stopped almost entirely with natural home care. Please see the following important steps in preventative dental care.

- **Diet** – feeding species-appropriate raw food is a very sensible option. If this is not possible then prescription dry kibble dental diets, which are tartar-control foods, can be tried. They are made with increased amounts of vegetable fibres that wrap around the teeth and prevent the food particles from adhering, or pull the tartar away when animals bite into them.

  Raw or steamed vegetables can also be given to pets to fight tartar. See Chapter 1: *Food Is Medicine*. Elizabeth recommends adding one teaspoon a day of 100 per cent ground seaweed to the food of both cats and dogs that have gingivitis (*see Resources section for stockists*) and also feeding the Bladderwrack K9/Feline sea biscuits (*see page 41*).

- **Chews** – tartar-control chews are a good choice and so are soft, gentle dental bones of good quality. Raw, meaty bones from the butcher that do not splinter can be given to dogs and cats regularly to stop tartar build-up. Knuckle bones for dogs and chicken necks for cats are also recommended. Pets must be supervised while they eat bones, to stop splintering and accidental swallowing. Use real deer antler treats.

- **Brushing** – for cats and dogs, a regular regime of twice-weekly teeth cleaning and brushing can go a long way in preventing dental disease. Lots of different, easy-to-use brushes are available. Special enzyme-based toothpastes and gels can be used. Natural toothpastes that have no known side effects are quite effective in cleaning out the tartar. Vets also recommend sprays and gels that prevent tartar formation – these can be rubbed onto the teeth.

- **Mouth inspections** – owners who regularly inspect their pet's mouth can usually tell if the smell or teeth appearance is abnormal. This is vital as gum disease and tumours can be identified early on.

- **Veterinary visits** – it is very important to arrange for regular oral exams by a vet who can then nip the problem in the bud by alerting the owner when there is a problem. A good home dental care regime can also be formulated, together with the owner's input, in the best interests of the pet concerned.

Dental problems pose a painful, chronic threat to the health of most of our domestic pets. They also tend to suppress the animal's immune system and render them more vulnerable to other degenerative diseases. More worrisome is the fact that bacteria from the infected teeth can enter the bloodstream, damaging the kidneys and/or the heart.

It is therefore very important to strengthen the whole constitution of our pets so they can fight dental disease from the inside out. By feeding a healthy, wholesome diet, and including regular home-based dental care and routine veterinary examinations, it is definitely possible to prevent dental problems.

⇨ *Healing & herbs*

Animal healing is a fantastic complement to veterinary care and can be safely given by you to your pet. See Chapter 5: *How to Give Healing to Your Pet* for instructions.

⨾ **Make your own** ⨽

The herb-infused honey (sage or thyme versions) – *see page 49* – and the sage toothpaste (*page 87*) are very beneficial and you can use them both for prevention and when your pet has a sore mouth. Elizabeth also recommends that you offer the bladderwrack-infused sunflower oil for self-selection (*page 50*).

DEPRESSION

Depression is defined as a condition of mental disturbance, typically with a lack of energy and difficulty in maintaining concentration or interest in life. It is characterized by a range of symptoms, such as persistent low mood, absence of positive effect (loss of interest and enjoyment in ordinary things and experiences), and a range of associated emotional, cognitive, physical and behavioural symptoms.

Because animals cannot communicate with us even if they have these kinds of experiences, the general opinion is that 'we cannot really say if an animal is depressed'. But this does not mean that animals do not suffer from depression. Most pet guardians have absolutely no doubt that their animals can be unhappy, angry, happy or fearful or even feel guilty.

According to psychiatrists, the core symptom of depression is anhedonia, which simply means an inability to feel pleasure and is defined as a psychological condition characterized by the inability to experience pleasure in acts that normally produce it. This also happens to be the only measurable symptom of depression in animals. Research shows that animals do suffer from depression, although not everyone is convinced. However, most people who work with animals have come across depressed ones.

Symptoms

Different animals exhibit different reactions to depression. A good guide to identifying the condition is to recognize out-of-the-ordinary behaviour. The most common signs are lethargy, lack of appetite or overeating, sleeping excessively, loss of initiative, moping, pacing, anxiety, aggression and even destructive behaviour. Some dogs may also stop playing, walking and participating in usually joyful activities.

Vets have noted that becoming withdrawn and excessive vocalization, barking or meowing can also be signs of depression. Cats tend to show some additional signs apart from the ones listed above, such as excessive grooming, not greeting their guardian and hiding in strange places. Regressive behaviour, such as when the animal was a puppy/kitten, and inappropriate urination and defecation may also be seen.

Causes

- **Grief** – this is the most common cause of depression in animals. The death of a favourite family member, losing an animal playmate, divorce in the family and family members moving out can all cause an animal to feel lonely and sad.

- **Changes in environment** – a new partner or a new baby, a new pet, moving into a new home, change of furniture, being kennelled. Any one of these changes can cause the pet to become disorientated and feel lost and depressed.

- **Changes in schedule** – dogs that are used to the owner being at home with them can become depressed when they take up a job. Separation anxiety can therefore be described as a big trigger to depression.

- **Mental state of the owner** – dogs definitely pick up on the emotions of their owners; depressed owners seem to have depressed pets. The animals respond to the grief of the owners.

- **Abuse** – most ill-treated pets are depressed.

- **Weather and seasonal changes** – seasonal affective disorder (SAD) has been observed in dogs, just as in humans, when winter begins. Similarly, prolonged bad weather, and hurricanes that change atmospheric pressure, seem to impact on the moods of pets.

- **Chemical imbalances** – as in humans, low levels of serotonin may be a predisposing factor to depression in animals.

- **Medical conditions** – most animals exhibit signs of depression when there is something physically wrong with them.

Diagnosis

As sick pets tend to show many of the same symptoms as depression, it is important to consult a vet and rule out physical ailments and life-threatening medical conditions before assuming that a pet is suffering from depression. Depression therefore tends to be diagnosed by vets through the process of elimination – after ruling out the possible medical causes for the symptoms exhibited.

A complete physical examination, blood tests, etc., may be necessary to rule out medical reasons for the depression. Obtaining a very thorough history goes a long way in the diagnosis of depression in animals. This usually reveals a trigger in the form of a coinciding event that may have started the cycle of depression. It is therefore vital to identify the cause. Once this has been established, it is a lot easier to confirm the diagnosis of depression.

Treatment

⇨ *Your vet and you*

In mild cases of depression I usually suggest some simple changes or common-sense interventions in the pet's lifestyle that can make a huge difference:

- **Increased attention** – giving you pet more attention, playing more games with him or her and cuddling more can help. Going on walking trips and holidays with dogs – as a way of re-bonding – is also a good idea.

- **Mental stimulation** – grief-stricken pets can be cheered up by hiding away things that remind them of the person who is not around, and just spending more time with them and distracting them with mental-stimulation activities like Kongs and games. Fishing pole-style toys or just an aquarium with fish can lift the spirits of our feline companions. Acquiring a new puppy or kitten can also help if the pet has lost its playmate or long-term animal companion.

- **Light treatment** – light and the functioning of the pituitary and endocrine glands are intimately linked. There is enough evidence that light stimulates the body to release hormones that can uplift the moods of animals, just as in people. So allowing the animal to sunbathe on a sunny porch or in a garden can make a big difference.

- **Drugs** – most responsible vets avoid using psychoactive drugs to treat pet depression. This is mainly because very few of these drugs are actually licensed for animal treatment – there is very little research and therefore a lack of data on animals. Vets are also aware that psychopharmacology can only be a valuable adjunct to more traditional environmental management and behaviour-modification programmes. Moreover, all of these drugs have side effects and if used in the wrong combination can cause central nervous system toxicity sometimes leading to death.

- **Pheromone therapy** – pheromones are a natural form of therapy based on the chemical signals used by animals for communication – for example, Feline Facial Pheromone (FFP) for cats and DAP (Dog Appeasing Pheromone) for dogs. There is evidence-based data to document their efficacy in many anxiety-based disorders, so they may help in depression.

They can be sprayed or diffused into the air in the pet's environment and have hardly any side effects, but they may confuse the pet by giving them mixed messages.

- **Dietary supplements** – L-tryptophan is being added to diets such as Royal Canin Calm as it is a precursor of serotonin (mood enhancer).

⇨ *You*

Apart from the diet there are useful complementary techniques that can help. Elizabeth has dealt with several cases where an animal's depression was related to diet. Therefore, offering natural foods as described in Chapter 1: *Food Is Medicine* (and reading the case study of Boris the Labradoodle on pages 13–17 of that chapter) and trying out the recipes in Chapter 2, such as K9/Feline Nature's Own Hotpot and K9/Feline fishcakes (*page 51*), and Catnip Feline biscuits (*page 41*) can help.

I have found music to be very effective in healing pet emotions. Although not every pet responds to music, some do respond to their favourite melodies. Music recorded at special healing frequencies is used to relax animals – as in, for example, the Animal Whispers Sound Therapy CD by Elizabeth Whiter and Tim Wheater.

⇨ *Healing & herbs*

Animal healing is a fantastic complement to veterinary care and can be safely given by you to your pet. See Chapter 5: *How to Give Healing to Your Pet* for instructions. Elizabeth documents several cases of grief-stricken pets that recovered as a result of healing in her first book, *The Animal Healer*.

⌇ Make your own ⌇

Elizabeth recommends offering calendula, catnip, chickweed, mint, nettle and rosehip infused in sunflower oil on a self-selection basis to your depressed pets (*see page 50*). Catnip-infused sunflower oil can cause feline euphoria and alleviate depression. For cats she also suggests rose petal water (*page 84*), the valerian and catnip toys (*pages 64 and 89*), and fresh and dried catnip (*page 64*). Ginger-infused honey (*page 49*) can also lift the mood. The plant St John's Wort has also been used in animals and so have skullcap and valerian, but their effectiveness in actual veterinary therapy is anecdotal.

Summary

There is a tremendous gap between a common-sense viewpoint and that of official science on the subject of animal feelings and emotions. So it is not surprising that very few scientists believe that animals can actually suffer from depression. As a vet, from personal experience with clients I can say with conviction that almost every single pet owner who brings his animal to me firmly believes that his pet has feelings. They not only believe it, but see evidence of it every single day.

Research on Zoochosis (abnormal behaviour patterns associated with animals kept in zoos or other artificial environments) in captive animals and evidence of clinical depression in the livestock population from a study by the US Food and Drug Administration confirms that animals *do* suffer from depression. Depression is a natural emotion but when it persists for a long time it can make a pet physically ill, so it is important to determine whether the depression has caused an illness or is a consequence of it.

Once the cause of the depression is established, it is possible to treat the depression quite easily in the majority of cases. In my view common-sense interventions, behaviour-modification techniques and complementary therapies should be attempted *before* treating animals with psychoactive drugs that have questionable efficacy and dangerous side effects. Only in the most serious cases, where there is concurrent aggression/self-trauma, is psychopharmacology justified.

DIABETES

Diabetes mellitus (DM) is a common condition that affects both cats and dogs. It is an endocrine disorder of carbohydrate, fat and protein metabolism that is caused by a deficiency of the pancreatic hormone called insulin. As in humans, diabetes is classified as type I (insulin-dependent) and type II (non-insulin dependent). Almost all of the dogs with diabetes and 50–70 per cent of the cats have type I. There is no complete recovery from diabetes, but it can be successfully controlled so that your pet can have a good quality of life.

Causes

Diabetes mellitus is caused by an absolute or relative lack of the hormone insulin, which controls the blood glucose level. Insulin deficiency prevents your pet from converting sugar (glucose) in its diet into energy. As a consequence, there is more glucose circulating in the blood and more sugar excreted in the urine of your pet. DM is more common in female dogs and male cats.

Genetic susceptibility, certain infections, pancreatitis, pre-existing Cushing's disease, immune-mediated destruction of the beta cells in the pancreas of dogs, amyloidosis in cats and the use of certain drugs are the main causes of DM. Obesity is a common cause of type II DM in bitches and cats, and entire female dogs are more at risk than spayed ones.

Symptoms

In the early stages of the disease, your pet will appear to be drinking much more than normal and urinating a lot more. It will also lose weight, despite eating a lot – it may be ravenous and constantly harass you for food. Recurrent cystitis, sweet-smelling ketotic breath and cataracts may be seen in later stages.

Ketoacidotic DM is a real emergency and your pet should be rushed to the vet. When this happens, apart from the above symptoms, your pet will also be very lethargic, weak and tired, and will stop eating. Poor haircoat, dandruff, an unkempt or shabby appearance and muscle wasting may also be seen in some pets.

Diagnosis

If your pet is drinking or urinating more than usual then it is always best to get him or her checked by the vet. DM needs to be differentiated from other diseases that may cause your pet to show these same symptoms. Your vet may request a urine sample and test for glucose in it with a dipstick or he or she may perform a blood test to check glucose levels. Blood tests may also be needed to rule out kidney and liver disease at the same time. If your pet has a persistent fasting blood glucose greater than 10mmol/l, it confirms DM.

Treatment

⇨ *Your vet*

Injecting your pet with insulin 1–2 times daily and regularly is necessary to treat DM. If your pet has ketoacidotic diabetes, it may be necessary to admit them and treat them as an inpatient first as this is a serious problem. If your pet is well in itself, and the vet is sure that the diagnosis is uncomplicated diabetes, they will start giving subcutaneous insulin injections and teach you how to administer them yourself using special insulin syringes with needles.

You may be required to visit your vet once or twice a day for injections, depending on the protocol selected, until your pet is stabilized and the vet is happy with your injection technique. Most vets will provide you with a DVD and leaflets explaining the procedure. It is important that you strictly follow the vet's advice and try your best to inject insulin at the same time every day.

⇨ *You*

Regulating your pet's diet is a very important part of the treatment. A diet based on high-quality complex carbohydrates (lentils, whole grains, broccoli, spinach, etc) with no simple sugars, restricted fat and moderate protein levels is necessary to prevent wide fluctuations of blood glucose. See Chapter 1: *Food Is Medicine* to learn about the hidden sugars in commercial pet foods.

Whether your pet is fed a home-made or a commercial diet, you must feed the daily ration in two divided meals before injecting your pet with insulin. Any extra titbits or treats will mess with the control of DM so care must be taken to avoid this. You can also try the following recipes: Elizabeth's chicken broth (*page 15*), K9/Feline Nature's Own Hotpot without the rice (*page 51*), Hard-boiled Egg and Eggshell K9/Feline treats (*pages 44–45*) and K9/Feline fishcakes without the honey (*page 51*).

Regular moderate exercise is beneficial, but you must not overly exert your dog. Diabetic coma, hypoglycaemic shock and ketosis are possible complications of DM so you will need to monitor your pet carefully and may be required to obtain a urine sample and check it every morning. Sometimes you may even be advised to check your pet's blood glucose regularly with a glucometer. Insulin must always be stored in the refrigerator and it is important to check the expiry date on it.

Using the right disposable syringes is vital as this can vary with the type of insulin. Always contact your vet immediately if your pet's symptoms are worse or it is losing weight. It is necessary to keep some source of concentrated glucose or sugar, like honey or sugar lumps, in case your pet goes wobbly or too quiet, as this may be due to low blood sugar – a result of too much insulin. In order for your pet to be a stable and happy diabetic, it is important to avoid making drastic changes to his or her environment, food or exercise regime.

⇨ *Healing & herbs*

Animal healing is a fantastic complement to veterinary care and can be safely given by you to your pet. See Chapter 5: *How to Give Healing to Your Pet* for instructions.

⁓ Make your own ⁓

Elizabeth recommends offering catnip- and chickweed-infused sunflower oil to cats (*see page 50*) and rosehip to dogs (*page 50*) on a self-selection basis. You can also try linseed cold-pressed oil for dogs (*page 76*).

DIARRHOEA

When faeces are passed from the bowels frequently and in liquid form, the condition is known as diarrhoea. It is a very common condition in both dogs and cats. If the diarrhoea started abruptly it is known as acute diarrhoea. If a change in faecal frequency and consistency, and the volume of faeces, has persisted for three weeks, or it seems to be happening intermittently, it is known as chronic diarrhoea.

Cause

The intestines are responsible for secretion, motility and absorption, so an imbalance of any of these functions can result in diarrhoea. Acute diarrhoea is common in puppies and kittens although potentially any animal can suffer with it. This is because young animals tend to eat anything, whether food or foreign bodies, and are also more prone to worms and infectious diseases.

Dietary indiscretion is the most common cause of acute diarrhoea. Excess food, spoiled food, garbage, dietary intolerance or even sudden food change can all cause sudden diarrhoea. See the table below for common causes of acute and chronic diarrhoea.

Acute diarrhoea	Chronic diarrhoea
Dietary (excess, sudden change, spoiled food, food intolerance, low fibre, etc).	Cancer/neoplasia – lymphomas and adenocarcinomas.
Metabolic – Addison's disease, liver/kidney disease, pancreatic disease.	Inflammatory bowel disease; malabsorption and maldigestion.
Intestinal obstruction and foreign bodies, intussusceptions, haemorrhagic gastroenteritis.	In cats: FeLV, FIV and FIP viruses. In dogs: clostridium, giardiasis, salmonella, campylobacter, etc.
Infectious – viruses such as parvovirus in dogs and feline pan leukopaenia in cats; canine distemper. Bacteria, worms, etc.	Foreign bodies causing partial obstructions.
Drugs – antibiotics, NSAIDs, steroids, anticancer and de-worming drugs.	Exocrine pancreatic insufficiency and hepatobiliary disease.
Poisons and toxins – lawn and garden feed, insecticides, weedicides, etc.	Hyperthyroidism in cats.

Symptoms

These vary, based on the underlying cause. In acute, mild diarrhoea, apart from frequent liquid stools, the pet is healthy and well. If the diarrhoea persists for days, especially in young animals, they can quickly become dehydrated and listless. The symptoms therefore vary with the severity of the disease. Fever, low blood pressure, vomiting, abdominal pain or discomfort and weakness may also be present.

Diagnosis

A complete physical examination by the veterinarian, a faecal sample examination and an assessment of the hydration status is necessary. If there is any suspicion of a foreign body or an obstruction, X-rays of the abdomen and/ or ultrasound exam may become essential. Endoscopy and biopsies may be required in cases of chronic diarrhoea.

Treatment
⇨ *Your vet*

The majority of dogs and cats with mild diarrhoea only (without vomiting) need minimal treatment and can get better with fasting them for 12–24 hours, and then feeding them a bland diet like chicken and boiled rice or some prescription diets for gastrointestinal health.

In some others, where the diarrhoea is causing discomfort or is messy, anti-diarrhoeal drugs that modify motility, probiotics and intestinal protectants may be prescribed. Antibiotics are not usually necessary in mild cases. Intravenous fluid therapy is warranted if your pet is dehydrated and also vomiting. In cases of parvovirus, where there is bloody diarrhoea, isolation and intensive care will be necessary.

Anti-emetics to control vomiting and supportive treatment will be given on an inpatient basis. If the cause is worms, anthelminthics or de-wormers are indicated. Bacterial infections will need an appropriate antibiotic course. Special diets will be necessary for malabsorption, exocrine pancreatic insufficiency (EPI) and pancreatitis. If your pet has eaten a foreign body then surgery will need to be performed to remove it, or any other obstruction. Chemotherapy may be advised if there is evidence of cancer.

⇨ *You*

Monitoring your puppy or kitten carefully and preventing them from scavenging or eating foreign bodies is the responsibility of every pet guardian. Similarly, feeding them good-quality food in the right amounts and identifying intolerances is also key to preventing gastrointestinal upsets.

In simple cases of diarrhoea, after a period of fasting them try feeding chicken and rice and any one of the following snacks: Charcoal K9/Feline D-Tox biscuits (*page 42*), Hard-boiled Egg and Eggshell K9/Feline treats (*pages 44–45*), Ginger K9 biscuits (*page 46*) and K9/Feline fishcakes (*page 51*). When the diarrhoea has stopped you can give them the chicken broth (*page 15*) for nourishment and try the Garlic K9 biscuits for dogs or the Chive Feline treat for cats (*page 46*).

⇨ *Healing & herbs*

Animal healing is a fantastic complement to veterinary care and can be safely given by you to your pet. See Chapter 5: *How to Give Healing to Your Pet* for instructions.

ᘒ **Make your own** ᘒ

Elizabeth avoids offering any infused oils to pets that have diarrhoea. Once the diarrhoea has abated offer separately either mint- or rosehip-infused sunflower oil for dogs, and for cats try calendula- or catnip-infused sunflower oil on a self-selection basis (*page 50*).

EAR DISEASE

Otitis externa is the inflammation of the external ear canal above the ear drum, or tympanic membrane, and is very commonly seen in practice. Otitis media (inflammation of the middle ear) and otitis interna (inflammation of the inner ear) are also seen but not as frequently. It is important to remember that most of the time, otitis is actually a secondary symptom of some other underlying disease.

Causes

Ear problems are more common in dog breeds that have hairy ear canals, pendulous ears or stenotic (narrow) ear canals. Bacteria, yeasts and ear mites can all cause ear infections. Food allergy, atopy (an inherited tendency to be hyperallergic or more prone to allergies) and hypothyroidism may also cause otitis. Frequent swimming can also increase the frequency of ear infections. Grass seeds, other plant materials or foreign bodies can be an important cause of otitis. Finally, polyps, cancerous growths and other obstructions in the ear canal contribute to otitis.

Symptoms

Head shaking and smelly or malodorous ears are common symptoms of ear disease. Cats and dogs can scratch their ears excessively and sometimes howl in pain after doing so. In severe cases, bloody discharge, redness and aural haematomas may be present. Head tilt (holding the head tilted to one side) is seen if there is vestibular syndrome (a balance mechanism disturbance) and middle ear involvement. Severe cases may also be lethargic and vomit.

Diagnosis

It is very important to have your pet's ear examined by a vet before randomly squirting ear drops, in case there is a foreign body or a cancerous growth inside it. Using an otoscope or an otoendoscope, your vet will make a diagnosis. Taking an ear swab for culture and conducting a microscopic examination of the discharge for mites and yeast may also be needed. If otitis media is suspected X-rays may be warranted.

Treatment

⇨ *Your vet*

After arriving at a diagnosis your vet will prescribe ear drops, which are usually a combination of different antibiotics and steroids. If your pet has very hairy ear canals, it may be necessary for him to be sedated to pluck the hair and also flush the debris from the ear canals. This is also important from a diagnostic point of view as it can be impossible to visualize the eardrum if the ear canal is occluded by hair and wax.

If a head tilt and vestibular syndrome is present, oral steroids and antibiotics are necessary. Treating the underlying cause, whether it is an allergy or hypothyroidism, for example, is crucial to prevent recurrent otitis. If the opening to the ear canal or the canal itself is obstructed, or stenosed (narrowed) then surgery to open up the ear canal or to remove the obstruction will be advised.

Aural haematoma is a blood-filled swelling which forms in the flap of the ear. If your pet has been scratching or shaking its head too vigorously, it can end up damaging small blood vessels in the ear flap, which bleed into the flap. The swelling can occupy some or the whole of the ear flap and may need surgery to correct it. Your vet may attempt to drain the swelling while your dog is conscious (if you have a very compliant, cooperative pet), but this is not always a success and the haematoma tends to recur.

⇨ *You*

It is important to inspect and clean out your pets' ears regularly – at least weekly. Using a good-quality ear cleanser from a vet or a herbal preparation is ideal.

⇨ *Healing & herbs*

Animal healing is a fantastic complement to veterinary care and can be safely given by you to your pet. See Chapter 5: *How to Give Healing to Your Pet* for instructions.

✢ Make your own ✢

For a small aural haematoma, to try to prevent further haemorrhage, and for the elderly dog that may not be a good candidate for surgical correction of a haematoma, Elizabeth recommends gently massaging the outside of the ear with the aloe vera basic gel with a clove of garlic crushed into it (*see page 59*) every day for a week. It relieves the tenderness. She also recommends the garlic oil remedy for prevention (*page 71*).

EPILEPSY

The term 'epilepsy' means recurrent seizures or fits. In general, if there is no identifiable cause for a seizural disorder then it is called epilepsy. Dogs, especially males, are more likely to suffer with classic or idiopathic epilepsy than cats.

Causes

Primary idiopathic epilepsy is a result of functional disturbances in a brain that is structurally normal, and therefore has no obvious cause, except maybe a hereditary predisposition. The exact mechanism of this dysfunction is still very much unknown, but is thought to be biochemical. True epilepsy is most common in dogs when they are aged between six months and five years. It is rare and very poorly documented in the cat.

Symptoms

Seizures or convulsions most commonly occur while the dog is asleep or resting, and therefore is reported often at night or in the early morning hours. Your pet may become stiff, salivate or drool profusely, chomp its jaw or clamp it shut. Some dogs urinate, defecate, howl and may paddle with all four limbs. After the seizure, the vast majority of animals may become confused and disorientated, drink lots of water and wander or pace aimlessly.

Diagnosis

Most pets are presented at the practice after the seizure has stopped, unless the seizure is very prolonged. Epilepsy is diagnosed after ruling out other causes of seizures, like poisoning, tumours, infection, fever and brain damage. The age at which the seizures start and their type and frequency provide important clues to a diagnosis of primary epilepsy. Pets suddenly developing seizures in old age may have metabolic disease or some brain lesion.

MRI and CT scans are necessary to confirm a suspicion of actual brain disease, like tumours or infections. Blood tests are necessary to ensure that liver function is good, so that medication can be safely commenced.

Treatment
⇨ *Your vet*
No treatment is required if the seizure is less than two minutes in duration and is not recurring. Dogs that have a cluster of seizures (two or more in 24 hours) and those that have seizures at regular intervals of one to four weeks have to be medicated. The drug of choice is usually Phenobarbital, but sometimes diazepam may be used by your vet in combination. There are newer drugs too, and your vet may decide on them after conferring with you.

If your dog has recurrent seizures and does not become fully conscious between them, or has seizures lasting more than five minutes, this is an emergency called status epilepticus. It can be life-threatening and needs immediate veterinary medical treatment. Your pet will have to be admitted and given intravenous medication and IV fluids, and be monitored carefully until stabilized.

⇨ *You*
It would be useful to video your pet while it is having a seizure, but that may not always be possible as a seizure can be a very distressing experience to your pet and to most pet guardians. It is also important to maintain a record of the number of seizures and their duration, as this can help with the diagnosis. Remember that your epileptic pet is unlikely to die of a seizure, but if it develops status epilepticus, it is a life-threatening emergency.

Also make sure your pet cannot injure himself on furniture or objects while he is having a fit. Most pets on anti-epileptic drugs tend to become overweight so this must be monitored. You should be aware of the side effects of the medications your pet is on and inform your vet if they are present. Regular blood testing to ensure there is no drug toxicity and no liver damage is necessary as your pet will most likely be on medication for life. Acupressure and homeopathy may help. Ask your holistic vet.

Healing & herbs

Animal healing is a fantastic complement to veterinary care and can be safely given by you to your pet. Do not attempt contact healing while your pet is having a seizure. Concentrate on keeping calm and offering distant healing until the seizure has stopped. See Chapter 5: *How to Give Healing to Your Pet* for instructions.

✿ Make your own ✿

Elizabeth recommends avoiding feeding any processed pet foods to epileptic pets and trying home-cooked diets including natural foods (*see ideas in Chapter 1*). You can also try feeding the following: K9/Feline fishcakes (*page 51*), Hard-boiled Egg and Eggshell K9/Feline treats (*pages 44–45*), K9/Feline Nature's Own Hotpot (*page 51*) and Linseed K9/Feline biscuits (*page 52*). For cats you can try the valerian cat toy and any form of catnip (*pages 89 and 64*).

EYE CONDITIONS

Any eye condition can be potentially serious and should therefore be checked by your veterinary surgeon. Immediate treatment is essential to prevent permanent damage to the eye, and blindness in many cases. This is mainly because more or less all eye conditions, from simple to serious, have the same signs and can look alike. There are more than 50 conditions that can affect the eye and the eyelids, but the most commonly seen eye conditions are conjunctivitis, corneal ulcers in certain breeds, foreign bodies in the eyes and cataracts. Blindness is rare but can be sudden.

Causes

Conjuctivitis is inflammation of the conjunctiva, which is the membrane lining the inner side of the eyelids and the external surface of the eyeball or globe. The third eyelid is also included. Allergy, infections and dry eye can all cause conjunctivitis. Dry eye, known as keratoconjunctivitis sicca (KCS), is a deficiency of tear film resulting in drying of the cornea and the conjunctiva. This is more common in certain dog breeds, such as the Cocker Spaniel, West Highland White Terrier, Shih Tzu and Lhasa Apso.

Corneal ulcers are basically craters on the surface of the cornea and can be a result of trauma from a foreign object or self-trauma by scratching at the eye, or even from grass seeds. In certain breeds like Boxers, and other breeds that have a bulbous or protruding eyeball, these ulcers are more common. Cataracts can be secondary to diabetes but are most often a sign of the ageing lens and occur in older dogs.

Symptoms

The most commonly seen symptom in most of the above eye conditions (except cataract) is a weepy eye with clear or greenish or yellowish discharge. Your pet may rub its eye, keep it partially or completely shut and avoid bright lights. Redness of the eye or bloody eye may also be seen. Sometimes the eye looks hazy or swollen. A tendency to bump into things is seen if your pet is partially or fully blind or has cataracts.

Diagnosis

After taking a thorough history from you and performing a general clinical examination, your vet will then perform a complete ophthalmic examination using a opthalmoscope. A fluorescein stain test to rule out ulcers and a schirmer tear test to rule out dry eye may also be performed.

If your vet suspects an increase in intraocular pressure, he or she will check this with a tono pen. Lash abnormalities such as ingrowing eyelashes will be ruled out and your vet will also check for any foreign bodies in the corners of your pet's eye and under the third eyelid. If the situation is more complicated, your pet may be referred to an eye vet for further investigation.

Treatment
⇨ *Your vet*

In simple, straightforward bacterial or allergic conjunctivitis, your vet will usually just dispense some antibiotic or steroid eye ointments or drops. If your pet has an ulcer that is large or non-responsive to topical treatment, then surgical procedures may be required. If your vet suspects a blocked nasolachrimal duct, then sedation and flushing of the ducts may be necessary. I have had to enucleate, or remove, a dog's eye on many occasions because of eyeball rupture and proptosis (eye pops out in front of the eyelids).

Cataracts are irreversible, and to improve your pet's quality of life, surgery may be necessary – especially if he or she is young. It must be remembered though that cataract surgery in dogs is undertaken by veterinary eye specialists only and can be expensive. Once diagnosed, they are better performed sooner rather than later. The procedure in dogs is more complicated than in humans as there is usually a lens-induced uveitis (an inflammatory response to rupture or injury to the lens) that decreases the success rate of cataract surgery.

⇨ *You*

Corneal ulcers will not heal if steroid eye drops are used, so it is dangerous to use any random leftover eye drops in your pet's eye without getting a diagnosis from your vet. Bathing your pet's eye gently with clean water can help remove the sticky discharge.

Some dogs I see in practice have hair covering their eyes. This can cause eye infections, tear staining and ulcers. Cleaning your pet's eyes regularly, and keeping the hair from falling into them, could be the single most useful thing you could do to help your pet. Please get your groomer to trim hair on the head, or if your pet will allow it, tie it up with a little bobble. Hair on the face can even make some dogs fearful and photophobic. The cornea is very slow to heal so it is best to prevent corneal damage. It can take weeks and even months for corneal ulcers to heal.

In certain brachycephalic breeds where the eye is quite protruding – Pug, Shih Tzu, Bulldog, etc.– trauma can easily dislodge the eye as the eye sockets are quite shallow. This is an *emergency* and your pet's eye can be saved only if you get them to the vet quickly. Delay will reduce the chances of saving the eye and your pet's vision.

⇨ *Healing & herbs*

Animal healing is a fantastic complement to veterinary care and can be safely given by you to your pet. See Chapter 5: *How to Give Healing to Your Pet* for instructions.

᪥ **Make your own** ᪥

Elizabeth recommends the chamomile soothing wash (cold compress) in simple cases of eye irritation (*see page 66*). You can offer on a self-selection basis the calendula-infused sunflower oil (*page 50*).

Please also refer to the superfoods shopping checklist on page 18 and also offer lightly steamed green leafy vegetables, carrots, peas and broccoli. Recipes that may be beneficial are Hard-boiled Egg and Eggshell K9/Feline treats (*pages 44–45*) and K9/Feline Nature's Own Hotpot (*page 51*).

FELINE INFECTIOUS DISEASES

There are certain infectious diseases that can spread between cats but do not infect dogs. Feline immunodeficiency virus (FIV), feline leukemia virus (FeLV), feline infectious anemia (FIA) and feline infectious peritonitis (FIP) are still seen in practice whereas, due to regular vaccinations, feline infectious enteritis and feline influenza, or cat flu, are rare now, especially in the UK. A brief knowledge of these diseases is important for any cat owner and the table below will be useful for this purpose.

Disease	Cause	Symptoms	Diagnosis	Treatment
FIV*	*Lenti virus FIV* Spread by cat saliva, cat bites, living together in same house.	Fever, stomatitis, gingivitis, diarrhoea, weight loss, lethargy, skin, respiratory and ocular signs.	Blood test for FIV antibodies.	Virus cannot be eliminated. Symptoms can be treated temporarily.
FeLV	*Feline leukemia virus* Congenital before birth and through saliva of infected cats by close contact. Breeding colonies are high risk.	Lymphosarcoma (tumour) and leukemia. Fever, wasting, reduced disease resistance, uveitis, vomiting, diarrhoea, coughing, kidney failure.	Blood test for FeLV antibodies, tumour biopsy, bone marrow tests, X-rays and ultrasound.	No treatment, but can be prevented by vaccination.
FIA	*Haemobartonella felis* Transmitted by fleas, mosquitoes, cat bites, and *in utero*.	Inappetance, weakness, pallor, third eyelid protrusion, jaundice.	Microscopic examination of the red blood cells for the parasite. Blood tests to confirm anemia.	Antibacterials. Diets, vitamins, minerals and blood transfusion in severe cases.
FIP	*Corona virus* Rescue cats or breeding colonies commonly affected. Cats less than three years of age affected.	Wet form with dyspnoea (laboured breathing) and abdominal distension and uveitis. Dry form with fever, wasting dyspnoea, vomiting, diarrhoea and dehydration.	Blood tests and biopsies in dry form. In wet form, examination of abdominal fluid obtained via paracentesis.	Antibacterials. Steroids and diuretics. A fatal disease most of the time and most cats die despite treatment.

* FIV belongs to the same group as the human AIDS virus and is usually referred to as Cat AIDS. However, there is no evidence that people can be

infected by cats with FIV. Because FIV and FeLV are spread by cat bites, your vet may advise you to keep your cat indoors to prevent spread.

Treatment

⇨ *You*

As cats with feline infectious diseases tend to have a poor appetite, it is vital to feed them a home-cooked diet for palatability, especially as their mouth can be sore. Also, they may have poor olfaction and be unable to smell their food, so strong-smelling food is better. Try feeding the K9/Feline Nature's Own Hotpot or K9/Feline fishcakes (*page 51*), Liver Cake K9/Feline bake (*page 52*) or chicken broth (*page 15*). You can also try the Charcoal K9/Feline De-Tox biscuits (*page 42*). Cats also enjoy a little lick of yeast extract when they are run down, as it is full of B vitamins.

⇨ *Healing & herbs*

Animal healing is a fantastic complement to veterinary care and can be safely given by you to your pet. See Chapter 5: *How to Give Healing to Your Pet* for instructions.

⁂ Make your own ⁂

Elizabeth recommends offering catnip- and nettle-infused sunflower oil on a self-selection basis (*see page 50*).

FLEAS

Fleas are common ectoparasites and can be very annoying to you and your pets. They are dark brown in colour and have droppings resembling charcoal dust that can be seen when you part your pet's fur. The life cycle of a flea is complex and there are four life stages – egg, larva, pupa and adult. If the environmental temperature and humidity levels are optimal the life cycle may last for weeks, but if not it can be less than a week.

Causes

Ctenocephalides canis (dog flea) and *Ctenocephalides felis* (cat flea) are the common fleas, although hedgehog and human fleas may also be the cause.

Fleas are responsible for the transmission of tapeworm (*Dipylidium caninum*) and some other infectious diseases. Seasonally warm climates or places where the weather is warm and humid all year round are ideal for fleas. Because of modern central heating, fleas are able to survive all year round, but they tend to peak in both spring and autumn.

Life cycle

Understanding the flea life cycle is crucial to the prevention of recurrent infestations. The life cycle begins when the adult flea sucks blood from a host like your pet and lays eggs. Each single female adult flea can lay up to 50 eggs a day. The eggs remain in your home and hatch when the temperature is warm and humid, so modern central heating is ideal for them. In cold and dry temperatures, they take longer to hatch.

Blind larvae emerge next and make up to 60 per cent of the flea population in the environment. They eat flea dirt (pre-digested blood) and when conditions become conducive, will spin a cocoon and form pupae. These pupae have a sticky outer coating so they can hide deep in bedding and carpets and cannot be cleaned out by vacuuming or sweeping. Only when a pupa or cocoon senses a host nearby will it hatch into a flea. The triggers are the vibrations of your pet walking, people moving about, a rise in CO_2 levels and body heat. The adult flea then starts the cycle again, as the following diagram shows:

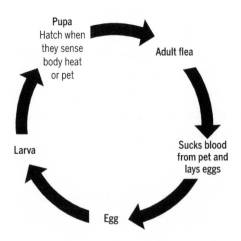

Symptoms

Your pet may bite or scratch itself compulsively on various parts of its body, especially on its rump or back area. Some tend to demonstrate corncob nibbling or chewing. Excessive licking and skin infections may also suggest fleas. If your pet is allergic to flea saliva, then just one fleabite is needed to cause severe flea allergic dermatitis.

Flea saliva contains a histamine-like compound that irritates skin. No flea needs to be present alive on your pet to cause flea allergic dermatitis (FAD). Young puppies and kittens may become pale, ill and debilitated if the flea infestation is severe because, if a large number of fleas suck blood, the animal can become anaemic.

Diagnosis

Flea dirt on the back and neck, hair loss from chewing and actual fleas when the fur is combed are all diagnostic of a flea infestation. As fleas are the intermediate hosts for both the dog and cat tapeworm, if your pet's faeces has tapeworms it suggests a flea infestation.

You can also try the **wet paper test**: take a wet piece of filter paper and gently rub it along the flea dirt on the back of your pet. If it is flea dirt, the black flecks will turn red – confirming fleas. Blood tests may be required to check the red blood cell count and haemoglobin levels if your pet becomes anaemic due to a severe flea infestation. If your dog suffers from allergic dermatitis/atopy, intradermal or antibody testing may be warranted to confirm flea allergy.

Treatment
⇨ *Your vet*

Your vet will treat flea allergic dermatitis with steroids or antihistamines and washes and may even have to prescribe antibiotics if there is a secondary bacterial infection on top of the FAD. You will then be advised to put proper flea control in place. There are a wide variety of flea treatments on the market, but the safest and least toxic ones are those supplied by your veterinarian.

The flea treatment must be fast-acting so the existing fleas on your pet are killed quickly. It should also have a long-lasting effect, to prevent re-infestation. Adult fleas need to be killed off before they lay eggs. Some flea treatments can also worm and kill mites but may not work on ticks. It is important to discuss your pet's lifestyle with your vet so that the right product can be used. Spot-on preparations are very popular as most pets do not like tablet preparations. However, it is still a matter of choice because some pets can have a localized reaction to the spot-on or lick it off.

⇨ *You*

Preventing a flea problem will save your pet the discomfort and you the hassle of spraying your whole house with chemicals. Both fleas on your pet and fleas in the environment have to be controlled in order to effectively treat a flea infestation. Environmental treatment is as important as treating your pet and is compulsory, especially if the fleas are biting you and your family. You will need to identify potential areas in your house that could be infested.

The eggs could have fallen in the rest areas of your house, like your living room or bedroom, or on garden furniture. As fleas survive in centrally heated houses, it is important to keep the flea treatment going all year round. There are some very good chemical preparations that you can use yourself, but if the infestation is bad then professional exterminators may need to be called in. Dips, shampoos and powders are now outdated, cause dry skin, and may contain organophospates, which should be avoided, especially in cats.

Elizabeth recommends feeding the Garlic K9 biscuits for dogs (*page 46*) and the Feline Chive treats for cats (*page 46*) once or twice a week, to ward off fleas. Feeding a tiny amount of yeast extract at the end of a teaspoon is recommended during peak flea season as it seems to deter some insects.

⇨ *Healing & herbs*

Animal healing is a fantastic complement to veterinary care and can be safely given by you to your pet. See Chapter 5: *How to Give Healing to Your Pet* for instructions.

ᕗ **Make your own** ᕃ

Elizabeth has had great success, both in the UK and on her trips abroad, with the neem insect repellent for dogs, and the neem-leaf tea insect repellent and the neem bark powder insect repellent for cats (*see pages 80–81*). The nettle-leaf K9 rinse (*page 83*) or the chamomile soothing wash (*page 66*) are great for symptomatic fleabite relief as they can be calming. Calendula ointment (*page 63*) is soothing when the skin is not broken but just a bit inflamed by scratching. In cases of eczema as a result of FAD, the yarrow and aloe vera gel is beneficial (*page 92*).

HEART DISEASE

Overall, approximately 10 per cent of dogs suffer with some form of heart disease. It can be present at birth (congenital) or can be acquired as an adult. Acquired heart disease is much more common than congenital. Congestive heart failure (CHF) is the most common manifestation of heart disease in dogs and cats and can be left or right sided.

Causes

Left-sided CHF affects the left side of the heart, and the most common cause for it is mitral valve disease (MVD). This is more common in older and smaller breeds – the Cavalier King Charles Spaniel is predisposed to MVD. The mitral valve of the heart becomes degenerate and nodular, preventing the valve from shutting fully so blood squirts backwards through the gap with every heartbeat, producing a 'heart murmur'.

Dilated cardiomyopathy (DCM) is the second-most common heart disease and tends to occur in larger dog breeds, especially males. Several large breeds, including Great Dane, Dobermann, Boxer, Golden Retriever and Newfoundland, are predisposed to DCM. In DCM, the major pumping muscle of the heart (the left ventricle) becomes weak and struggles to pump blood. As a result the left ventricle cannot empty fully and becomes dilated and stretched.

In cats, hypertrophic cardiomyopathy (HCM) is the most common acquired heart disease and can cause sudden death. Any cat can suffer from it, but it is more common in middle-aged to older castrated male cats. A blood clot or emboli – arterial thromboembolism – is a complication seen in 50 per cent of cats that have HCM. Taurine deficiency can cause heart disease in cats so if your cat is on a home-cooked diet, do supplement it with taurine (see Chapter 1: *Food Is Medicine*).

Right-sided CHF affects the right side of the heart and may be caused by tricuspid valve disease, DCM and pericardial effusion (fluid around the heart), which may be due to a pericardial bleed. Pericardial bleeds can occur due to a cancerous growth of the heart or pericarditis (inflammation of the pericardium – the membrane surrounding the heart).

Congenital heart disease can be hereditary and there are certain breeds that are more prone to certain heart defects. There is also a hereditary element to some adult heart diseases like DCM. Heartworm disease is caused by a parasite called *Dirofilaria immitis*, which is spread by mosquito bites. This is uncommon in the UK, but prevalent in other countries.

Symptoms

Most dogs with heart disease present with some common signs. Coughing, laboured breathing or panting excessively, reluctance to exercise and sometimes abdominal enlargement. Some dogs may also go off their food and lose weight if the loss of appetite goes undetected. They might become lethargic and tire easily.

Cats with HCM have similar signs. Although they tend not to cough, their breathing is worse. Both dogs and cats with cardiac disease may have sudden spasms and collapse, and then recover completely within minutes. These episodes are known as syncope. Cats with thromboembolism may collapse and be unable to use or drag their back legs. They are paralyzed in their back end and have cold feet. These cats will also be in a lot of pain and tend to vocalize. This is an *emergency* and you must take your cat to a vet immediately.

Diagnosis

Your vet will take into account several factors, like your pet's species, age, sex and breed. After obtaining a thorough history of the symptoms, he or she will check your pet's heart with a stethoscope to listen to murmurs, heart sounds, heart rate, etc. Your pet's respiratory rate is an important clue, and the colour of their tongue and gums will also provide valuable information.

After a full clinical examination, your pet may need blood tests, X-rays, ECG and/or echocardiography in order to get a concrete diagnosis. Other causes of cough, like bronchitis, kennel cough and lung problems will also need to be ruled out. This will usually be done step by step, to get a full picture.

The table below shows the parameters for normal heart and respiratory rates for dogs and cats. By counting the number of times your pet's chest or abdomen rises up and down in one minute, you can count their respiratory rate. By sliding your hand along the chest between the front legs, towards centre-left, you can feel your pet's heart and can count their heart rate.

Normal heart rate and respiratory rate	Cat	Dog
Heart rate	140–240 beats per minute	65–150 beats per minute
Respiratory rate	20–40/minute	20–30/minute

Treatment

⇨ *Your vet*

Treatment of cardiac disease will depend on how critical or stable your pet is when diagnosed. If your pet is critical, he or she will have to be admitted for cage rest and oxygenation. They may need to be sedated for X-rays if they are distressed, and intravenous medication may also be given.

If your pet is stable and a proper diagnosis of the heart condition has been made, he or she will be started on two to three types of medication, such as diuretics (water tablets), ACE inhibitors to reduce water and sodium retention, and other drugs. In DCM cases, special drugs to enhance the ability of the heart to contract better will be prescribed.

Antiarrythmic drugs like digoxin, and blood pressure-lowering drugs may also be necessary. In cats with HCM, calcium channel blockers are the first choice of treatment. The main aim of veterinary treatment with drugs is to improve the quality of your pet's life by alleviating the clinical symptoms of heart disease, and to prolong their life. Heartworm disease can be treated with some monthly injections but sometimes if there are too many adult worms, surgical removal may be necessary, which is risky.

⇨ *You*

Rest and regulated exercise are key to helping your pet's heart cope with heart disease. Excessive exercise is dangerous and must be avoided. Obesity is a well-known cause of increased cardiac workload, especially if your pet is running or playing, etc., so feeding your animal the right food and in the right amount to enable weight loss is vital. It is very important that you feed your pet a low-sodium diet. High-salt diets exacerbate fluid retention and that is a problem in heart failure. Salty treats should also be stopped.

Elizabeth recommends home-prepared natural diets with plenty of vegetables, so please refer to the superfoods shopping checklist on page 18. Many processed pet foods have a high salt and fat content so they are best avoided. Cats need taurine for a healthy heart, and that is naturally available in fresh meat. Avoid commercial cat foods, which have synthetic taurine instead.

Try the following: the chicken broth recipe on page 15, lean cuts of meat, K9/Feline fishcakes or K9/Feline Nature's Own Hotpot *(page 51)* with added fresh parsley, Linseed K9/Feline biscuits *(page 52)*, Garlic K9 biscuits or Chive Feline treats *(page 46)*, adding wheatgrass to the biscuit recipes in Chapter 2, Nettle K9 biscuits and Prairie Woof Jacks *(page 53)*.

⇨ Healing & herbs

Animal healing is a fantastic complement to veterinary care and can be safely given by you to your pet. See Chapter 5: *How to Give Healing to Your Pet* for instructions. Holistically speaking, heart problems, especially acquired disease, may be a result of energy imbalances in the body so stimulating acupoints HT 7, located just above the wrist on the outside of the forelimbs, and points BL13–15, on either side of the spine between the shoulder blades, can be beneficial. See Chapter 6: *Fingers and Thumbs*.

⸎ Make your own ⸎

Elizabeth recommends calendula-, catnip- and rosehip-infused sunflower oils on a self-selection basis (see *page 50*).

HIP DYSPLASIA

Hip dysplasia is predominantly a common inherited orthopaedic disorder of large and giant dog breeds, but it can also affect a wide range of other mammals. The hallmark of this condition is the abnormal formation of the hip socket and the abnormal development of the structures that make up the hip joint, leading to subsequent joint deformity.

In its severe form hip dysplasia causes crippling lameness and painful osteoarthritis of the hip joints. It is therefore one of the most studied veterinary conditions in dogs and probably the single most common cause of canine osteoarthritis affecting the hip joint. See *Arthritis* above.

Causes

- **Genetic factor** – hip dysplasia is primarily a hereditary condition so puppies of parents who had the disorder are more likely to inherit it. However, because it is a polygenic trait, it can skip generations; also, some puppies in the same litter may not inherit it.

- **Environmental factors** – over-nutrition, leading to rapid growth and obesity; too much exercise too young, like jogging with a pup under one year of age; and over-exertion of the hip joint and injury or ligament tear at a young age can all contribute to the development of hip dysplasia. The debate continues as to what degree the problem is inherited and to what extent environmental, man-made influences contribute to this condition.

- **Breed predilection** – large and giant breeds, such as Newfoundland, Mastiff, German Shepherd Dog, Labrador and Golden Retriever, Rottweiler and large hounds are over-represented. Some small breeds, like Pug, Bassett Hound and Bulldog, can also suffer from this condition.

Normal hip vs dysplasic hip anatomy

In a normal hip joint, the ball-shaped femoral head is supposed to fit snugly into the socket of the pelvic acetabulum or socket. In dogs with hip dysplasia, the normally tight-fitting hip joint is much looser, allowing the femoral head to 'rattle around' in the acetabular fossa.

The reason for the laxity, or 'loose fit', could be a shallow hip socket (acetabulum) or a misshapen femoral head (caput) or a combination of both. In either case, there is abnormal wear and tear of the joint that results in the pathology observed in hip dysplasia. The constant rubbing leads to degenerative changes and ultimately, to osteoarthritis.

Symptoms

- **Puppies and young dogs** – if there is major hip dysplasia, pups can show signs from as early as five to 10 months of age. They bunny hop like a rabbit, rest quickly after exercise, and after play they hesitate to get up quickly and instead sit on their haunches with one or both legs splayed outwards like a frog. They also avoid negotiating stairs or slopes. Some of them avoid jumping and carry their back legs slightly forward so as to rely more on their front legs.

- **Adult dogs** – dogs with very mild dysplasia may not show any symptoms, except slight lameness after over-exertion or stiffness first thing in the morning. Even this limping may not start till they are four to five years old. Only dogs that have severe hip dysplasia will show pain or limited mobility prior to maturity.

Severely dysplastic dogs exhibit symptoms ranging from stiffness or soreness after rising from rest, reluctance to exercise, bunny-hopping gait (legs move together at run, rather than swinging alternately), swaying or wobbly gait, lameness, pain, reluctance to climb stairs or jump up into cars, refusal to stand on hind legs, and sudden dislocation of the hip joint. Some dogs cry or wince when the hips are touched. In advanced cases, there is atrophy of the muscles adjoining the hip and thigh areas.

As different dogs have different body weights, pain thresholds, lifestyles and exercise routines, there is a lot of variation in symptoms. Some dogs with the same extent of hip dysplasia start showing signs early while others may be asymptomatic. Each dog is therefore unique in its capacity to adapt and live with hip dysplasia.

Diagnosis

When a puppy or an adult dog is presented to a veterinarian with the above symptoms, based on the history, signalment, physical examination and palpation, he or she will suspect a hip problem. A confirmed diagnosis of hip dysplasia would require X-rays of the hip taken in a certain position, with the dog lying on his/her back and the hips positioned in a specific way. Sedation is compulsory to obtain a good X-ray. Hip scoring may be carried out to evaluate the extent of hip dysplasia and to provide guidance regarding use for breeding – this is mainly owing to hip dysplasia being an inherited disorder.

Treatment
⇨ *Your vet*

There is no complete cure for hip dysplasia but it is possible to alleviate the symptoms and in most cases provide a good quality of life for your dog by using a combination of the following:

- **Enforced rest or exercise control** – rest is crucial, especially when there are acute episodes like dislocations, and also when there is significant arthritis. By resting, there will be a reduction in the wear and tear of the hips.

- **Mild analgesics or painkillers** – hip dysplasia can go from being non-painful to being very painful depending on the extent of arthritis in the joint, so most dogs will need some painkillers, such as tramadol, codeine, etc.

- **Anti-inflammatory drugs** – as in osteoarthritis of any joint, your vet will most probably prescribe NSAIDs (non-steroidal anti-inflammatory drugs), which double up as painkillers as well as reducing inflammation. Meloxicam, carprofen and robenacoxib are a few popular ones. See Chapter 8: *Which Drugs and Why* for side effects and uses of NSAIDs.

- **Surgery** is usually the last choice and is opted for only when medications fail to provide an adequate quality of life. There are two main types of surgery – those that aim to modify or repair the abnormal hip joint and those that replace the hip completely:

- **Triple pelvic osteotomy** is exclusively performed in young animals aged between five months and one year. It can only be performed by a specialist veterinary orthopaedic surgeon and it is vital that there should be no evidence of any arthritis at the time of surgery. The procedure involves rotating the pelvic acetabulum (socket) in such a way that it is better aligned with the femoral head and enables the head to sit snugly in the socket.

- **Femoral head excision** is considered a salvage procedure and is performed in dogs with significant pain and irreversible arthritis. The surgery involves the removal of the femoral head. As a consequence scar tissue fills the defect between the femur and the acetabulum, which forms a false joint and gives back 70 per cent hip function without any pain.

  It is a relatively inexpensive procedure and can be performed by an experienced vet. It works best in dogs that weigh less than 20kg (45lb). I have performed several of these operations and found it quite beneficial; most dogs do quite well on it.

- **Total hip replacement** involves removing both the ball and the socket and replacing them with implants. It is very similar to the operation in humans. The success rate is 95 per cent and optimal joint function is reinstated. It is currently the best surgical procedure recommended to correct hip dyplasia in large-breed dogs and needs to be performed by a specialist orthopaedic veterinary surgeon.

More research is being conducted, and other surgical procedures – like DARthroplasty, pubic symphysiodesis and capsular neurectomy – are also being explored. BioScaffold implant procedures are also being tried out. Surgery for hip dyplasia should not be taken lightly and various other options should be discussed with your vet before deciding.

⇨ *You*

Weight control is definitely the single most important thing you can do to help your dysplastic dog. Reducing weight can really make a phenomenal difference to the progression of hip dyplasia to the severely arthritic form. Low-calorie prescription diets are usually recommended by vets.

Overweight dogs may be advised to go onto obesity management and other weight-loss diets. If you are committed to cooking for your dog, you can make balanced recipes or use raw food, low-carb and low-fat diets and add joint supplements (*see Chapter 1: Food Is Medicine*).

Both conventional and holistic vets recommend nutritional supplements that help rebuild cartilage and/or promote joint surface lubrication. Supplements containing chondroitin sulphate, glucosamine, glycoflex and collagen are all very effective, in both early and advanced cases.

Dog hip braces, special harnesses, orthoses and other mobility aids are being marketed. These can be very useful where hip dysplasia has caused severe muscle wastage. Pressure-reducing ortho beds, foam bedding, ramps, stairs and car hoists can really help these dogs move from place to place and alleviate their pain.

Regular moderate exercise is the key to keeping your dog mobile, but at the same time ensuring they are not over exercised. Large-breed pups under 18 months of age must not be pushed to walk too far or exercised for too long.

⇨ *Healing & herbs*

Animal healing is a fantastic complement to veterinary care and can be safely given by you to your pet. Read Chapter 5: *How to Give Healing to Your Pet* for instructions. Healing per se can therefore be an excellent tool in pain management when used with other appropriate healing modalities. See *Musculoskeletal* section below for herbs, and for the home-cooked food recipes that can really help.

- **Acupressure** – make a three-finger tripod with the thumb, index and middle finger, and position them over the hip bone on three acupressure points – BL 54, GB 29 and GB 30 – pressing for 30 seconds at a time. This has been found to be immensely beneficial. I have used acupressure on my own dog, who has hip dysplasia, and others have found it quite helpful. See Chapter 6: *Fingers and Thumbs*, for image and further details.

Giving dysplastic dogs a daily massage relaxes the tight muscles and relieves pain by increasing circulation. The aim is to massage the muscles, not the bones. A heat massage using a hot water bottle/heating pad wrapped in a thick towel applied to achy hips for 10 minutes once or twice a day helps.

Hydro- and physiotherapy can also be very beneficial. Hip hammocks have been found to be affective in aiding dogs suffering from hip dyplasia to regain their mobility. Several companies are now designing orthotic and prosthetic solutions to help stiff dogs get moving. Ask your vet for details.

⇨ *Summary*

Hip dysplasia is a complex orthopaedic problem affecting the hips of primarily large to giant-breed dogs. It is caused by a combination of both genetic and environmental influences. The abnormal development of the hip joint leads to hip laxity and gradually results in osteoarthritis of the coxo-femoral joint.

The condition has a major welfare impact on the lives of the dogs who suffer from it. By following a good dietary and therapeutic plan, it is possible to provide a good quality of life for dogs with hip dysplasia. Careful, selective, sensible breeding is the only way to prevent hip dysplasia in the future.

KIDNEY DISEASE

The kidneys are responsible for the removal of waste products and excess water from the bloodstream in the form of urine. Kidney disease can be acute (sudden) or chronic (over time). In the acute form, referred to as acute kidney injury (AKI), there is an abrupt drop in kidney function but there is a chance of recovery. In chronic renal failure (CRF), there is a progressive loss of kidney function in stages, and if left undiagnosed and untreated, it is not possible to repair the kidney.

Causes

AKI can be caused by accidents in which there may be trauma to the kidneys; by poisoning with poisons such as lilies, grapes or antifreeze; by infections such as leptospirosis; by acute pancreatitis; by the use of non-steroidal anti-inflammatory drugs; and by renal lymphoma.

Chronic kidney failure may be idiopathic (unknown or spontaneous), or due to ageing, high blood pressure, diabetes mellitus, urinary tract infections, polycystic kidney disease, kidney stones or cancer. There can be many other less common causes too. CRF is more prevalent in cats over nine years of age and dogs who are more than seven years old, but may affect an animal of any age.

Symptoms

- **Acute kidney injury (AKI)** – your pet may suddenly start drinking more, go off its food, develop diarrhoea and vomit. Sometimes the vomit may have pieces of lily if the cause is lily poisoning. Neurological signs like seizures and tremors may be seen in antifreeze (ethylene glycol) poisoning. Halitosis and difficulty urinating may also be present. Dehydration can occur.

- **Chronic renal failure (CRF)** – poor appetite, weight loss, increased urination and thirst, vomiting, uraemic breath or bad breath and blood in the faeces due to gastrointestinal ulceration are some of the symptoms seen. Most of these signs are not seen in the early stages of CRF.

Diagnosis

It is not easy to distinguish between acute and chronic renal disease and veterinary attention is a must to get a diagnosis and initiate treatment. Acute renal failure is not as common as the chronic form but is rapidly progressive. In AKI, your pet is most likely to have been fine one day and then really sick the next. This is usually the case if there is exposure to a toxin or a poison.

After taking a full history and examining your pet clinically, the vet will palpate the kidneys to check their size. In general the kidneys are painful and enlarged in AKI but small and shrunken in CRF. Blood tests to check the levels of urea, creatinine and phosphorus are very important.

The vet will examine your pet's urine under the microscope for crystals and casts, check if his or her urine is dilute or normal and look for the amount of protein being voided. Ultrasound examination, X-rays, both plain and contrast radiography, may be necessary to rule out kidney stones, obstruction, cysts and tumours.

Treatment
⇨ *Your vet*

Early recognition is crucial to the successful treatment of AKI so it is important to seek veterinary help sooner rather than later. Specific treatment can be given as antidotes if the poison is known. However, in most cases the cause is unknown, making treatment difficult. Sometimes it is also too late to make the pet vomit or to treat. Antidotes need to be given within three hours. Supportive treatment with intravenous drip, anti-emetics to stop the vomiting, supplying the correct nutrition and providing pain relief in AKI is the mainstay of treatment.

Your pet will have to remain an inpatient until he stops vomiting and is eating. CRF can only be managed but cannot be cured. In CRF, after initial hospitalization your pet can go home on a proper prescription diet. In cats with CRF drugs to treat high blood pressure and ACE inhibitors may also be prescribed and are very effective. ACE inhibitors have been proven to delay the progression of chronic renal insufficiency in cats, provided they are also on a renal diet.

⇨ *You*

Omega-3 fatty acids and vitamin B are useful nutrients to supplement. Phosphate binders may need to be added to the diet to reduce phosphate intake, which comes from protein; restricting the protein intake is therefore crucial. Also, drugs may be prescribed to reduce the protein lost in your cat's urine, as this is associated with a shorter life span. It is important to remember that the biggest challenge in pets with CRF is getting them to eat. See feeding tips above, under *Appetite Loss*.

So a prescription diet designed for kidney disease management, or a home-made one with the following features, is necessary. See also Chapter 1: *Food Is Medicine*.

Key features of a renal diet:

- Must be tasty.

- Must be low in phosphorus.

- Must contain a low amount of high-quality protein, like eggs, chicken, sardines.

- Must be high in omega-3 fatty acids, vitamin B and antioxidants.

- Must have moderate salt content.

- Must be high energy – with calories from non-protein sources such as brown rice, basmati rice and millet.

Elizabeth recommends home-prepared natural diets with plenty of vegetables: see the superfoods shopping checklist on page 18. Try the following: chicken broth (*page 15*), lean cuts of meat, Hard-boiled Egg and Eggshell K9/Feline treats (*pages 44–45*), K9/Feline fishcakes (*page 51*), K9/Feline Nature's Own Hotpot, with added fresh parsley (*page 51*), Linseed K9/Feline biscuits (*page 52*), Garlic

K9 biscuits or Chive Feline treats (*page 46*), nettle seeds or Nettle K9 biscuits (*page 83*), adding wheatgrass to the biscuit recipes in Chapter 2 and Prairie Woof Jacks (*page 53*).

⇨ *Healing & herbs*

Animal healing is a fantastic complement to veterinary care and can be safely given by you to your pet. Read Chapter 5: *How to Give Healing to Your Pet* for instructions.

⁂ **Make your own** ⁂

For dogs, Elizabeth recommends the linseed cold-pressed oil as it is full of omega-3 and omega-6 fatty acids (*see page 76*), or nettle-infused sunflower oil on a self-selection basis (*page 50*). Cats do not seem to self-select linseed cold-pressed oil. Instead, you can try catnip- and chickweed-infused sunflower oil on a self-selection basis (*page 50*). Milk thistle is excellent for kidney and liver disease (*page 77*).

LIVER DISEASE

The liver is the largest organ in the body, both in animals and humans. It is very important and has many critical functions. Liver disease is a diagnostic challenge to any veterinarian because of the organ's ability to regenerate, and because 70 per cent of the liver needs to be damaged before signs of liver disease are observed. The good news is that even if severely damaged, the liver can regenerate if given the right nutrition.

Causes

Liver disease may be caused by infections such as leptospirosis and infectious canine hepatitis. Both of these are relatively less common nowadays because of regular vaccinations. Liver shunts and fibrosis can be the cause of liver problems in very young animals. Liver cancer is more common in older animals.

Copper-associated liver disease is seen in West Highland White Terriers and Bedlington Terriers. Cocker Spaniels are more predisposed to cirrhosis. Cats are different to dogs with respect to liver functions and suffer more with fatty liver and cholangiohepatitis. Sometimes liver disease is secondary to other diseases like diabetes mellitus, Cushing's disease and cancer spread from other parts of the body.

Symptoms

Many of the symptoms seen in liver disease are also found in other diseases, making it difficult to diagnose. Most animals stop eating or get picky with their food. They appear tired and may drink and urinate a lot. Vomiting and diarrhoea are quite common in liver disease. Yellow gums and yellow conjunctiva indicate jaundice, which is a symptom of liver disease with or without gall bladder involvement. Ascites or fluid accumulation in the abdomen is a common feature of liver disease.

Not all of these signs will be seen in the same animal. Poor tolerance to drugs and weight loss are seen in advanced liver disease. Seizures, fly catching and even aggression may be seen in animals that have developed hepatoencephalopathy.

Diagnosis

After taking a full history and performing a clinical examination of your pet, your vet may want to confirm liver disease by performing some blood tests. Checking liver enzyme levels, to see how much of the liver may be damaged, and performing liver function tests will be necessary. Routine haematology to check the blood count may also be needed.

Ultrasound examination of the liver will enable the vet to rule out tumours and check for liver enlargement, gall bladder problems, etc. Liver biopsy is the only way to get a definitive diagnosis in most patients. X-rays are also part of the investigation, as they can help rule out any obstruction. Faecal and urine samples may also need testing. As the liver is responsible for manufacturing clotting factors, the clotting time of blood may be increased.

Treatment

⇨ *Your vet*

Liver disease is very difficult to treat with drugs but it can be managed by diet. If your pet's liver disease is caused by another disease like diabetes, then treating that should help. Similarly, leptospirosis and other causes should be treated and removed. The aim of treatment is to stimulate regeneration and prevent hepatoencephalopathy from developing. Your pet may need to be admitted and cage rested to improve hepatic circulation, reduce pain and stimulate their appetite.

Steroids may be necessary in certain types of liver disease. A nutritional supplement called S-adenosyl-L-methionine has proven to be very effective due to its anti-inflammatory and cytoprotective properties. Antibiotic therapy may be commenced in hepatitis and cholangiohepatitis. Liver cancer is difficult to treat.

⇨ *You*

Starvation is the worst thing to do in liver disease, in both cats and dogs, so every attempt must be made by you to get your pet eating. Good-quality protein in the right amount is very important. Soya and egg protein is preferable to meat. A commercial prescription diet for liver disease, supplemented with cottage cheese, is probably the safest option, provided your pet will eat it. See the information on a home-made diet in Chapter 1: *Food Is Medicine*. Vitamins B and E should be increased in the diet but not A, C or D.

Key features of a liver diet:

• Moderate levels of high-quality protein, such as chicken, fish and turkey.

• Easily digestible carbohydrates, such as basmati rice.

• Increased fibre and zinc levels and B-complex vitamins.

• Low in copper.

• Moderate salt content.

Elizabeth strongly advocates a home-prepared, natural diet with plenty of vegetables, so please refer to the superfoods shopping checklist on page 18. Processed pet foods contain high levels of salt, fat and additives etc., which are highly detrimental to the liver. As the liver is an important organ for detoxification, when it is damaged it is very important to keep the diet simple.

Feed a home-cooked diet consisting of the chicken broth (*page 15*), fresh meat such as chicken, turkey, venison or rabbit, or the K9/Feline Nature's Own

Hotpot with added fresh parsley (*page 51*). Try snacks such as the Charcoal K9/Feline D-Tox biscuits (*page 42*), K9/Feline fishcakes (*page 51*), Linseed K9/Feline biscuits (*page 52*), Garlic K9 biscuits or Chive Feline treats (*page 46*), wheatgrass added to any of the biscuit recipes in Chapter 2, Nettle K9 biscuits and Prairie Woof Jacks (*page 53*).

You can also feed soya milk and oat porridge with added milk thistle from time to time. If your pet is having chemo- or radiotherapy, the Charcoal K9/Feline D-Tox biscuits can help with detoxification.

⇨ *Healing & herbs*

Animal healing is a fantastic complement to veterinary care and can be safely given by you to your pet. Read Chapter 5: *How to Give Healing to Your Pet* for instructions.

MANGE

Mange is a common skin problem caused by microscopic parasites called mites. Sarcoptic mange and demodectic mange are seen regularly in practice, but lately, due to modern flea-control products that also control mites, it is probably on the decrease. Most modern spot-on flea-control products can also prevent mite infestation so make sure you buy the right ones.

1. SARCOPTIC MANGE

This is a contagious dermatosis that affects dogs primarily and is seen very rarely in cats. It is caused by the mite *Sarcoptes scabiei*. When this mite tunnels under the skin and leaves secretions, it triggers an allergic or hypersensitivity reaction that can be intensely itchy.

Symptoms

Tiny papules and greyish-yellow crusting on the ear pinnae, elbows, hocks and on the skin adjacent to them are usually seen in this type of mange. By scratching, your pet may make them worse and also end up losing the hair or fur in these areas.

Diagnosis

A diagnosis is made by identifying the mites or their eggs under a microscope. Multiple skin scrapings from the affected areas have to be examined and some other flotation/concentration techniques may be necessary.

Treatment

⇨ *Your vet and you*

Organophosphates and amitraz treatments will be prescribed to kill the mites. Ivermectin injections may also be given, unless your pet is a Border Collie or Collie cross, or a breed in which this drug is contraindicated. You may also need to treat your home and consult your doctor if you develop lesions – as scabies can be contagious to humans, this is very important. Not just the pet that is affected but those that are in contact with him or her should also be treated.

2. DEMODECTIC MANGE

This is also known as red mange and is quite different from sarcoptic mange because it is not a contagious disease – i.e. it does not spread to others. The mite *Demodex canis* is present in small numbers on the skin of healthy dogs without causing any symptoms at all, but if an animal is immunosuppressed or is genetically predisposed, these mites increase in numbers and cause clinical disease.

Symptoms

Localized demodicosis is seen in young dogs (three to 11 months). The face and forelimbs are usually affected and you may see focal areas of hair thinning, scaling, alopecia and even some redness. Most of these cases do not need treatment and usually self-cure.

The generalized form is seen in adult dogs and can look quite horrendous, with severe skin lesions. As the mites burrow, the hair follicles rupture and a foreign body reaction to these mites results, causing widespread redness, itching, crusting and even furunculosis, which is a chronic skin disease.

Dogs affected may also look quite miserable, stop eating and even develop a fever. Microscopic examination of deep skin scrapes obtained from affected areas will usually reveal a large number of cigar-shaped mites. If the lesions have become too thickened, then a skin biopsy may be needed.

Treatment

➪ *Your vet*

Once diagnosed treatment involves clipping or shaving the areas, bathing every two weeks with amitraz solution or benzoyl peroxide shampoos. Your pet may be prescribed oral milbemycin or ivermectin injections. Skin scrapes must be performed every two weeks, to check if the mites are decreasing in number, and treatment must be carried on for a good four weeks after a negative skin scrape.

Steroids must not be used, even if your pet is very itchy, because they will cause further immunosuppression and exacerbate the infestation. This is one of the more serious skin conditions – second only to skin cancer.

➪ *You*

Foods that boost immunity, such as the K9/Feline Nature's Own Hotpot (*see page 51*), are very beneficial. You can also feed Bladderwrack K9/Feline sea biscuits and Calendula biscuits (*page 41*), Mint K9 biscuits (*page 53*), Garlic K9 biscuits or Chive Feline treats (*page 46*) and garlic-infused honey (*page 49*). You can also try a tiny bit of yeast extract as it seems to repel flies.

➪ *Healing & herbs*

Animal healing is a fantastic complement to veterinary care and can be safely given by you to your pet. Read Chapter 5: *How to Give Healing to Your Pet*, for instructions.

⚘ Make your own ⚘

Elizabeth recommends the topical aloe vera gel with some crushed garlic and two drops of tea tree oil (*see page 59*). You can also offer bladderwrack- and calendula-infused sunflower oil on a self-selection basis (*page 50*).

MUSCULOSKELETAL PROBLEMS

There are a large number of muscle, bone and joint problems that can affect dogs and cats. A few of the most common disorders are outlined in this chapter. In general, dogs and cats have a hardy musculoskeletal system but disorders can occur for several reasons. Please see table below for a brief list, with causes, symptoms, diagnosis and treatment options. As arthritis and hip dysplasia are common and involve a lot of guardian input, I have written in detail about them in separate entries above.

Disorder	Causes	Signs	Diagnosis	Treatment
Arthritis	Wear and tear, injury and diet.	Pain, stiffness, lameness.	X-rays and joint fluid analysis.	See *Arthritis* above.
Disc protrusion	Degeneration, trauma; breeds such as Dachshund, Pekingese.	Depends on location of protruded disc; pain: paralysis, loss of bladder control, poor reflexes.	MRI and CT scans, X-rays.	Steroids, NSAIDs, painkillers, surgery, massage, hydrotherapy, acupuncture.
Fractures*	Accidents, especially road traffic accidents, old age, poor bone quality.	Pain, crepitus, lameness, swelling, not able to use limb or bear weight, and awkward appearance of limb.	X-rays or radiographs.	Cast or plaster, external fixation, pins and plates, wires and other orthopaedic surgery.
Cruciate disease	Tear of the cruciate ligament in the knee joint by trauma, slipping, and accidents while running. More common in large dog breeds.	Hind limb lameness, toe touching or dragging back leg, or lifting leg up while running; hobbling on one leg, etc.	History, clinical examination by vet and manipulation of knee joint and X-rays.	Rest and restricted exercise, surgery to perform cruciate ligament repair.
Hip dysplasia	Breeds such as German Shepherd, Labrador, etc., genetic.	Lameness, pain, bunny hopping, etc.	X-rays.	See *Hip dysplasia* above.
Patellar luxation (slipped knee cap).	Congenital or traumatic displacement of the patella to one side of the knee. Seen in toy breed dogs. Rarely in cats.	Limping, hopping on three legs with affected leg carried. May be intermittent.	By feeling the knee joint, and by X-rays to confirm.	Rest in mild cases. Corrective surgery to fix the patella in the groove by deepening the groove, TCT (tibial crest transposition), etc.

* Fractures are best treated early rather than late. They may not be life-threatening most of the time but the outcome is much better if fixed early on. See symptoms above.

Treatment

⇨ *You*

Good nutrition is key to joint and bone health. As the guardian, you can play a key role in preventing musculoskeletal disorders. Just like us, animals cannot manufacture omega fatty acids 3, 6 and 9 and so it is paramount that their diet contains them. A natural diet containing oily fish and ground, natural nuts is good.

Elizabeth recommends the chicken broth recipe for dogs and cats on page 15, the Hard-boiled Egg and Eggshell K9/Feline treats (*pages 44–45*), K9/Feline Nature's Own Hotpot (*page 51*), Linseed K9/Feline biscuits (*page 52*), and K9/Feline fishcakes (*page 51*).

⇨ *Healing & herbs*

Animal healing is a fantastic complement to veterinary care and can be safely given by you to your pet. Read Chapter 5: *How to Give Healing to Your Pet* for instructions.

⁂ Make your own ⁂

Elizabeth recommends offering, on a self-selection basis, the calendula-infused sunflower oil to dogs and cats that are recovering from a fracture (*see page 50*). Offer cold-pressed linseed oil for dogs that have had cruciate disease or other ligament problems (*page 76*). For painful muscles and joints, you can try the comfrey topical ointment (*page 68*) and use rosemary massage oil (*page 86*) for acupressure points (see also Chapter 6: *Fingers and Thumbs*).

PANCREATITIS

Pancreatitis is a very painful, life-threatening and commonly under-diagnosed condition affecting both cats and dogs. It is defined as inflammation of the pancreas. This inflammation causes leakage of the digestive enzymes from the pancreas and as a result the pancreas literally starts digesting itself. Pancreatitis can be acute (sudden) or it can be chronic (slowly occurring over a period of time). While both forms are life-threatening, the acute form is more serious and painful.

Causes

In the majority of cases the cause is unknown and dogs seems to suffer more than cats. The acute form is more common in dogs and is very painful, while cats seem to suffer from the chronic form, exhibiting milder symptoms. The incidence of pancreatitis is more common among obese, middle-aged or elderly dogs and more common in bitches than males.

The trouble in dogs usually starts when they eat something too rich and too high in fat (like a whole birthday cake), or something too foreign (a dead bird) that is too challenging for their digestive system. The pancreas is then overburdened and becomes inflamed. Instead of sending the digestive enzymes described above to the duodenum, it starts to leach them into the abdomen and raises the enzyme levels in the blood, causing severe pain.

The chronic form of pancreatitis in dogs maybe due to hyperlipidaemia, high-fat diets, viral or bacterial infections, contaminated food and water, concurrent diabetes mellitus and also the use of certain drugs like organophosphate parasiticides, antibiotics and diuretics. In cats there is an increased prevalence in those animals that already have cholangiohepatitis, hepatic lipidosis and concurrent inflammatory bowel disease. This is often referred to as triaditis.

Symptoms

The main problem with pancreatitis is that the symptoms are very vague, making it extremely difficult to diagnose, especially in cats. In acute cases, the abdomen becomes painful and distended, vomiting and nausea follow, the animal stops eating and becomes depressed and lethargic.

The signs can range from the aforementioned classic signs of a gastrointestinal upset to that of collapse and death. Some dogs adopt a 'praying mantis' posture – stretching because of the pain. Cats may present with inappetance and even jaundice. It is this lack of specific symptoms that makes the diagnosis of pancreatitis challenging.

Diagnosis

Veterinary attention should always be sought because potentially a pet can die from pancreatitis. The vet will obtain a full history (dietary indiscretions like scavenging, eating garbage, cakes, fatty food, etc. must be mentioned) and then perform a thorough clinical examination. By a process of elimination and differential diagnoses he or she may arrive at a provisional diagnosis of acute/chronic pancreatitis.

Following this, a diagnostic blood test called CPLI (canine pancreatic lipase immunoreactivity) in dogs and FPLI (feline pancreatic lipase immunoreactivity) in cats may be indicated. Ultrasound of the abdomen and X-rays may also be necessary. A general health profile may also be requested.

Treatment

⇨ *Your vet*

The treatment of pancreatitis is primarily supportive, meaning that there is not usually a direct cause and cure. The animal needs to be sustained while allowing natural healing to occur and to help the pancreas recover. The veterinary team will take care of the animal's fluid needs via IV or drip, and will address any other disease processes (infection, diabetes, etc.) while letting the pancreas heal on its own. In cats the treatment varies, depending on whether there is concurrent jaundice, cholangiohepatitis, etc.

- **Nil by mouth or NPO** *(non per os)* used to be the rule of thumb in pancreatitis. Basically it means NO FOOD. By doing this we were essentially 'switching off' the pancreatic enzymes to prevent autodigestion. Resting the pancreas and gastrointestinal system is key to recovery.

  It can mean no food or water by mouth for one to five or more days while on IV fluids. This is dependent on the severity of each case, and the animal must be on fluids and other support to survive and heal the pancreas while off oral food and water. Nowadays, pets can be fed special low-fat food via a naso-gastric tube (straight into the stomach), thereby by-passing the pancreas.

- **Pain relief** is always provided. Antibiotics, antacids, anti-emetics, etc., may also be prescribed, depending on the case.

- **A low-fat diet**. After recovery, a low-fat prescription diet like Hill's ID or Royal Canin low-fat gastrointestinal diet is recommended. Acute cases are always admitted and treated as inpatients to provide supportive treatment until the pet can eat and keep down substantial amounts of food for sustenance.

⇨ *You*

It is possible that years and years of feeding commercial pet food lacking in natural digestive enzymes can overload a pet's digestive system and this additional stress can cause the pancreas to malfunction. So feeding dogs and cats high-quality, all-natural foods after recovery is very useful.

During the initial illness, apart from the IV drip, the pet could be put on a liquid fast and fed a chicken or vegetable broth as multiple small feeds with ad lib distilled water. Home-made diets, low in fat and oils with chicken or turkey and grains like brown rice or millet, may serve the same purpose and work out healthier and cheaper. Try recipes such as the chicken broth (*page 15*) or the K9/Feline Nature's Own Hotpot (*page 51*). It is very important to keep the diet simple and not overload the body. See Chapter 1: *Food Is Medicine*.

⇨ *Healing & herbs*

Animal healing is a fantastic complement to veterinary care and can be safely given by you to your pet. Read Chapter 5: *How to Give Healing to Your Pet* for instructions. Giving distant healing to a pet while he or she is an inpatient at the vet's could go a long way in helping a quick recovery – the animal will also be less distressed in the hospital. Acupressure is beneficial.

Hands-on healing can then be done when the pet returns home, especially focusing on the solar plexus, which rules the pancreas. Healing can help with the quick return of homeostasis because it promotes calm, peace and deep relaxation, which hasten recovery in any disease process.

⁘ Make your own ⁘

Nettle K9 biscuits (*see page 53*) are a safe option when your pet has recovered from pancreatitis. The Woof Berry and Yoghurt dog treats can be tried as a quick pick-me-up if your pet is refusing all types of food (*page 54*).

Summary

Pancreatitis causes a lot of suffering to the animal concerned – it is not only painful but can cost the life of a valued pet. Viewed holistically, the pancreatitis is less often a distinct condition but more a part of a larger disease complex. Rather than pumping drugs into an animal on diagnosis, it is better to focus on the larger disease complex and ease it with holistic measures. Natural, low-fat diets and good supplements can prevent flare-ups.

PYOMETRA

Accumulation of pus in the uterine cavity or uterus is referred to as pyometra and is therefore a condition that only occurs in females, both in queens and bitches. The uterus becomes infected in unneutered females, especially in older dogs, and is regarded as an *emergency*. It occurs in the luteal phase of the oestrus cycle, between 5 and 80 days after the end of a season or oestrus.

Causes

It is not uncommon to get bacterial infection in the uterus from time to time but this infection can be persistent and become pyometra if there is underlying cystic endometrial hyperplasia – build-up of the uterine lining without a pregnancy. Use of hormones like estrogen to control season or to cause abortions can also increase the risk of pyometra.

These bacteria find their way into the uterus by the anogenital route and can persist there if the endometrial lining is abnormal. If your pet has been spayed, it is possible for her to develop pyometra of the uterine stump at any time. Elderly bitches that have never had pups are predisposed to pyometra.

Symptoms

Lethargy, inappetance, drinking more (polydipsia) and urinating more (polyuria), with or without vomiting, are the common clinical signs. There may be an obvious swelling of the abdomen as the uterus becomes distended with pus. In later stages, there may be a smelly vulva discharge that can be a light chocolate-brown colour, or sometimes blood tinged and yellowish cream in colour.

Some animals also have a high temperature. If left undiagnosed, animals can die within 14–21 days from the beginning of clinical signs as described above. The uterus may rupture due to the large amount of pus inside and cause septic shock.

Diagnosis

This condition can be diagnosed by a vet on the basis of the symptoms alone, but whenever possible an ultrasound scan or an X-ray is necessary to confirm it and to detect an enlarged, pus-filled uterus. Leukocytosis is seen frequently in closed-cervix pyometra so performing a blood test to check leukocyte numbers is important but not always necessary.

Pyometra should be differentiated from metritis, which is also a uterine infection but occurs in bitches that have just had pups. A general health profile is helpful to rule out other common causes of polyuria and polydipsia like diabetes, liver and kidney disease.

Treatment

⇨ Your vet

Ovariohysterectomy or neutering is the treatment of choice if your pet has pyometra. The success rate is quite high if she is diagnosed quickly after the symptoms develop. I have successfully performed a large number of these operations and have had no problems, even in very elderly pets that are otherwise healthy. In most animals the distended uterus is at least four to five times the size of a normal uterus.

Intravenous fluid therapy prior to surgery is very beneficial, especially if there is renal dysfunction due to the increased thirst. A course of antibiotics is usually prescribed to combat the infection. Prostaglandins and antibiotics have been tried in combination in bitches where surgery is not possible due to some other serious health condition, or because the bitch is used for breeding. These are not always successful and most pets have required spaying at some point. More recently a drug called Aglepristone has been tried in pyometra, with limited success.

⇨ You

If you do not intend to breed from your pet then it is a good idea to get her neutered in order to prevent pyometra, a life-threatening condition that is best prevented. The cost of performing a routine ovariohysterectomy (OVH) is much lower than surgery for pyometra. Observing your pet and monitoring her seasons is also very important, to enable early diagnosis and treatment.

You can feed your pet the chicken broth (*page 15*) and K9 Nature's Own Hotpot (*page 51*) and try the Garlic K9 biscuits (*page 46*), the Linseed K9/Feline biscuits for dogs (*page 52*) and the Chive Feline treats for cats (*page 46*).

⇨ *Healing & herbs*

Animal healing is a fantastic complement to veterinary care and can be safely given by you to your pet. Read Chapter 5: *How to Give Healing to Your Pet* for instructions.

৯ Make your own ৯

Elizabeth recommends garlic- or thyme-infused honey on a self-selection basis (*see page 49*) and calendula- or nettle-infused sunflower oil (*page 50*). The yarrow and aloe vera gel (*page 92*) can be gently massaged around the suture line and over the abdomen in the post-op period.

RINGWORM

Dermatophytosis, commonly known as ringworm, is an infection of the skin, hair or nail caused by fungi such as *Microsporum, Trichophyton* or *Epidermophyton*. Ringworm can easily spread to humans, especially children, who tend to be in very close contact with the infected pets. It also spreads from pet to pet, but it should be noted that most of the cases of ringworm seen in people are *not* from pets.

Causes

The fungus *Microsporum canis* is responsible for approximately 50 per cent of the cases seen in both dogs and cats. Young animals less than 12 months of age seem to be more susceptible, maybe because their immune response is still quite poorly developed. Persian cats seem to suffer more too. Old and immunocompromised pets may also be more predisposed. Cats in colonies are at high risk as the fungal spores are shed in the cattery and can remain alive for 18 months.

Symptoms

Circular, rather damp, areas of skin appear as the hair becomes damaged and falls out. These focal areas are primarily seen on the face, head and feet. Lesions also tend to be strikingly symmetrical and not itchy. In cats just a dull hair coat and some patchy hair loss may be the only symptoms.

Diagnosis

Your vet will need to differentiate ringworm from other skin diseases causing similar symptoms like pyoderma, FAD, eczema and other mite infestations. A wood's lamp is used for diagnosis as the lesions fluoresce under this UV light, but it is not definitive, as only *Microsporum canis* infections tend to be positive. Hair plucks from the suspected area are cultured in a special dermatophyte test medium (DTM) to obtain a definitive diagnosis.

Treatment

⇨ *Your vet*

Your vet is not allowed to dispense treatment without a definitive diagnosis, so these tests are compulsory. All long-haired cats with lesions have to be clipped and the clippings burned so as to reduce environmental contamination. Systemic treatment with drugs like griseofulvin or ketoconazole may be necessary in cats and can be very prolonged and expensive.

Griseofulvin is contraindicated in pregnant queens and has several side effects. Washing with antifungal shampoos and applying topical antifungal agents like clotrimazole and micanozole may be useful alongside lime sulphur or enilconazole dips.

⇨ *You*

Catteries will need to put in strict protocols and management changes as ringworm is a difficult disease to contain. Areas used by your pets at home should be vacuumed daily, to get rid of contaminated hair and spores. 1:10 diluted household bleach solution should be used to clean all cages and surfaces where your cat has been. Enilconazole sprays are available and can be used as an environmental agent. See your doctor if you find circular lesions on your own skin.

⇨ *Healing & herbs*

Animal healing is a fantastic complement to veterinary care and can be safely given by you to your pet. Read Chapter 5: *How to Give Healing to Your Pet* for instructions.

⚓ **Make your own** ⚓

Elizabeth has had fantastic results in dogs with aloe vera topical gel with two drops of tea tree oil added to it (*page 59*). Avoid tea tree with cats.

SENIOR PETS

Pets live a lot longer these days due to the advances in veterinary medicine. Ageing itself is inevitable but certain disease conditions become more common as your pets age. The following table lists these conditions, along with their incidence.

Disease	Incidence	Clinical signs	Treatment
Dental disease	Affects 85 per cent of pets over three years of age.	Bad teeth, halitosis, inappetance, oral tumours.	See *Dental disease*, above.
Kidney disease	Chronic renal insufficiency (CRI) is more common in cats; chronic kidney disease (CKD) in dogs. Average age of onset is seven years.	Increased thirst, decreased appetite, vomiting, lethargy and weight loss.	See *Kidney disease*, above.
High blood pressure	Common in cats and secondary to Chronic renal insufficiency (CRI), hypertrophic cardiomyopathy (HCM), hyperthyroidism or primary systemic hypertension.	Blood pressure is greater than 200mm Hg. Eye damage (including detached retina, blood in eye).	Usually treating primary disease, and with drugs such as amlodipine, etc.
Arthritis	Mainly dogs; less common in cats. Hip dysplasia, osteochondrosis (OCD), ruptured cruciate ligament increase incidence.	Lameness, stiffness in the morning after rest, cannot jump into car or climb stairs, etc.	NSAIDs, joint supplements, weight loss. See *Oestoarthritis*, above.
Senility	Seen in most pets at varying age.	Aimless, confused behaviour, going blind and deaf, Incontinence, disturbed sleep and vocalizing at odd hours.	Special diets and some supplements. See *Senility*, below.

(continued)

Disease	Incidence	Clinical signs	Treatment
Tumours	Common in all ageing pets and can be benign or malignant (cancerous).	Growths on body, signs based on which organ is affected.	Depends on the type of tumour, its location, and speed of diagnosis. Chemotherapy or surgery if possible. Palliative if not.
Respiratory disease	Upper airway diseases like tracheal collapse and laryngeal paralysis increase with age. Lower airway diseases like feline asthma and old dog bronchitis.	Coughing, wheezing, abnormal breathing noises.	Depends on the cause. Surgery in laryngeal paralysis. See Cough, above.
Endocrine disorders	Hyperthyroidism in cats over 10 years of age. Hypothyroidism in dogs. Cushing's disease mainly in dogs. Diabetes mellitus in both cats and dogs.	Depends on condition.	See appropriate condition above.
Prostate problems	Benign prostatic hyperplasia in male entire dogs only. Prostate cancer.	Haematuria (bloody urine), difficulty passing faeces and urine.	Hormone injections or castration in benign prostatic hyperplasia. Chemotherapy for cancer. See Cancer, above.
Incontinence	Urinary incontinence in neutered bitches as they age. Faecal incontinence in both dogs and cats.	Urine leakage while asleep, defecating indoors	See Incontinence, above. No treatment for faecal incontinence.
Liver failure	Hepatitis, cirrhosis, liver cancer; seen in both dogs and cats.	Senile behaviour, inappetance, vomiting, jaundice.	See Liver disease, above.
Vestibular geriatric disease	Incorrectly called stroke. Common acquired disease of old dogs aged over eight years.	Sudden imbalance, disorientation, falling or leaning to one side, head tilt and irregular eye movements, wide stance or ataxia and vomiting.	Sedatives like diazepam, anti-emetics or motion sickness medication, steroids and antibiotics. May need to be an inpatient if not eating. Self cures in two to three weeks.

Most of the conditions above are chronic and get progressively worse as your pet gets older. They may be incurable. Nowadays, veterinary practices have geriatric clinics for the ageing pet that are worth attending. Your vet will check your pet's urine, perform blood tests and check blood pressure after performing a thorough clinical exam to rule out the conditions listed.

In general small breeds have a longer life expectancy than large breeds. Overweight pets tend to have a shorter life span because their systems are overloaded. These animals also tend to be exercised less, and develop arthritis, heart disease and diabetes. The drugs used to treat them can give them a reasonable quality of life but may compromise their life span.

Indoor pets tend to live longer than their counterparts who go outdoors, because they are less likely to be involved in road traffic accidents, pick up infections or get bitten, etc. On average, it can be said that castrated male cats live five years longer than entire Toms, while spayed female cats live four years longer than entire females. It is surmised that this could be because they expend less energy in reproductive and birth-related activities.

SENILITY

Senility occurs to an extent in dogs and cats, just like in people. Your dog may appear confused and wander aimlessly around the house, stand with his head in the corner for a while or void faeces and urine inappropriately. It is almost as if he has forgotten where to urinate or defecate.

Cats may forget to use the cat flap or go out through the cat flap only to appear on the window sill a few minutes later, asking to be let in, and then repeat the process almost immediately. Your pet may otherwise appear normal, eat, drink and have a decent quality of life.

Causes

A gradual reduction in nerve cells and neurotransmitters is thought to be the cause of senile behaviour.

Symptoms

Your pet may act as described above, and may also have deafness, blindness and a disturbed sleep pattern. They may lose their sense of time and wake you up at unearthly hours, and even vocalize or bark or howl. House soiling is common. Some may stop grooming themselves and become distant.

Diagnosis

You can usually tell by the symptoms but it is important to get your vet to give a full clinical exam to rule out any other conditions that may be amenable to treatment.

Treatment

⇨ *You*

As it is a natural process, ageing cannot be treated but it can be managed. Most senior animals are very fussy with their food and really enjoy home-prepared meals and snacks (see Chapter 1: *Food Is Medicine*, and the recipes in Chapter 2). You can try the chicken broth recipe on page 15, K9/Feline Nature's Own Hotpot (*page 51*). K9/Feline Liver Cake (*page 52*) and the Woof Berry and Yoghurt dog treats (*page 54*).

⇨ *Healing & herbs*

Animal healing is a fantastic complement to veterinary care and can be safely given by you to your pet. Read Chapter 5: *How to Give Healing to Your Pet* for instructions. A wellness acupressure massage can help (see Chapter 6: *Fingers and Thumbs* for further guidance).

⚶ Make your own ⚶

Elizabeth recommends offering on a self-selection basis either bladderwrack, calendula, catnip, chickweed, mint, nettle or rosehip infused in sunflower oil, depending on the condition (*page 50*).

STOMACH DISORDERS

Stomach or gastric disorders are quite common in dogs and less common in cats. Cats seem to suffer with fur balls mainly, whereas dogs can have many conditions. Gastric disorders can be acute or chronic.

Causes

The following table lists the common disorders and their probable causes.

Acute	Chronic
Gastritis – very common and may be due to eating decayed materials, toxins, bones, grass, drug treatment, infections like parvovirus, leptospirosis, worms and even food allergies.	Gastritis – due to kidney failure or liver failure.
Gastric dilation and volvulus (GDV)/torsion. Bloating due to aerophagia; eating cereal-based foods too quickly; overeating and pyloric obstruction. Gastric torsion – a condition common in deep-chested dogs who eat a large amount in one meal and then exercise.	Tumours – benign polyps or gastric adenocarcinoma. Gastric ulceration – due to chronic drug use such as NSAIDs; renal and kidney failure.
Pyloric obstruction – due to a foreign body/polyp.	Pyloric stenosis in young Boxers.
HGE – haemorrhagic gastroenteritis, as in parvovirus.	Foreign bodies – like bony pieces or gravel or balls, etc., that have not been passed.
Overeating in puppies.	
Fur balls in long-haired cats.	
Pyloric stenosis in Boxers, Bull Terriers and Oriental cats.	

Symptoms

Vomiting is a very common symptom in both acute and chronic stomach disorders. Bloating and abdominal swelling are seen in gastric dilation and volvulus (GDV) with torsion. Inappetance, increased thirst but bringing water back up. Hematemesis or vomiting blood may also be seen. In chronic disease, the vomiting may be intermittent and there may be waxing and waning appetite, depression, melaena (black faeces) and abdominal pain.

Diagnosis

If your pet cannot keep anything down, you need to seek veterinary attention to stop dehydration. Radiographs or X-rays, barium meal studies, gastroscopy, exploratory laparotomy and a gastric biopsy may be necessary depending on the cause.

Treatment

⇨ *Your vet*

Surgery is necessary to remove gastric foreign bodies and tumours and for obtaining biopsies. Gastric dilation and volvulus (GDV) is an *emergency* and a stomach tube may be passed to deflate the stomach. This will not be possible in torsion, where the stomach twists on itself and closes the esophageal sphincter. Then, after stabilizing your dog on fluids, etc., surgical correction will be necessary, which can be quite complicated. If gastric ulceration is diagnosed, antacids, gastroprotectants and anti-emetics may be prescribed. Feeding your pet little and often is advisable.

⇨ *You*

Simple gastritis can get better on its own, so simple steps like starving your pet for 24 hours and then offering a bland diet such as boiled fish or chicken and rice may be enough. Water should be offered in small quantities, otherwise your pet will vomit it all back up. GDV is an *emergency* and needs urgent veterinary attention.

⇨ *Healing & herbs*

Animal healing is a fantastic complement to veterinary care and can be safely given by you to your pet. Read Chapter 5: *How to Give Healing to Your Pet* for instructions. Massaging acupoint ST 36 can help (see Chapter 6: *Fingers and Thumbs* for location and technique).

⚞ Make your own ⚟

Try the following recipes: Mint biscuits (*page 52*), or Garlic K9 biscuits or Chives Feline treat for cats (*page 46*). Elizabeth recommends offering catnip-infused sunflower oil (*page 50*) for cats that suffer with fur balls. She also recommends Ginger K9 biscuits (*page 46*) and ginger-infused honey (*page 49*) if your pet is nauseous.

In simple cases of gastritis, when your pet is on the mend and where the veterinarian has ruled out GDV, FB, etc., you can offer calendula-, mint-, or catnip-infused sunflower oil on a self-selection basis (*page 50*).

THYROID DISORDERS

The thyroid gland releases the thyroid hormone under the control of the pituitary and hypothalamus. This hormone controls metabolism, activates hair growth and is necessary for growth and development. Hypothyroidism is a condition seen primarily in dogs, whereas hyperthyroidism is common in cats and is also the most common endocrine disorder seen in cats.

Causes

Hypothyroidism is a clinical condition, affecting dogs mainly, where there is inadequate production of the thyroxine hormone because of thyroiditis, thyroid atrophy or (rarely) cancer. Hyperthyroidism on the other hand is a pathological condition seen primarily in cats where there are increased levels of circulating thyroid hormones.

This could be because nodules in the thyroid gland are hypersecreting or, rarely, due to a thyroid carcinoma or cancer. Hyperthyroidism is very rare in dogs but extremely common in late middle-aged and elderly cats.

Symptoms

Hypothyroid dogs present with dullness, lethargy, inactivity, excessive moulting and hair loss, as well as weight gain (they cannot lose weight even when put on a diet). They may also suffer with recurrent skin infections and ear problems and intolerance to cold may also be observed.

Hyperthyroid cats are very hungry, drink a lot, show weight loss, may vomit and have diarrhoea. Some may become aggressive and hyperactive and appear to be breathing with difficulty. They also appear shabby, unkempt and have thickened nails.

Diagnosis

Hypothyroidism has to be differentiated from other conditions, such as skin or endocrine conditions. Your vet will take a full history, perform a full clinical exam and then perform a blood test to check your dog's thyroxine levels and that of the thyroid-stimulating hormone. Low T4 levels are consistent with hypothyroidism.

In most cats with hyperthyroidism, your vet will be able to feel the enlarged thyroid gland, at least on one side of the neck. A heart murmur is usually present and there may be some other abnormalities on auscultation. The age of your cat and its appearance will give your vet important clues. A full blood test to rule out other diseases with similar symptoms and a test to check thyroxine levels will be carried out. If there is suspicion of underlying renal and myocardial disease, an ultrasound exam of the kidney and X-rays of the heart may be needed.

Treatment

⇨ *Your vet*

Hypothyroid dogs will need to be given Levothyroxine twice a day, to deal with the low thyroxine levels. Dosage will be adjusted by response to therapy so regular blood testing to check thyroxine levels will be advised. In cats with confirmed hyperthyroidism, drugs like methimazole or carbimazole, which interfere with the synthesis of the thyroid hormones, are prescribed and must be taken life long. These are to be taken by mouth, and in practice, I have found this difficult for the majority of cat owners as their cats are not easy to medicate by mouth.

In such cases, thyroidectomy (surgically removing the enlarged thyroid) may be the only choice. I have performed several of these operations with a very good success rate. Surgical treatment of thyroid carcinomas is mainly palliative and usually not curative.

While drug treatments have side effects, surgery can have complications too, like hypoparathyroidism. As the parathyroid is attached to the thyroid it may not always be preserved during a thyroidectomy. Radioiodine therapy for hyperthyroidism is very effective but expensive.

⇨ *You*

For hypothyroid dogs, Elizabeth recommends K9/Feline sea biscuits (*page 41*), Hard-boiled Egg and Eggshell K9/Feline treats (*page 44–45*), K9/Feline fishcakes and K9/Feline Nature's Own Hotpot (*page 51*), and Liver Cake K9/Feline bake (*page 52*).

⇨ *Healing & herbs*

Animal healing is a fantastic complement to veterinary care and can be safely given by you to your pet. Read Chapter 5: *How to Give Healing to Your Pet* for instructions.

✿ Make your own ✿

For hypothyroid dogs Elizabeth recommends offering bladderwrack-infused sunflower oil on a self-selection basis (*page 50*). In cases of severe moulting try cold-pressed linseed oil on a self-selection basis (*page 76*). Hyperthyroid cats usually self-select catnip-infused sunflower oil (*page 50*) and you can also try Catnip Feline biscuits (*page 41*).

VOMITING

Vomiting is the forceful reflex expulsion of the contents of the stomach through the mouth. It is a symptom of many conditions in the dog and the cat. Vomiting may be acute (less than one day's duration), chronic (intermittent vomiting on and off) or persistent (vomiting for weeks or months).

Causes

The following is a list of possible causes for acute and chronic vomiting in dogs and cats.

Acute vomiting	Chronic vomiting
Food indiscretion (eating rapidly and scavenging), food allergies, including sudden diet change.	Diseases of the oesophagus, such as hiatal hernia, reflux or inflammation.
Drugs like NSAIDs, steroids, chemotherapy.	Infections – like helicobacter.
Inflammation of the stomach or intestines due to viruses like parvo, canine distemper, bacterial disease, campylobacter, etc.	Metabolic disease like kidney, liver, gall bladder, diabetes, chronic pancreatitis and electrolyte abnormalities. Cats – cholangiohepatitis and hyperthyroidism.
Worms – puppies and kittens may vomit worms.	Inflammatory bowel disease.
Gastrointestinal obstruction, foreign bodies in the stomach or intestine, GDV, cancer, intussusception and constipation.	Partially obstructing gastrointestinal disease – gravel, foreign bodies, or bony pieces and intussusception
Infections in the abdomen – pyometra, pancreatitis, peritonitis, hepatitis.	Neoplasia – cancer, polyps, etc.
Poisons or toxins, including household plants, antifreeze, etc.	Neurological problems such as brain tumours or vestibular syndrome.
Liver or kidney failure.	Post-surgical motility disorders.
Endocrine disorders like diabetic ketoacidosis, Addison's disease.	Food allergies and intolerances.
Heat stroke, motion sickness, fear, etc.	Toxicity and constipation.

Diagnosis

As vomiting can be caused by a whole host of conditions, unless it is just temporary and one-off, you must get your pet checked out. After taking a full history and performing a clinical exam your vet may advise blood tests to rule out metabolic and infectious causes. X-rays and/or ultrasound may be required if there is suspicion of a foreign body or obstruction.

Endoscopy is very useful to rule out foreign bodies in the oesophagus, stomach or duodenum. It can also diagnose ulcers. If Addison's disease is suspected then an ACTH stimulation test may be necessary – this is a blood test to check cortisol levels. Other tests may also be required, depending on the suspected cause.

Treatment
⇨ *You*
As the most common cause of vomiting is dietary indiscretion, fasting your pet for 12–24 hours, followed by small amounts of water, ice cubes and bland food, is usually sufficient. Elizabeth recommends chickweed ice cubes (*page 67*), ginger-infused honey (*page 49*) and Ginger K9 biscuits (*page 46*). In cats that vomit fur balls, offering catnip-infused sunflower oil can be very beneficial (*page 50*). Please read the tips under appropriate conditions if the cause of vomiting has been ascertained by your vet.

⇨ *Your vet*
If vomiting persists then your pet will need veterinary treatment and hospitalization. Fluid therapy with anti-emetics, antacids and H2 antagonists like Ranitidine may be necessary until your pet can keep food and water down. Proton-pump inhibitors like omeprazole are prescribed in chronic cases.

Anti-emetics like metaclopramide are contraindicated if there is an obstruction so will not be given until X-rays have confirmed its absence. Inflammatory Bowel Disease (IBD) cases may need steroids and antibiotics, and also worming if there is concurrent worm infection. Symptomatic therapy, supportive therapy and if necessary surgery to remove foreign bodies is the approach to vomiting cases.

⇨ *Healing & herbs*
Animal healing is a fantastic complement to veterinary care and can be safely given by you to your pet (see Chapter 5). Stimulating acupoint ST 36 can also help (see Chapter 6 for location and technique).

WORMS
Worms infect most dogs and cats at some point in their lives and are quite a common problem in pets. Most puppies are born with worms and will need

regular worming depending on the risk of re-infection. Worms can infect people and their larvae pose a health risk, especially to children. There are two main types of worms that commonly infect cats and dogs – the roundworms (or *Nematodes*) and tapeworms (or *Cestodes*).

The roundworm *Toxocara canis* can actually cause blindness if transmitted to humans. In general roundworms are more common in puppies and kittens whereas tapeworms are common in adults. Cats that hunt are more likely to get worm burden. There are also other less common worms like lungworms, heartworms, whipworms and hookworms.

Causes

The dog roundworm (*Toxocara canis*) lives in the small intestine of dogs and can be picked up by the puppy in the womb of the bitch by the transplacental route. They can also be infected through the milk, or by eating eggs that all parasites lay. The cat roundworm (*Toxocara cati*) is not picked up by the kitten in the womb but by intramammary transfer – suckling the mother's milk. It can also be infected by eating the eggs of the worms or by the cat eating small rodents. Roundworms look like pieces of string or vermicelli.

Tapeworms have very complicated life cycles involving passage through an intermediate host or second animal (the flea or a small rodent or rabbit, depending on the particular tapeworm concerned) before they can again infect their main host animals such as the dog or cat.

Tapeworms are flat and can be 50cm (19in) long, but the tapeworm segments that become detached from the end of the worm and fall out in the faeces resemble grains of rice. *Dipylidium caninum* is the most widely diagnosed tapeworm in both cats and dogs and is transmitted by fleas.

Dogs become infected from contaminated soil, which may contain faeces from an infected animal. The worm eggs or larvae can survive in the faeces for a whole year and fox droppings are an important source of tapeworm larvae. Swallowing fleas infected with *Dipylidium caninum* while grooming is another potential cause.

Cats and dogs can be infected by tapeworm when they eat infected small mammals like rabbits or mice. As tapeworms infect grazing animals like sheep, feeding on a sheep carcass can also be a source of infection.

Lungworms

The lungworm (*Angiostrongylus vasorum*), which is spreading at an alarming rate in the UK, is actually a type of nematode. An increase in the number of slugs and snails, increased pet movement and urbanization of foxes have all been declared as significant factors, resulting in increased risk all year round rather than a seasonal problem.

The lungworm larvae are carried by slugs and snails and the problem occurs when dogs accidentally eat them from dirty puddles, grass, outdoor water pools or bowls, or deliberately eat them if they are sat on their toys or bones, etc. Frogs carry larvae and foxes can also get infected and spread the disease.

The lungworm larvae migrate via the digestive tract, and via the bloodstream they actually enter the lungs and the heart. The disease was first discovered in France and is found in other countries all over Europe, America and Africa. Younger dogs less than two years of age are more susceptible.

Symptoms

Symptoms differ, depending on the age of your pet and the worm. Kittens and puppies may actually pass roundworms that look like strings in their stools. They may be pot-bellied, lethargic and have vomiting and diarrhoea. Some pets vomit whole worms. Adult pets scoot their bottom across the floor or lick or groom excessively around their bottom.

Worms should not be taken lightly as excess worm burden can actually kill a kitten or puppy. In lungworm disease, your pet may show no symptoms at all. However they might tire easily, cough, bleed excessively when injured, have nose bleeds, become anaemic, lose weight and appetite, vomit and have diarrhoea. Occasionally seizures and depression may also be symptoms. Sudden death is also possible with lungworm disease.

Diagnosis

In most cases, the worms may go unnoticed and are only spotted because the animal vomits whole roundworms or passes them when it has diarrhoea. Tiredness and poor growth in spite of eating well may suggest worms. Tapeworms for example, may be seen as rice grains around your pet's bottom but most of the time they are invisible and stay in the intestines – sucking away valuable nutrients and blood, which eventually causes weakness and tiredness.

As the same symptoms can be caused by various other health conditions, it is important to take your pet to the vet so he or she can rule out the other causes. Most vets will enquire about worming during your pet's annual check or during any visit. If there is a suspicion of worms, you will be asked to collect a three-day pooled faecal sample, which will then be tested for worm segments, larvae, etc. Lungworms are diagnosed by a Baermann test, faecal examination and X-rays. A blood clotting test may also need to be performed.

Treatment
⇨ *Your vet*
Depending on the worm that is the cause of the infection, your vet will provide the correct product; this is why it is important to seek veterinary attention. Many modern flea treatments also contain worming products so do check what the product does. The dosage is different if your pet has an active infection than if they are fine and just need prevention. Similarly, the dosage for worming treatments is calculated based on the weight of your pet, so it is important to get your pet weighed.

⇨ *Worming protocol*
- Puppies and kittens need to be wormed every two weeks from two weeks of age until they are 12 weeks old.

- They should be wormed monthly till the age of six months and then wormed every three to six months, based on the product used and their lifestyle. Some products may only last for one month so do check the pack.

- As roundworm larvae can be transferred to the pups from day 42 of pregnancy, Fenbendazole treatment should be given every day from day 40 of the bitch's pregnancy until two days after she has whelped.

- Lungworm treatment should be given by your vet and then prevented by using products regularly. Advocate is a very popular product used for prevention in the UK.

➪ *You*

There are many safe and effective treatments for roundworms available in the shops but be sure you understand them and are sure of the diagnosis. Discuss your pet's lifestyle, your lifestyle, kids involved, your pet's hunting habits, etc., with your vet so they can advise the correct product. If your pet does not take tablets then you may be given a syrup or a spot-on wormer. Most vets will be happy to give the wormer to your pet manually if you find it difficult.

➪ *How to reduce the risk of worms*

- Pick up your pet's faeces regularly and dispose of them safely.
- Regularly pick up your dog's toys at the end of each day and store them in a snail-tight box.
- Check and clean your pet's water bowl, in case snails target it.
- Worm all new pups and kittens.
- Stop your pet from scavenging carcasses and hunting.
- Avoid feeding unsterilized pet food.
- Feed food with added garlic.
- Use regular flea treatment for all your pets.

➪ *Healing & herbs*

Animal healing is a fantastic complement to veterinary care and can be safely given by you to your pet. Read Chapter 5: *How to Give Healing to Your Pet* for instructions. Feeding small amounts of K9 Garlic biscuits or Feline Chive treats (*page 46*) from time to time as part of a balanced diet may help.

⚘ Make your own ⚘

Elizabeth recommends offering on a self-selection basis the calendula- and nettle-infused sunflower oil (*page 50*).

Part 3

EMPOWERING THE PET GUARDIAN

Chapter 8

~⌒

Which Drugs and Why –
Pros and Cons of Medication

In this chapter we will be looking at the three most common classes of drugs that may be prescribed by your veterinarian, their uses and most likely side effects. When used intelligently and safely after a proper diagnosis, drugs can really enhance the quality of your pet's life. Some of them are life-saving and are compulsory in emergency situations. However, when they are prescribed indiscriminately and unnecessarily, drugs can cause more harm than good.

An impatient owner who wants quick results can force even the most well-meaning, holistically minded veterinarian to prescribe needless medication, while a well-informed pet guardian who has the long-term wellness of her pet in mind will request and choose the more natural options, which are safer and have no known side effects.

The Collins dictionary defines 'drug' as 'any synthetic or natural chemical substance used in the treatment, prevention or diagnosis of disease'. Medicines, agents and compounds are all synonyms for drugs. Any one drug can have many names, unfortunately, which can be very confusing.

All drugs have at least two nonchemical names: a *generic* name, which has been officially approved, and a *brand* name, which is the commercial name chosen by a pharmaceutical company. In most cases the generic name will provide a clue to the pharmacotherapeutic action and/or classification, but not in all cases.

To make matters more confusing, these generic names can vary between countries and so can brand names. If you are in any doubt, always contact your vet to check if you have the correct drug. Today a lot of pet owners buy drugs from online pharmacies, so it is vital they have some knowledge of drugs, their names, benefits and side effects.

ANTIBIOTICS/ANTIBACTERIALS

Antibacterials are undoubtedly the most important therapeutic discovery made in the 20th century. Today, these medications are probably the most frequently used and abused in conventional veterinary practice. Antibiotics are by-products of other microorganisms, like moulds, and are used to treat infections caused by bacteria.

Antibiotics are known to have selective toxicity, as they interfere with a vital function of the bacterial cell such as cell wall synthesis, DNA replication, protein synthesis, folic acid metabolism, etc., but have minimal or no effect on the host (animal or human) cells. It is because of their selective toxicity that antibiotics have what is called a high therapeutic index (the ratio of the toxic dose to the therapeutic dose) or, in simple terms, excellent safety profiles.

It is important to know that an antibiotic's ability to inhibit or kill bacteria will depend on its concentration, and that its bactericidal (killing) property can be both concentration-dependent or time-dependent, which is why your vet will insist on using an antibiotic at the same time each day and with the correct time intervals (for example: use twice daily, 12 hours apart).

Sometimes your vet may prescribe more than one antibiotic. This is because certain antibiotics may act together synergistically. In the same way, some may act antagonistically, or oppose each other, so it is best not to medicate your pet with antibiotics yourself.

Some of the most commonly used antibiotics in small animal veterinary practice, along with their popular brand names, are listed in the following table.

Antibiotic	Brand name
Amoxicillin	Amoxycare, Betamox, Clamoxyl
Amoxicillin-clavulanate	Noroclav, Synulox, Kesium, Clavaseptin
Cefalexin (cephalexin)	Ceporex, Rilexine, Therios, Cephacare
Cefovecin	Convenia
Cefuroxine	Zincacef, Zinnat
Chloramphenicol	Chloromycetin
Clindamycin	Antirobe, Clinacin, Clindacyl
Doxycycline	Ronaxan, Doxyseptin 300, Vibramycin
Enrofloxacin	Baytril, Enrocare, Enroxil
Fusidic acid	Canaural, Fuciderm, Fucithalmic
Gentamicin	Clinagel Vet, Easotic, Otomax, Tiacil
Marbofloxacin	Marbocyl, Aurizon
Metronidazole	Stomorgyl, Metronidazole, Flagyl
Oxytetracycline	Oxycare, Engemycin
Trimethoprim/Sulphonamide	Duphatrim, Trimacare, Tribrissen, Septrin

Vets consider several factors before deciding on a particular antibiotic for your pet. Sometimes though, many pets are treated with them for prolonged periods of time – intermittently or continuously – without even a proper diagnosis to justify their use. In my experience, this usually happens when the pet owner cannot afford the tests required to arrive at a diagnosis and would rather just spend on treatment.

Side effects

Gastrointestinal symptoms, like vomiting and diarrhoea, are probably the most common side effects of antibiotics. Very rarely, just like humans, pets can also suffer a severe allergic reaction to an antibiotic, usually after taking one or two doses. When antibiotics are taken for prolonged periods your pet may also become more susceptible to yeast infections.

Vets and pet owners should both insist on culture and sensitivity testing to ensure the appropriate antibiotic is being prescribed. It is also very important that the correct antibiotics are used at the right dose, at the right time each day and for the right length of time. Pet owners have a tendency to stop using the antibiotic as soon as the pet appears to be back to normal. The course *must be completed* even if the pet appears to be well, as otherwise relapse is very common.

Resistance

Antibiotic resistance is a real problem today. It happens when bacteria are no longer killed by the antibiotics that have previously been effective. There is increasing fear that this resistance will spread to such an extent that we might return to the 'dark ages', when there was no treatment for many of the infections that afflict both humans and animals.

The improper and overzealous use of antibiotics by vets, and poor compliance by owners, are considered as contributing factors. The UK's Veterinary Medicines Directorate (VMD) has called for responsible antibiotic use by vets, farmers, animal keepers and pet owners. The focus should be on improving pet health through good nutrition, and as far as possible avoiding antibiotic use.

Complementary therapies

There are several herbs, spices and foodstuffs with antibacterial properties. Aloe vera, garlic, tea tree and turmeric can be tried (see Chapter 3, *A–Z Pet-Friendly Herbs*). I also prefer to use antibacterial shampoos rather than systemic antibiotics for recurrent skin infections.

NON-STEROIDAL ANTI-INFLAMMATORY DRUGS (NSAIDS)

NSAIDs are the second-most commonly prescribed medications and are used extensively in small animal practice, especially in dogs. These drugs are sometimes referred to as *aspirin-like* drugs, as their actions are very similar to those of aspirin, which was introduced into human clinical medicine way back in the 1890s. The three main therapeutic effects of NSAIDs are:

- An anti-inflammatory effect: they modify the inflammatory reaction present.

- An analgesic effect: they reduce certain types of pain, especially pain caused by inflammation.

- An antipyretic effect: they can lower the body temperature if it is increased during disease or fever.

Vets tend to prescribe NSAIDs for symptomatic relief from pain and swelling, which is present in chronic joint disease like osteoarthritis, and also to alleviate pain caused by acute inflammatory conditions such as dog or cat bite injuries, fractures, sprains and other soft tissue injuries. They are also used to provide relief from post-surgical pain, dental procedures and any minor aches or pains.

While most NSAIDs bring about their drug action in a similar way, there are striking differences in their toxicity and the degree of tolerance between dogs and cats – and even within dogs and cats. *It is very unwise*, therefore, to try and use them without veterinary advice. For example, Paracetamol *must not* be used in cats, as they lack the special enzyme called glucoronyl transferase that is required to metabolize this drug and can therefore die if given it.

The table below gives the most common NSAIDs used by vets in small animal practice, and their popular brand names.

NSAIDs	Brand names
Aspirin	Acetylsalicylic acid, Aspirin BP
Carprofen	Rimadyl, Carprodyl, Carprieve, Norocarp
Firocoxib	Previcox
Ketoprofen	Ketofen
Mavacoxib	Trocoxil
Meloxicam	Metacam, Meloxidyl, Loxicam, Rheumocam
Paracetamol	Paracetamol, Pardale V (with codeine)
Phenylbutazone	Companozone
Piroxicam	Piroxicam, Feldene
Robenacoxib	Onsior
Tolfenamic acid	Tolfedine

Most NSAIDs are metabolized in the liver and excreted by the kidney. To a large extent they all share the same types of mechanism-based side effects. All these effects are thought to be due to their primary action – inhibition of the fatty acid COX enzyme, and thus inhibition of the production of prostaglandins and thromboxanes.

Their anti-inflammatory action is thought to be due to their inhibition of COX-2, and their unwanted side effects, particularly the gastrointestinal disturbances like gastric irritation, are said to be largely a result of their action on COX-1.

Side effects

Gastrointestinal ulceration and irritation are common side effects of almost all NSAIDs, but some of them can cause gastrointestinal bleeding, neurological and behavioural problems and even anaemia. Most vets will advise that if there are signs of adverse reaction, like severe vomiting and diarrhoea or bloody stools, these drugs must be stopped immediately.

When possible vets will avoid prescribing NSAIDs to pets that are elderly, have a previous history of gastrointestinal ulcer or bleeding or have kidney, liver or heart problems. A very important precaution or contraindication with NSAIDs is that they must not be administered concurrently or within 24 hours of giving another NSAID or a steroid. It is important to mention that prolonged use of any NSAID is not in the best interests of your pets, especially if they are on it for several years in conditions such as arthritis.

Complementary therapies

It is a good idea for pet owners to try complementary therapies for chronic pain and inflammation, such as herbs (see Chapter 3, *A–Z Pet-Friendly Herbs*) and joint supplements such as Synoquin EFA – containing glucosamine and chondroitin sulphate with Dexahan krill oil, antioxidants and omega-3 fatty acids. A good, balanced diet is very beneficial and acupuncture and acupressure can also be very useful to help with chronic pain (see Chapter 6, *Fingers and Thumbs*).

CORTICOSTEROIDS

The correct name for these drugs is Glucocorticoids but they are more commonly referred to as 'steroids'. They have been abused frequently, both by vets and doctors, in the past. However, recently there has been more awareness and as a result, their use is now much more prudent.

Steroids are not as 'horrible' or 'evil' as most people think. They are wonderful, life-saving drugs that have huge benefits when used properly. Corticosteroids are very good as anti-inflammatory and pain-relieving medications. However, it is their ability to relieve itching that has led to their long-term use in the allergic skin conditions that afflict pets.

In emergency situations, where the pet is in severe shock or has neurological signs because of injuries to the brain or spinal cord, steroids were thought to be beneficial. On the contrary, recent research seems to suggest that their use could in fact be detrimental and should be avoided. Their use in emergencies is therefore still a very grey area among vets and is a subject of controversy.

In autoimmune diseases like lupus, pemphigus, immune-mediated anemias, etc., where the pet's immune system is fighting itself, steroids have proven to be very effective because of their immunosuppressive properties. Steroids are also used in the treatment of Addison's disease, chronic atopy, inflammatory bowel disease and some cancers.

The table below lists the commonly used steroids used in small animal veterinary practice, along with their brand names. They may be in the form of tablets or gels or creams or powders, and so on, but they contain the steroid mentioned as the active ingredient.

Steroids	Brand names
Betamethasone	Fuciderm, Otomax, Betnesol, Maxidex
Dexamethasone	Aurizon, Dexadreson, Dexafort, Maxitrol
Hydrocortisone	Efcortesol, Hydrocortisone
Hydrocortisone aceponate	Cortavance, Easotic
Methylprednisolone	Depo-medrone, Medrone, Solu-medrone
Prednisolone	PLT, Prednicare, Prednidale, Pred forte

On the flip side, the very same properties that make steroids useful can make them harmful, which is why they should be used with care and consideration. They can impair wound healing and bring about delayed recovery from infections, so they should be used with caution in these situations.

Pets that are on long-term steroids must therefore be carefully monitored for infections. Steroids are no longer being used orally in the treatment of arthritis but are still being used as intra-articular or joint injections in worst-case scenarios. Their immunosuppressive nature, while useful in immune-mediated disease, is detrimental to the immune system as it renders the body more susceptible to infections.

Side effects

Both short- and long-term side effects are observed as a result of steroid use. A transient increase in appetite, water intake and urination is seen mainly in dogs that have been given steroids. Cats seem to have better tolerance to the drugs, and exhibit relatively fewer side effects, but equal care should be taken to prevent unnecessary steroid use.

The short-term side effects are not really harmful when compared to the long-term ones. Prolonged steroid use can suppress the HPA (hypothalamic-pituitary axis) and cause adrenal atrophy. Iatrogenic Cushing's disease may also develop with prolonged steroid use. Other effects, such as vomiting, diarrhoea and gastrointestinal ulceration, may also occur. Excessive use of steroid skin cream and gels has been known to cause epidermal atrophy or thinning of the skin with wrinkling.

Osteoporosis (thin bones), high blood pressure, water retention, hair loss, infertility, birth defects, fatty liver, obesity, cataracts, thromboembolism (blood clots in lungs) and raised liver enzymes are the less likely side effects of steroids. It should be noted that not all pets and not all steroids will exhibit all these possible side effects.

Steroids should not be prescribed for conditions affecting pregnant animals, pets with diabetes mellitus and those with renal/kidney disease. Pets that have ulcerative keratitis/corneal ulcers should not be prescribed eye preparations that contain steroids. All vets are aware of these contraindications and will try their best to adhere to them.

Most veterinarians will therefore prescribe steroids in *supraphysiologic* doses – to maximize the therapeutic benefit but minimize the dose-related side effects. Systemic steroids (oral/injections) are therefore started off in high doses and then gradually tapered to give the minimal effective dose. Giving steroids every two days is enough in most cases – especially in chronic skin conditions to control the itching – rather than giving them every day.

The key point here is that steroids may be the best therapy for some pets, for certain conditions, in order to ensure a decent quality of life. The aim of this chapter is not to frighten you or put you off steroids completely, but to help you make an informed choice.

There is no doubt that long-term steroid use may reduce the life span of your pet for the reasons mentioned above. However, a well-informed risk-to-benefit assessment must be made before deciding against them. This is where complementary therapies can be beneficial.

Complementary therapies

Usually, any skin condition that responds to steroids will also respond to a proper natural diet or a hypoallergenic diet. Supplementing with raw foods, antioxidants, omega-3 fatty acids, oil of evening primrose, cleansing hypoallergenic shampoos and herbal remedies (*see Chapter 3*) will go a long way in alleviating chronic dermatitis or itchy skin problems. Acupuncture, glucosamine and chondroitin sulphate, krill oil and herbal remedies, hydrotherapy and massage can alleviate chronic arthritic pain.

Inflammatory bowel disease responds very well to dietary management (see Chapter 1, *Food Is Medicine*) and probiotics. Herbs, good diets and immune-strengthening food supplements may benefit animals with immune-mediated disease by at least helping them to do well on lower steroid doses. Immunotherapy vaccines tailor-made after allergy testing are a good alternative to steroid use in chronic allergic skin disease but can be expensive.

The bottom line is this – 'use drugs with caution'. An open discussion with a holistically minded veterinarian will help you make the right choice for your pet.

Chapter 9

Chapter 9

~~~

The Vaccination Debate – Should Companion Animals Be Vaccinated?

Vaccination is defined as the administration of antigenic material (a vaccine) to stimulate an animal's immune system to develop adaptive immunity to a particular or combination of pathogens. The very first vaccine was developed in 1796, against smallpox in humans, by British doctor Edward Jenner.

Over the years, the effectiveness of vaccines has been widely studied and verified, and vaccinating has been considered the most effective method of preventing infectious diseases. Just like humans, animals suffer from a wide range of infectious diseases, and with the advancement of veterinary medicine it became of vital importance that they should also be protected against them. Creating immunity to certain diseases in animals became a priority, and as a result animal vaccinations were introduced.

THE VACCINATION CONTROVERSY

As a veterinarian, I have recently observed an increase in negativity and fear among clients about pet vaccinations, and about the perceived dangerous effects of over-vaccinating animals; the vaccination debate is also rife on the internet. There seems to be a lot of confusion among vets and pet guardians over this subject. I therefore felt it was important to examine the main concerns and evaluate them to see if there is any real justification for this.

The history of animal vaccinations is quite confusing. The lack of clarity – and not enough research into the correlations and adverse reactions – is highly disconcerting. When animal vaccinations were first developed, they were primarily against four killer diseases, but in recent years the list of diseases has increased dramatically. Animal vaccine manufacturing is now a multibillion-dollar industry.

But do we really need so many vaccines? There is no doubt that vaccine manufacturers started off with honourable intentions, responding to the common health epidemics, but now it seems as if there is a market for new vaccines to fight milder diseases that can easily be treated.

Holistic veterinarian Jean Dodds says: 'It is the vets' fault, really.' She, along with many other vets, believes that we have stopped practising medicine and started focusing more on vaccines and pills. Over time, vaccines became a major chunk of any conventional veterinarian's income and in the 1970s the tradition of annual revaccinations was born. What most pet owners find odd is the fact that while they themselves are only vaccinated rarely, their pets are vaccinated every year. It is a very valid question. Are annual boosters really necessary, or is it a trap to make money?

According to the vets, this vaccination protocol ensured that pets were brought in to be checked annually. If boosters were not compulsory, they argued, most owners would just ignore the annual checks, which are vital to an animal's wellbeing. I can see their point of view, but if a responsible pet guardian is willing to bring their pet in every year for an annual health check, should we insist on the annual booster?

THE ANNUAL BOOSTER: ESSENTIAL FOR HEALTH OR HARMFUL?

Most conventional vets seem to be confused about the vaccination schedule, and the differences between the guidelines set by the Vaccination Guidelines Group (VGG) of the WSAVA (World Small Animal Veterinary Association), and what is mentioned in the data sheet provided by the pharmaceutical companies who produce the vaccines. The questions are: 'Are vaccines really causing enough adverse reactions that one should take over-vaccination so seriously?' What is the ideal protocol? How often is safe and enough?

The majority of vets tend to follow the data sheet as this protects them from any litigation and the onus is then on the vaccine companies. The pet guardians, on the other hand, are more concerned with the adverse effects of vaccinating their pets, the cost of vaccinations and, most importantly, over-vaccinating.

Are the adverse reactions only those listed in the vaccine manufacturer's data sheet or is there more to it? Are the vaccinations actually making the pets ill? If so, do we have proof? These are important questions that we need to address.

Several holistic vets were interviewed by the UK's *Dogs Naturally* magazine in June 2012 and most of them felt that vaccines did more harm than good. Some felt that most of the diseases that have an immunological basis can be triggered by vaccinating.

Allergies, atopy, asthma, autoimmune diseases, pancreatitis, cardiomyopathy, epilepsy, cancers like lymphoma, kidney failure, anal gland problems, cystitis, colitis and even behavioural problems, to name just a few, have all been related to 'vaccinosis' (a term coined by the late 19th-century British homeopath J. Compton-Burnett to describe subtle chronic conditions triggered by vaccinations).

In horses, colic, laminitis and anorexia have all been connected to recent vaccinations. Most of the vets interviewed for the magazine believed that their observations were not just anecdotal and that it was happening too often to be dismissed as a coincidence.

Vaccine-related fibrosarcomas in cats are a well-documented adverse reaction, and so is the fact that rabies vaccines can cause terminal cancer in cats. Vaccinating cats with the feline leukemia vaccine can also predispose them to cancer, according to many holistic vets.

When the immune system is compromised, all sorts of germs can attack from all sides. It is very difficult, therefore, to prove that it is the vaccine that caused the subsequent disease. From her own research, vet Jean Dodds found enough evidence to link the onset of polyneuropathies (nerve disorders), muscular atrophy (deterioration of muscle), incoordination and seizures to distemper, parvovirus and rabies vaccinations. She also established a link between vaccinating for Lyme disease and consequent kidney and liver failure.

Similarly, in cats, a suspicious link still exists between using the feline distemper vaccine in a combo vaccine and the increased incidence of hyperthyroidism.

The important question here is: has any of this been taken seriously? Studies conducted in mice and human infants have shown that early vaccinations stimulate humoral immunity, which helps fight specific diseases but at the same time decreases cell-mediated immunity, which is necessary to fight cancer. This pattern can continue into an animal's adult life, resulting in an increased risk of cancer development in old age.

VACCINATION GUIDELINES

In 1997, the first Veterinary Vaccines and Diagnostics symposium of some 500 vets, scientists, physicians, immunologists and epidemiologists convened at the University of Wisconsin, USA, and reached a landmark conclusion. The mixture of conventional and alternative experts agreed that vaccine boosters should not be given more than every three years. They also said that instead of annual vaccinations, annual blood tests/titer testing should be undertaken in the interim to confirm protection.

The WSAVA Vaccination Guidelines Group (VGG) was convened in 2006 with the task of producing global vaccination guidelines for dogs and cats that would consider international differences in economic and societal factors that impact on the keeping of these small companion animals. The guidelines were launched at the 2007 WSAVA Congress. Since then the VGG have convened in 2009 and in 2010. They looked into two major concepts regarding vaccinating companion animals:

- **Re-evaluation of vaccination practice and the importance of herd immunity**. The VGG observed that even in developed countries, only 30–50 per cent of the pet animal population was vaccinated, and this was significantly less in developing nations. In small animal medicine, they felt that there had been a slow realization regarding the concept of 'herd immunity' – that vaccination of individual pet animals is important, not only to protect the individual, but to reduce the number of susceptible animals in the regional population, and thus the prevalence of disease.

  Herd immunity with the core vaccines that provide a long (many years) DOI (duration of immunity) is highly dependent on the percentage of animals in the population vaccinated and not the number of vaccinations that occur annually. They concluded therefore that every effort should be made to vaccinate a higher percentage of cats and dogs with the core vaccines.

- **Reduce the 'vaccine load' on individual animals in order to minimize the potential for adverse reactions to vaccine products**. For that reason, the VGG prepared vaccination guidelines based on a rational analysis of the vaccine requirements for each pet, and the proposal that vaccines be considered 'core' (compulsory) and 'non-core' (optional) in nature.

Species diseases controlled by vaccines

According to the UK's National Office of Animal Health (NOAH), companion animals can be vaccinated against several diseases:

⇨ *Dogs*

Distemper, infectious canine hepatitis, leptospirosis, parvovirus, kennel cough (*Bordetella bronchiseptica*) and canine parainfluenza virus. Also, rabies for dogs going abroad as part of the Pet Travel scheme (PETS).

⇨ *Cats*

Feline infectious enteritis (or panleucopenia), feline leukaemia, chlamydia, cat 'flu' (feline herpes virus and feline calcivirus). Also rabies for cats going abroad as part of the Pet Travel scheme (PETS).

⇨ *Horses*

Equine herpes virus 1, influenza, tetanus, viral arteritis. Also rabies (not routinely used in the UK).

⇨ *Rabbits*

Myxomatosis, viral haemorrhagic disease.

Most of the above diseases, except rabies, are endemic in the UK, and most are also killer diseases in which death occurs despite veterinary treatment. These diseases also cause unnecessary suffering, and sometimes irreparable damage, to affected animals that could easily have been prevented by responsible vaccination by the owners.

Natural immunity can develop without vaccination but for this to happen an animal must first encounter the disease and then survive it. Due to the potentially life-threatening nature of the above diseases, is it worth taking the risk?

The most important message of the VGG is therefore encapsulated in the following statement: 'We should aim to vaccinate every animal with core vaccines, and to vaccinate each individual less frequently by only giving non-core vaccines that are necessary for that animal.'

The WSAVA vaccination guidelines state:

'Core vaccines should not be given any more frequently than every three years after the 12-month booster injection following the puppy/kitten series, because the duration of immunity (DOI) is many years and may be up to the lifetime of the pet. In order to ensure the existence of the duration of immunity, titer testing may be used.'

RONALD D SCHULTZ, PH.D, PROFESSOR AND CHAIRMAN, DEPT. OF PATHOBIOLOGICAL SCIENCES, SCHOOL OF VETERINARY MEDICINE, UNIVERSITY OF WISCONSIN, MEMBER OF WSAVA AND AAHA VACCINE GUIDELINE GROUPS

'Only one dose of the modified canine "core" vaccine (against CDV*, CAV-2 and CPV-2) or modified live feline "core" vaccine (against FPV, FCV and FHV), when administered at 16 weeks or older, will provide long-lasting (many years to a lifetime) immunity in a very high percentage of animals.'

SCHULTZ 1998, SCHULTZ 2000 AND SCHULTZ 2006

*CDV refers to canine distemper virus, CAV to canine adeno virus, CPV to canine parvovirus, FPV to feline panleukopaenia/parvovirus, FCV to feline corona virus and FHV to feline herpes virus.

The reason why it is necessary to vaccinate again at 14–16 weeks is because before this period, in most puppies and kittens, there are circulating maternal antibodies (immunity passed on by the mother) that can prevent the vaccine from working. So it would be good practice to give the first vaccination at 10 weeks or older and the second at 14 weeks.

Fortunately, this is filtering into practice now and many veterinarians give core vaccines as a puppy/kitten course, a full annual booster of core vaccines and then do not give them again until the third year. The leptospirosis vaccine is still given yearly, mainly because the disease is zoonotic (it can spread to humans) and also because not much information is available to find out if there is a risk of the disease in the area or if the dog in question is at risk.

Toy breed dogs are more prone to adverse anaphylactic reactions after the administration of the leptospirosis vaccine, so unless the dog is at a very high risk of exposure it is best avoided. The kennel cough vaccine is very much optional, according to the WSAVA, and certainly not compulsory. In cats the feline leukemia vaccine is not a core vaccine but it should be given to high-risk groups such as outdoor cats who are more likely to get into fights and become infected by the virus.

Some holistic vets recommend 'nosodes' instead of or after vaccinations. These are a potentised homeopathic remedy prepared from diseased tissue or from an infected discharge. They may have a role as an alternative to orthodox vaccines, but at present there is no scientific evidence that they offer the same protection as the conventional vaccines.

For owners who are totally opposed to the idea of annual vaccinations, it is good practice to at least administer nosodes and then titers can be run following the nosode administration to evaluate whether it was effective in stimulating the immune system.

Summary

There is no doubt that there is a controversy right now on companion animal vaccinations and that a lot of vets and the general public are concerning themselves about vaccine protocols. Unfortunately, in spite of the concerted efforts of many vets, both holistic and conventional, and guidelines from the VGG, annual vaccinations are the norm, predominantly for financial and legal reasons.

Vets do not want to lose the money gained from vaccinating and are also scared of being sued if they advise against annual vaccines – insurance companies insist on them and so do pet travel schemes and kennels. The pet guardians find the annual vaccinations cheaper than titer testing.

They also worry about the insurers, boarding kennel regulations and compulsory travel requirements. Many pet guardians cannot wait to take their puppies for a walk or to puppy classes. They want them to have early vaccines from six weeks onwards and finish at 10 weeks, rather than keep the pups at home till they are 14–16 weeks old.

A paradigm shift is therefore required in the mentality of both pet guardians and vets. Pet guardians need to pick the right vet for their pet, and be willing to wait till their pup is older before taking them out.

The guidelines stated above are not compulsory and your veterinarian does not have to follow them – they just guide us to use vaccines efficiently. But the ultimate decision is down to the individual veterinarian. Vets therefore need to stop succumbing to financial and pharmaceutical company pressure and do what is in the best interests of the pet in their care.

Vaccine data sheets do specify that their vaccines should not be used in animals that are unhealthy/immunocompromised. This should be enough to waive vaccines in the elderly (seven to ten years or older, based on breed) and those animals who have chronic health problems. I discuss the options with my client and tailor them to suit their needs and that of the pet.

Hopefully, with the development of quicker and more economical titer testing kits, which are now available, blind vaccination will be replaced by 'evidence-based boosters'. Only give a booster vaccine if there is a low antibody titer and the pet is at risk. Instead of calculating how much money can be made per animal by vaccinations, vets need to focus on encouraging age-appropriate regular pet health checks and educating guardians on how best to care for their pets in a holistic and realistic way.

Chapter 10

~⌒

How to Vet Your Vet – Choosing the Right Vet for You and Your Pet

When I was growing up in India, before swallowing any medicine I would recite the ancient Sanskrit prayer *Vaidhyo Narayano Harihi*. This translates as 'The doctor is God himself', but in context it means when the body is diseased, the medicine is like healing holy water and the doctor is God himself. It represents the faith one has in the goodness of the medicine taken and the trust in the doctor who prescribed it. Healing is bound to follow.

It can also mean that if you have no faith in your vet or doctor you will subconsciously delay or even stop healing. This is precisely why you need to find the right vet for your pet. Your pet's wellbeing can only be ensured if there is a trustworthy partnership between you, your pet and your vet. When it comes to your health, or that of your pet, you need to consider your level of commitment, your economic circumstances and your belief system.

The fact that you are reading this book means you are very likely to be a proactive pet guardian who wants to have an active input in your pet's healthcare. While most vets will be happy to listen to your point of view, some will misconstrue this as a challenge to their authority and resent it. Others can be dogmatic and conventional, or simply do not have the time or the patience to consider that there are other options.

I believe that becoming a doctor for humans or animals should be a calling or a vocation rather than a career. You need to be able to care, to empathize, to understand and to strive to relieve pain and suffering with knowledge, expertise and compassion. The majority of vets and doctors start out with honest intentions, and most of them continue to have those ideals, but unfortunately there are quite a few who succumb to other practice pressures – such as financial targets and drug company incentives – and lose sight of their true mission.

WHY VETERINARY CARE CAN BE EXPENSIVE

Integrity and honesty are two very important qualities you need to look for in both your doctor and your vet. It is sad that many vets today have forgotten that ours is a service profession and instead treat it just as a lucrative business. Veterinarians are given monthly financial targets by their practice managers, which they are under pressure to meet. This is more common in the large practices owned by corporate companies.

These vets are forced to act like salespeople and hard-sell commercial diets that have better profit margins for the practice; they also carry out unnecessary blood tests, X-rays and scans and even perform unnecessary surgical procedures to meet their targets.

I strongly disagree with this and am proud never to have succumbed to this sort of pressure. I have always acted with honesty and integrity. This especially seems to be a big problem for young, inexperienced vets who are forced into this by their practices.

Many end up losing their jobs if they do not meet their targets. It must be soul-destroying to work under these conditions. No wonder there is such a high rate of suicide and drop-out in the veterinary profession, especially among new graduates.

Most young vets have spent at least six years studying and have invested a lot of money (thousands of pounds or dollars) to qualify. They have put in several years of hard work, from school to university level, to follow their dream of becoming a veterinarian. If their job is at risk because they are not financially minded, they have no choice but to give in and let their conscience take a back seat. It is a general misconception that veterinarians are highly paid: their income is not in the same league as doctors or dentists.

However, none of this justifies bad practice. I have heard from other vets that some practices make a point of finding out how much the pet's insurance will cover and make sure to use it all up, leaving no money for future emergencies or treatment. I find this shocking and unethical. As an experienced vet, I can usually tell what the problem is just by obtaining a good history and performing a clinical exam.

To confirm my diagnosis, I may decide on some blood tests or perform some imaging, such as X-rays. Most of the time, this is adequate. Yes, technology has advanced a lot and it is wonderful that we have a lot of equipment that can help, but we have to be judicious in its use. It is wrong to perform every possible test under the sun to confirm something that you already know.

In conventional veterinary medicine, most of the expense today is due to the investigation or the process of diagnosis, rather than the actual treatment. This is all very well if you, the pet guardians, have an infinite amount of money to spend, but when finances are tight this can be crippling. On the flip side, we veterinarians find it quite puzzling that many pet owners seem just to acquire pets without considering their financial or health circumstances.

I love animals very much. But I am not irresponsible and I do not condone collecting a large number of them when you cannot afford to feed them or spend time with them, or even give them veterinary attention when they are ill. Your pets are your responsibility and it is unfair to blame veterinarians or the cost of living or society if you are not able to provide for them. Please consider this before getting another pet.

If your pet is referred to a teaching or a university hospital, the staff there have to perform many tests and follow strict protocols as they need to publish research data and teach vet students, so be prepared for an expensive work-up. In routine practice, I know that it is possible to diagnose most conditions and treat them without extensive and expensive investigations. Some vets are scared to do this because their clients then accuse them of not being thorough or performing enough tests or scans.

You need to make your requirements clear and be open with your vet. If you are not happy, feel bullied, or feel that nothing is working, communicate this to your vet or change your vet. If you want 'instant' solutions to your pet's health problems, your vet will be forced to inject steroids or resort to other quick methods that will help in the short term but leave your pet with long-term problems. So, essentially, the choice is yours. Listen to your gut feeling and always get a second opinion if you are not happy.

VETTING YOUR VET CHECKLIST

Here is a useful checklist to help you choose your vet:

- Make sure your main conventional or integrative veterinarian is as near as possible in the event of an emergency.

- If it is not an emergency, then be prepared to travel with your pet if you trust a particular vet, in order to get correct, honest care.

- Find out if your local vet will do house visits if you are unable to transport your pet.

- Check that your veterinary practice is reasonably priced for your needs. The cheapest practice is not necessarily bad, nor is an expensive one guaranteed to be good. The price generally reflects the practice location rather than the quality of veterinary care.

- Make sure that the vaccination protocol of the practice is tailor-made to suit your pet's lifestyle.

- Ensure the practice has adequate, modern equipment, expertise and good inpatient care.

- Choose a vet who is open-minded, approachable and happy to explain the reasoning behind a test – and also how the test will affect the treatment options for your pet.

- Make sure your regular vet is willing to refer you to both conventional specialists like oncologists and orthopaedic surgeons, and other holistic vets or therapists if necessary.

- Do not be bullied by your vet into buying commercial diets, unless they are prescription diets essential for serious health conditions.

- Ensure your vet is open-minded and happy for you to home-cook or buy natural diets or try raw food diets, as long as it suits your pet's health.

- If you are holistically minded then do try and find a holistic vet.

- Finally, make sure YOU and YOUR PET like YOUR VET.

I believe that holistic integrated veterinary care will become the norm in the near future. More and more vets and pet guardians want a well-rounded approach. There is no doubt that conventional veterinary medicine is excellent and a must for emergencies, serious injuries and acute conditions but this Western approach does not seem to work for long-standing or chronic conditions.

In a 10–15 minute appointment, it is perfectly possible for a conventional veterinarian to diagnose and treat most symptoms, but not enough to look at the problem in a holistic way. There is just not enough time to get the full picture of your pet's emotional and physical problems.

I believe that to effectively prevent and maintain a pet in good holistic health, it is important to get to know you and your pet – including your pet's personality, lifestyle, diet and health condition. A good one-hour consultation with a holistic integrated vet can be life-changing for your pet.

I strongly recommend that you find a holistic integrative vet who can provide the best of both worlds. If this is not possible, then look for a holistic vet who will refer you to a conventional one when your pet needs it. Otherwise find an open-minded conventional vet who will refer you to a holistic vet or a trained complementary veterinary therapist if necessary. Together we can work miracles and help your pet heal.

Part IV

RESPONSIBLE
PET
GUARDIANSHIP

Chapter 11

~⌒

Give a Pet a Home – Adopting a Rescued Animal

If you are thinking of extending your family with the addition of a rescued pet in need of a loving home, then read on for some helpful tips for choosing the one for you. We have enlisted the help of Ruth from the RSPCA, the UK's leading animal welfare charity, to help guide us through.

WHY CHOOSE A RESCUED PET?

Animals find themselves in rescue centres through no fault of their own. It may be that:

- Their owner has passed away.

- Their previous family has broken up.

- Their owner has become unemployed and cannot afford to keep them.

- Their previous family has found themselves homeless/evicted.

- Their owner has had a change in lifestyle – for example, working long hours.

- They have been removed from their previous home for their own good, because of neglect or cruelty.

There are many places to buy a pet, but there are many reasons to proceed with caution. Buying from an unrecognized breeder will only encourage the puppy trade and could mean more animals requiring help. You could be putting your money into the hands of people who are only breeding animals to make money and who do not have their best interests at heart.

Buying from a pet shop does fuel the trade in animals. Many of the animals for sale come from puppy farms where conditions are often bad and where adult dogs are used as breeding machines. All too often the animals do not get to live a normal life and their basic needs are not met.

Adopting a rescue animal will not only give that animal its forever home with you, but it will also make some space in the rescue centre, allowing it to accept another animal in need of help. Please do not be tempted to take an animal that is advertised as 'free'. There is normally more than one reason behind the rehoming of these animals, and you may not get the truth until it is too late and it has cost you a lot of money – you might end up buying an animal in ill health, and then need to pay huge vet bills.

Are you ready to adopt an animal?

Here are some things to consider before starting your search:

⇨ *Your lifestyle*

Do you have the time that is needed to do the following:

- Settle in your new companion?

- Give it the exercise it needs?

- Attend training classes?

⇨ *Costs*

Do you have the financial security your pet needs for:

- Initial outlay – equipment, cost of buying the animal?

- Vet bills – pet insurance does not cover all bills?

- Insurance – cover for ill health and third-party liability?

- Food – this cost varies a great deal depending on the individual animal?

- Holiday boarding?

- Grooming – for some breeds, this is required on a regular basis?

⇨ *Energy levels*

Your energy levels must match those of your pet. Do you like to run? How energetic is the pet and could he or she keep up with you? What type or breed are you adopting and how much exercise do they need? For example, larger dogs need less exercise than smaller terrier types. Try thinking about what job the breed used to do, as that might help you understand their needs.

Also, if you are thinking about taking on a puppy, remember that it is like having a new baby in your home. They need feeding every few hours, house-training and attention by the bucketload.

⇨ *Environment*

Is your home suitable for a new pet? What about the other animals in your home? Will they accept a new companion? Do you have children and is the animal compatible with children their age?

⇨ *Needs of the animal*

Your pet may also need:

- A safe environment away from busy roads.

- Access to a cat flap.

- A suitable diet – this should include fresh food if at all possible – as we learned earlier in the book, processed food is as bad for our pets as it is for us.

- Understanding of their personality – we all have a past.

- Compatibility with the other animals and humans in the home.

- A quiet area where they can rest, away from the hustle and bustle of the household.

- Stimulation with toys, exercise and training.

- Daily grooming with the correct equipment – to include claws, teeth and coat.

- Socializing with other animals and people.

- Your time for companionship.

- Boundaries – your new pet needs to know the rules of their new home. And all the occupants need to be using the same rules – so as not to confuse the animal.

WHERE TO FIND THE RESCUE PET THAT NEEDS YOU

If you have visited an animal rescue centre and feel sorry for the animals staying there, STOP and think carefully before going ahead with an adoption. Sympathy does not help these loving creatures. We all understand empathy but if you have visited an established and well-known rescue society, the animals in their care are the lucky ones: these are the animals that will get loving, caring forever homes – eventually.

A word of warning – not every rescue centre is a charity! Anyone can set up an animal rescue centre and run it as a business. Many of these places are not run for the wellbeing of animals, but as a money-making setup for the owners. An animal may not have had a full health check or an assessment to see if it is suitable for your home. If you are not sure whether a rescue centre is a charity or not, you can check it out on the UK's Charity Commission website.

There are many wonderful rescue centres to choose from. Do choose wisely, though, as you do not want your donation to go into the pocket of someone who uses animals for money. If you do visit a place where you see an animal being cruelly treated or in distress, do not remove the animal, but report the centre to the RSPCA or a similar organization, who will investigate it. If you remove the animal, evidence that is essential to ensure a prosecution might be compromised.

Visiting a reputable rescue centre

Once you have chosen the place then visit and ask about their homing procedure, which can vary. Your new companion should have been:

- Neutered if old enough – or you should be given a voucher for when it is old enough.

- Micro-chipped – and registered to you.

- Wormed with a product from the vet.

- Given a flea treatment with a product from the vet.

- Given a full health check by a qualified vet.

- Had its personality and suitability for rehoming assessed.

The staff will be able to assist you in choosing the right rescue animal for your family and lifestyle. Make sure that all family members meet a potential companion before you take it home – remember to choose your pet for its personality, not its looks.

Taking your new companion home

This is where your aura and state of mind will help: all animals pick up on whatever energy is around them. Keeping your energy calm and relaxed will help your new friend during this very scary time of going to new places with new people. This is very difficult when you and your family are all so excited, so try practising beforehand. Mindful meditation and deep breathing can help.

Remember: your new companion has a past and a memory – so be aware of their behaviour in different situations. Hands-on healing sessions will help you and him or her greatly, by creating a calm, relaxing environment and developing a closer relationship built on trust and love. Enlist the help of a registered animal healer at www.healinganimals.org.

Please enjoy your new friend and remember to recommend to others that rescue animals make a great addition to any family.

Chapter 12

⁓

When it is Time to Let Go –
Dealing with the Loss of Your Pet

We associate the word 'bereavement' with loss, death and mourning. All of us who have loved an animal know that sometimes the sadness actually begins as we realize that our friend is getting older or perhaps is experiencing a chronic or terminal illness. The first tears fall when we realize that time is limited. While loss can be difficult and emotionally trying, especially if we are presented with a critical decision concerning our animal companion, ultimately it is a natural part of life. That is, after all, how animals view it.

A LIFELONG FRIEND

Like it or not, most of us outlive our animal companions. Having been blessed with the gift of many years with a beloved friend does not make it easier to say goodbye or let go. It is a bittersweet time, one that is not always understood by those who have not enjoyed the enduring company of an animal. At the Healing Animals Organisation (HAO) we believe that joy can be found in all phases of life, and we are able to help you and your friend walk this path together.

When we bring a new animal into our life, we sign up for the duration, and that is easy to ignore when a youngster is gloriously thriving and playing.

Yet in the same way that he is dependent on us for food, shelter, love and healthcare, he is also dependent on us when the play is slower, the naps are longer and the walks are shorter. True love requires that we look with honest eyes upon our friend, and meet his needs at every step.

Care for the carer

To be truly present and willing to be a champion for our animals requires that we care for ourselves. It is important to be honest and to communicate our feelings to our animal friends. Being a source of calm, love and care is one of the greatest gifts we can give them. Though our journeys are intertwined, our pets are individuals.

Is your animal in pain?

When we are so closely bonded to our animal, our judgement may be too clouded with emotion for us to recognize whether he or she is in pain or discomfort. Our vets are experts who can guide us. If you notice your animal friend has developed any unusual behaviour your vet is your first call for care.

Put your pet's needs ahead of your own

Our animal companions love us and want us to be happy. If their health fails and we become afraid of losing them, they may choose to struggle on, at all costs. This can mean that despite constant pain or infirmity they will fight to stay with us when they know we cannot yet let go.

It is important to stand back and consider whether this situation is developing in your home. Our animals are very proud, and to really love and honour your friend may require putting your desires aside. This acknowledgement is true, unconditional love, and the essence of true love never dies.

If your pet needs help to leave

We all desperately hope that we will never need to make such a decision for our pet. However, the hoped-for passing during a good nap is rare. The bottom line is that we all have to let go of something. As guardian to our beloved, the time may come when the question of euthanasia has to be considered with a vet.

Having done all you can for your pet throughout his or her life, you need to do all you can at the end to make it a smooth, gentle transition. Your ability to put your animal's care and comfort before your own fear of loss is a great responsibility and also a great gift. It can be a decision that demonstrates the amazing amount of love you have for your pet.

Talk it through with your vet, your pet and your family. This can help reduce much of the anxiety, and you may find that it brings an understanding of what your animal friend feels and needs. You may find that they completely understand and actually welcome your help – they appreciate the fullness of a life lived well. A HAO Animal Healer can be especially valuable during this period. Healing and relaxation can replace turmoil with comfort and calm.

Choosing the time

If you make the decision to help your friend pass over, you can choose a time and place for a peaceful and even beautiful transition. If you choose to go to your vet's surgery, ask them for the best time at the end of their day when you will have a peaceful space. Talk with your animal about what will occur, and explain that the vet is going to help them gently let go. Think ahead about taking a favourite blanket or toy.

You may tell your vet that you want to be present at the moment of passing, or if you feel you simply cannot handle this you can choose to say your goodbyes fully and let your animal know that the vet will give him or her ease. Remember that your animal friend will feel your anxiety, so do your best to focus only on the love, which is more powerful than all the rest.

If possible, consider letting your friend pass on in the bosom of hearth and home. You can ask your vet to come outside of surgery hours, family members can be present and your lovely animal will be surrounded by all the comforts of his or her life. You can have gentle music playing, and a home filled with love.

Whatever arrangements are made, this is another time when asking a HAO Animal Healer to assist you can be a tremendous help. Planning the passing, setting the environment and bringing a state of beautiful calm to all is a privilege that our organization always feels honoured to accept. Vets welcome the presence of a Bereavement Healer to help facilitate a calm environment.

Once your friend's spirit has passed, you are left with the items they used and played with, and their body. You have several options. You may have already decided on burial or cremation – and whether you need to have the remains returned to you. There is no one answer for everyone.

If you choose cremation, you may decide between an individual or a group cremation. If you want your animal to be buried on your property you must choose a place away from underground utilities or bodies of water, and ensure you can prepare a hole appropriately deep for the size of animal. In the UK dogs and cats require a depth of at least 1 metre (3ft) and of course, larger animals need special consideration.

Celebrate your pet's life

All beings have their time on this Earth. If you ever remember a day when your animal friend moped about and worried about yesterday or tomorrow, then by all means hold fast to your grief. If, however, your friend woke each day with a wagging tail or any other joyful hello, take the lesson and honour it with a celebration of the amazing friend who shared your life. Having a ceremony with family and friends to reminisce and laugh over silly antics, funny stories and special moments helps celebrate a life well lived and allows the healing to begin.

The 'process' of grief

People vary widely in the way they cope with feelings, and grief affects us in many ways. Anxiety, fear, agitation, restlessness, anger, blame, resentment, depression, shock and feelings of detachment are all very normal responses. As is guilt. With so much responsibility and the desire to do the right thing, we automatically question our judgement and decisions.

The phases of dealing with grief are highly individual, and some people also experience physical pain or illness. It is important to recognize that it is a natural way to deal with loss, to be kind to ourselves and allow time to let these emotions flow. Often the depth of the pain comes as a surprise, even to the most ardent animal lover.

Other family members go through their own individual process. Many children have a deep bond with their animal friend, and it is important never to lie to a child by way of explanation. Our animals are honest creatures; their journey is a wonderful lesson in love and life for us all. It is important to respect this and be truthful. Having someone to help us through this period can be of tremendous benefit.

Do animals mourn?

Do animals mourn their own frailty or mortality? Animals recognize that getting older and slower is a natural part of the life cycle, yet they do not bemoan this. It is much more important to our animals that we accept their abilities and limitations. To adjust the routine and environment to be ever more comfortable and restful is one of the best gifts we can give.

Do animals mourn another animal when it passes on? In many ways, yes, they do. They have shared the same home and time as you have, and when a companion dies the animals who remain demonstrate their own emotions as they adjust to the different energy in the home. What we often fail to see is that our own reactions of grief, and our inability to accept or let go, often cause real emotional pain in our other animals.

If we realized it, would we ever choose to hurt our friend simply by our own need to grieve? Again, having the help of a HAO Animal Healer can bring calm and soothing relaxation to all family members.

A gentle request

Please do not shun your other animals as you miss the one who has just passed; rather, draw them close – they are feeling the loss as well. Appreciate their uniqueness and let their unconditional love form a renewed bond. A HAO Animal Healer can help all family members during this adjustment by honouring and releasing the sorrow and finding the way to move forward together.

If you have no other animals, you may feel that you can never, ever open your heart to more guaranteed heartache. The pain of loss can be incredible, but balanced against the years of joy, would you honestly have said at the start that it was not worth the journey?

Give yourself time, and then consider what your animal friend would want for you. Having experienced your love and care for so long, their greatest wish would be to have another animal enjoy such an amazing life. It is never possible to replicate the missing friend, nor would you really want to, yet when the time is right, and the perfect pair of eyes gaze into yours, another animal may find their way into your tender heart and show you their magic.

Contacting a Healing Animals Organisation Animal Healer

The Healing Animals Organisation is a professional body of UK and international qualified healers for both humans and animals. Go to www.healinganimals.org to find a graduate in your area of the UK, Europe, USA or Asia. Many specialize in celebrating senior animals and in helping both humans and animals travel the last steps of their journey together. When enlisting the aid of a Bereavement Healer, a donation towards their time and transportation is welcome.

Case study: Keymos, the Warrior Dog

In the following case study, Susan, a graduate of my Diploma in Animal Healing, tells us in her own words about the incredible journey she undertook to save her two dogs, who battled a series of life-threatening conditions. Anyone reading this will feel truly inspired by Susan's positive attitude, which she maintained even when times were tough.

There was an incredible bond of friendship between Susan and her dogs, and Keymos implicitly trusted in his mistress's judgement call, time and time again. It was such an honour for me to work with this beautiful family of souls.

'It was 2009, and I'd just attended Elizabeth Whiter's presentation on Animal Healing at a talk in London. Everything she showed us made sense to me. Afterwards I followed her downstairs to buy her book, *The Animal Healer*. I was hopeful that she could help my dog, Shadow, who had just been diagnosed with terminal cancer.

'I was also excited to learn that I could train to be an Animal Healer through her Diploma course. As I looked into Elizabeth's eyes, I felt an immediate connection. I knew, innately, that one of the reasons my dog had got cancer was to put me on the path with this woman.

'A few months later Elizabeth was treating Shadow, and I was studying with her. Although Shadow's cancer diagnosis was quite advanced, with Elizabeth's healing, the best possible nutrition and support, and learning to recognize and respect Shadow's wisdom as he showed me his own self-selection, he exceeded the vet's prognosis by 10 times. When he passed, I knew that we had done everything possible. It is a tremendous gift to have no regrets.

'Six months later we got another cancer diagnosis, this time for our senior dog, Keymos. At age 12, he was diagnosed with Hemangiosarcoma. The odds were against us. His best prognosis was five months: *if* we were very lucky.

'Because of Shadow, we were already feeding Keymos healthy, natural foods, as both Elizabeth and Dr Dressler, the US dog cancer vet, recommended. We had the best nutraceuticals, hope and healing. Keymos attended the Diploma modules and monthly healing evenings with me. Elizabeth's students added Keymos to their healing lists.

'My vet did not expect miracles, but at the six-month mark, he stood back and said, "Whatever you are doing, keep doing it, because he's thriving." We celebrated Keymos's 13th birthday and stopped all conventional treatment. He was happy, healthy and well – a cancer survivor! I received my Diploma in Animal Healing, started work as a healer and I was on my way to recognizing my dream of working with and really helping animals.'

'In his 14th year, Keymos encountered more challenges. First, he had laryngeal tie-back surgery. The cartilage in his throat had become brittle, making it difficult to breathe when he was excited. He had the recommended surgery, again supported by healing. Again, he sailed through.

'Several months later he experienced two successive bouts of gastric torsion: a life-threatening condition. We rushed him to the vets on the first occasion, and with emergency surgery he was saved. Forty-eight hours later his stomach began to turn again. I remember the scene at the overnight emergency vet office vividly. Keymos being prepped by the nurse, while the vet, who I'd never met before, advised me that she could operate, "if that is the option we wanted to take".

'For a moment I thought she had some new, innovative treatment up her sleeve, so I asked her what she meant. "Well, he's a senior dog and he's been through a lot this week. You may just want to let him go."

'I took a deep breath, looked at my dog, at my partner, Dave, and looked back at this woman. I said, "I understand that is your opinion, and I respect that you needed to share it with me. You do not know this dog. He's a fighter. Our job is to give him every opportunity to heal. It is his decision whether he takes it or not. So, I am asking you to operate, but before you take a step towards him, I need you to get on our team. I need you to have the energy of 'come on, boy, let's get you through this'."

'She blinked and nearly took a step back, stammering, "Well of course we always aim for survival.' I said: "I know, but I need you to hear me, and I need to know that you are really aiming for recovery."

'Two years earlier I may not have questioned her opinion, but I had learned so much. This was Keymos's journey. Twenty-four hours later in the hospital, his vital signs dropped, and he wasn't expected to pull through. We stayed with him, talking to him and giving him permission from our hearts to go if he needed to go.

'Our need to keep him with us was secondary to his choice. Elizabeth and dozens of healers were sending him healing energy, and as we lay next to him through the long night, his vitals started to rise. When dawn broke they were back to normal and he was looking for breakfast. The nurses who had monitored him all night were talking about the "medical miracle" that had occurred. Two days later he came home.

'Later that year, a disc in Keymos's lower spine compressed: more surgery, more healing. There was never any doubt that he wanted to be here, so we did what you do for family. We loved him, took him to hydrotherapy, walked him with a special cart to support his back legs. With that cart he ran and played stick with us, and tug with our other dogs. He still led his pack, only now he had wheels!

'By this point he was a senior lecturer in his own right at the Healing Animals Organisation. Students learned from him the dignity and gentle energy of a senior dog; that age is not a disease. His 15th birthday came, then his 16th. Our motto became: *It is not the dog in the fight, it is the fight in the dog.*

'Just after Christmas 2013, Keymos passed away in our arms – peacefully, painlessly, and with complete ease. It was simply time for the warrior to stop. We rejoiced through our tears, knowing it was right. Having no regrets.

'Life and death are personal journeys. Shadow, Keymos and Elizabeth have taught me that loving animals means respecting that their lives are their own. My animals are not "mine": I am merely blessed to share my life with them. Whatever form healing takes, whether medicine, food, surgery, prayer or play, it should always be offered with love, and the respect of the animal to accept it, or not. We would ask for no less for ourselves.'

Bibliography

The 5-minute Veterinary Consult: Canine and Feline, 2nd edition, Larry P. Tilley and Francis W.K. Smith, Jr. (Lippincott Williams & Wilkins, 2000)

Acu-Dog: A Guide to Canine Acupressure, Amy Snow and Nancy Zidonis, 1st edition (Tall grass publishers, LLC 2011)

Animal Acupressure Illustrated: Vol 1, Deanna S. Smith (CreateSpace Independent Publishing Platform, 2011)

The Animal Healer, Elizabeth Whiter (Hay House, 2010)

BSAVA Manual of Canine and Feline Behavioural Medicine, 2nd edition (British Small Animal Veterinary Association, 2010)

BSAVA Manual of Canine and Feline Emergency and Critical Care, 2nd edition (British Small Animal Veterinary Association, 2007)

BSAVA Small Animal Formulary, 7th edition (British Small Animal Veterinary Association, 2011)

A Colour Handbook of Skin Diseases of the Dog and Cat, Richard G. Harvey and Patrick J. McKeever (Manson Publishing, 2003)

Cakiroglu D, Meral Y, Sancak AA and Cifti G (2007) Relationship between the serum concentrations of serotonin and lipids and aggression in dogs. *Veterinary Record* 161, 59-61

The Dog Cancer Survival Guide, Dr Demian Dressler, DVM, with Dr Susan Ettinger, DVM, Dip. ACVIM (oncology) (Maui Media, 2011)

Dogs Never Lie About Love, Jeffrey Masson (Vintage, 1998)

The Emotional Lives of Animals, Marc Bekoff (New World Library, 2008)

Everyday Homeopathy for Animals, Francis Hunter (Beaconsfield Publishers Ltd, 2004)

Four Paws Five Directions, Cheryl Schwartz, DVM (Celestial Arts, 1996)

Health in Your Hands – Acupressure and other Natural Therapies, Vol. 1, Devendra Vora (Navneet publications, 1997)

The Henston Companion Animal Veterinary Vade Mecum, 21st edition (Nestlé PURINA, 2002)

Integrated Pharmacology, 2nd edition, Page, Curtis, Sutter, Walker and Hoffman (Mosby, 2002)

Love, Miracles, and Animal Healing, Allen M. Schoen, DVM and Pam Proctor (Prentice Hall & IBD, 1996)

Natural Health Bible for Dogs & Cats, Shawn Messonnier, DVM (Three Rivers Press 2001)

Nature Cure for Common Diseases, Dr D.R. Gala, Dr D. Gala, Dr S. Gala (Navneet Publications (India) Ltd, 1999)

The Nature of Animal Healing, Martin Goldstein, DVM (Ballantine Books Inc., 2001)

New Choices in Natural Healing for Dogs & Cats, Amy D. Shojai (Rodale Press, 2001)

Notes on Canine Internal Medicine, 2nd edition, P.G.G. Darke (Wiley-Blackwell, 1991)

Rang and Dale's Pharmacology, 6th edition (Churchill Livingstone, 2011)

When Elephants Weep – The Emotional Lives of Animals, Jeffrey Masson and Susan McCarthy (Vintage, 1996)

https://en.wikipedia.org/wiki/Vaccination
http://www.dogsnaturallymagazine.com/vets-on-vaccines/
http://www.wsava.org/guidelines/vaccination-guidelines

Further reading

Communication With All Life: How To Understand And Talk To Animals, Joan Ranquet (Hay House, 2008)

Edible Wild Plants & Herbs: a Compendium of Recipes and Remedies, Pamela Michael (Grub Street Publishing, 2007)

The Goldsteins' Wellness & Longevity Program, Robert S. Goldstein, VMD and Susan J. Goldstein (TFH Publications, USA, 2006)

Healing Foods, Margaret Roberts (Briza, 2012)

Herbs for Pets, Mary L. Wulff-Tilford and Gregory L. Tilford (5 Publishing, 2009)

How to Meditate with your Dog, James Jacobson (Maui Media, LLC, 2011)

My 100 Favourite Herbs, Margaret Roberts (Struik Nature, 2012)

Sacred Healing: A Soul-based Approach to Subtle Energy Medicine), Jack and Jan Angelo (Piatkus, 2001)

You Can Heal Your Life, Louise Hay (Hay House, 2004)

~⌒

Resources

Elizabeth Whiter, MHAO MNFSH IIZ ITEC Dip. WSA, teaches the professional Diploma in Animal Healing, animal herbal workshops, and Certificate in Natural Food Animal Remedies, and facilitates international animal welfare workshops with Dr Rohini Sathish.

She can be contacted at:

Elizabeth Whiter
PO Box 25, Hassocks, West Sussex BN6 8WN

www.healinganimals.org
www.elizabethwhiter.com
elizabeth@healinganimals.org

Diploma in Animal Healing
with Elizabeth Whiter MHAO MNFSH IIZ ITEC Dip. WSA

1-year part-time courses
- Small animal
- Equine

Email elizabeth@healinganimals.org
for further details and booking forms

To find a registered Animal Healer near you who has trained in the Diploma in Animal Healing with Elizabeth, please visit: www.healinganimals.org.

Dr Rohini Sathish, BVSC & AH MSC MRCVS MHAO MCIVT, is nominee Vet of the Year 2015 and a holistic integrative veterinarian with more than 21 years' experience. She is based in Cheshire, UK, and is a practising veterinarian, surgeon and Animal Healer. Dr Rohini also conducts workshops on holistic integrative vet care: please check the website for dates and booking forms.

For holistic, conventional and integrated consultations, contact Dr Rohini at www.rohinisholisticvetcare.com or via email vetdoc@rohinisholisticvetcare.com.

A selection of videos showing Dr Rohini demonstrating acupuncture and other treatment modalities, plus animal care tips, etc., can be seen on her YouTube channel, Dr Rohini's Holistic Integrated Vetcare.

A range of videos explaining how to make animal herbal remedies and tasty recipes with Elizabeth and Rohini can be seen at www.youtube.com/healinganimals.

Recommended UK stockists of herbs, oils, food products and equipment

(All the suppliers listed will deliver overseas)

G Baldwin & Co

+44 (0)207 703 5550; www.baldwins.co.uk
Bottles, jars, kitchen equipment, beeswax, dried culinary herbs, health foods.

www.animalchoices.co.uk

+44(0)1273 891472
Herb-infused sunflower oil for animals; cold-pressed linseed oil and meal; fresh aloe vera; animal healing and meditation CDs.

Lakeland Ltd

+44 (0)15394 88100; www.lakeland.co.uk
All manner of kitchen equipment.

Neal's Yard Remedies
www.nealsyardremedies.com
Beeswax, bottles, dried oils, essential oils.

The Neem People
+44 (0)1437 764415; www.theneempeople.com
Cold-pressed neem oil, dried neem leaves and bark.

Dolphin Sea Vegetable Company
www.irishseaweeds.com
A range of seaweeds, including dulse and sea lettuce.

Norfolk Herbs
www.norfolkherbs.co.uk
A fantastic range of online nursery herb plants.

www.wheatgrass-uk.com
Organic wheatgrass seeds, shoots, and plants.

Recommended US stockists of herbs, oils, food products and equipment
(All the suppliers listed will deliver overseas)

Starwest Botanical
www.starwest-botanicals.com
An incredible range of dried herbs, equipment for harvesting herbs, and kitchen equipment such as scales, funnels and bottles.

Horizon Herbs
www.horizonherbs.com
A fantastic range of fresh nursery herbal plants and dried herbs.

www.eddieswheels.com
Premier resource for wheelchairs for dogs, and other assistance items.

www.animalacupressure.com

Tallgrass equine and small animal acupressure course providers.

www.headspace.com

An app offering mindful meditation and relaxation techniques to still the mind.

Holistic integrative veterinarians

A directory of international Integrative Veterinarians is available on the website of the College of Integrative Veterinary Therapy: www.civtedu.org.

A directory of US holistic veterinarians is available on the website of the American Holistic Veterinary Association: www.ahvma.org.

Charities

www.charitychoice.co.uk/charities/animals/animal-rescue-centres-and-homes

The premier guide to animal rescue and rehoming.

RSPCA www.rspca.org.uk

Blue Cross www.bluecross.org.uk

Cat Protection www.cats.org.uk

Celia Hammond Animal Trust www.celiahammond.org

Dogs Trust www.dogstrust.org.uk

Animal Care Egypt www.ace-egypt.org.uk

World Animal Protection www.worldanimalprotection.org.uk

Compassion in World farming www.ciwf.org.uk

Compassion Unlimited Plus Action India www.cupabangalore.org

Friends of Birkenhead Kennels FOBK www.fobk.org

People's Dispensary for Sick Animals www.pdsa.org.uk

American Society for Prevention of Cruelty to Animals www.aspca.org

Adopt a pet, rescue and care USA www.humanesociety.org

Acknowledgements

ROHINI SATHISH

I grew up reading the work of British vet and writer James Herriot, who said: 'If having a soul means being able to feel love and loyalty and gratitude, then animals are better off than a lot of humans.'

As I write this, my heart is brimming with love and gratitude for the many people and animals who have been part of my journey over the years. It would be impossible to name every one of them – my friends, colleagues, my teachers, my mentors, all the wonderful vets, pets and pet guardians who have enriched my life and taught me valuable lessons along the way.

I am deeply grateful to my dear husband Sathish and our wonderful daughter Sanjana, for their remarkable patience and support while I was engrossed in my book writing. Thank you both for always being there for me.

I am indebted to my beloved parents, who have always inspired me to be the best I can be, and to my mother-in-law for her loving prayers. I thank my dear sister Nandini, my brother Srinath and my dear friends Rebecca, Nitya, and Mangala for their constant encouragement and pep talks.

My special thanks to Nirad and Vijay, for their words of wisdom and guidance. Thank you so much.

To Loges, my friend, my vet-mentor and teacher – I thank you with all my heart for always being just a phone call away.

I am thankful to our wonderful veterinary nursing team, especially Noreen, Marion, Claire and Kirsty, for their encouraging words and constant supply of tea. I am grateful to Nick Whieldon of Cvets for supporting my holistic clinic and to Kimm, our practice manager, for her encouragement.

My gratitude to Sylvia Bates, who first recognized the healer in me. I am also thankful to Paul and Geoff at Alder Vets for their support and for enabling me to prescribe natural remedies.

I am ever so grateful to Brian Clifford, Susan Whiter and Holly Woodward for their fantastic work with the photographs for the book.

I give thanks to dear Silky, my dear departed cat, who started me on this healing journey, and to my pets Frodo and Troy, who are willing guinea pigs to my crazy experiments, be it food, needles, herbs or massage.

Lastly, but most importantly, my heartfelt thanks to Elizabeth – my healing Guru, co-author and kindred spirit – who made this book possible. Loved working on this book with you, and looking forward to many more.

ELIZABETH WHITER

First and foremost, my thanks go to my husband Brian, for supporting and encouraging me through this writing process. It has not been easy, as you have seen so little of me, or our wonderful dogs. Most nights we have all been holed up in the healing barn: Morris, Frank and Lily curled up around my feet, keeping me company while I write. You are my rock, my life, and I love you.

To my magnificent and talented sister Susie, whose love and support knows no limit.

Heartfelt thanks to my wonderful team in the office, who have been so understanding when I have needed to focus and concentrate on writing this wonderful book. Juggling my time between the animal clinic, teaching, planting and harvesting herbs and our rescue and rehabilitation work: thank you for putting up with me! Love and gratitude to my earth angels: Catherine, Holly, Lee, Susan, Diane and Gina.

Enormous thanks and gratitude to the beautiful, precious animals that share my life: Lily, Frank, Morris, Taiyo, Iris, Betty and Dancer. Your friendship and company make my life so complete.

Special thanks to my dear friend Janice Barry at Hay House, South Africa. Witty and beautiful inside and out! You are a guiding light and champion of helping animals great and small.

To all my students and graduates at the Healing Animals Organisation, who inspire me every day with their loving kindness to animals in need.

I'm profoundly grateful and thankful to all the wonderful animals that have come into my life – you are my greatest mentors and teachers and I hope I can continue to serve you and champion your needs for the highest good.

There are so many people I would personally like to thank, but I cannot mention you all. Just know I am hugely indebted to you for being part of my life.

Finally, to Rohini, my wonder co-author and friend: you are a shining star and a great inspiration. I have loved working with you on this book and I am so looking forward to good times ahead.

ELIZABETH AND ROHINI

We are both so grateful to everyone at Hay House, especially to Amy Kiberd for commissioning this book, our editors Julie Oughton and Debra Wolter, to Michelle Pilley, Jo Burgess, Diane Hill, Duncan Carson, Tom Cole, Leanne Sui Anastasi and the many wonderful people who worked behind the scenes to help bring this book to you.

Special thanks to our 'Buddha boy', Morris, for sharing your wisdom, love and healing to all. You were the perfect model for our photoshoot for the step-by-step guide for the *Fingers and Thumbs* chapter and the animal healing session.

To all the wonderful people who work with animals, especially Ruth for her contribution to the chapter on pet rescue.

To dear Francis Hunter, for generously sharing your wisdom, love and happiness. You are always in our hearts and we will always be inspired by your love and devotion to animals.

Index

ABOUT THE AUTHORS

Brian Clifford

Elizabeth Whiter MHAO MNFSH IIZ Dip. WSA is a professional animal complementary therapist, specializing in energy healing, animal nutrition, Zoopharmacognosy and emotional balance techniques for animals. She has a complementary animal and human clinic in Sussex, and is author of *The Animal Healer*, founder of The Healing Animals Organisation and principal lecturer for the professional Diplomas in Animal Healing, Equine Healing and the Practitioner Certificate in Natural Food Remedies.

In 2005, Elizabeth established her animal training faculty, where students from around the world, including vets, attend lectures, workshops and her Diploma courses. She travels worldwide to work at animal sanctuaries and fundraise for them, and collaborates with animal charities on specific rehabilitation projects. Elizabeth is regularly invited to appear on radio and BBC TV, and lectures at colleges and wildlife charities.

Dr Rohini Tirumala Sathish BVSC & AH MSC MRCVS MHAO MCIVT is an award-winning, highly experienced holistic integrative veterinarian. She has a proven 21-year track record as a successful veterinary surgeon and popular clinician, and is a nominee Vet of the Year 2015.

Dr Rohini graduated from SV Veterinary University in India and the University of Reading, UK, before obtaining her MRCVS. After training in acupuncture, healing and herbal medicine, she now actively integrates conventional veterinary treatments with complementary therapies. Dr Rohini is Senior Veterinary Surgeon at Cvets Merseyside and the Veterinary Adviser for the Healing Animals Organisation. She also conducts holistic integrative clinics and workshops worldwide, and regularly appears on tv and radio. Dr Rohini currently resides in Cheshire, UK, with her scientist husband, Dr J.G. Sathish, daughter Sanjana, their dog, Troy, and cat, Frodo.

www.healinganimals.org
www.rohinisholisticvetcare.com

Lightning Source UK Ltd.
Milton Keynes UK
UKHW040845160119
335655UK00001B/206/P